Bui

AN IRISH STUDIES JOURNAL

General Editor
Ray Ryan

Co-Editors
Rónán McDonald, Jim Smyth

Asssitant Editor
Julie Costello

Advisory Editors and Patrons
Toby Barnard
Seamus Deane
Terry Eagleton
Roy Foster
Christopher Fox
Seamus Heaney
John Kelly
Bernard O'Donoghue
Tom Paulin
Fiona Stafford
Jon Stallwothy

Production Manager
Sean O'Brien

Volume 4 Number 1   **Autumn 1998**

Editorial

Bullán is an independent, interdisciplinary journal of Irish studies. Published twice-yearly, it seeks to make available in an accessible form new research from established and emerging scholars. Aimed at both an academic audience and the interested general reader, *Bullán* is committed to challenging the ways in which we view all aspects of Irish culture through a deliberately eclectic approach.

All correspondence and queries should be addressed to Bullán, c/o Sean O'Brien, 1148 Flanner Hall, University of Notre Dame, Notre Dame, IN 46556-5611.

Subscription rates: (UK & Ireland)
(incl. p&p) Individuals – £7.50 per issue, £15.00 per year (two issues), £25.00 per two years.
Institutions – £25.00 per year.

(USA)
Individuals – $15.00 per issue, $30.00 per year, $55.00 per two years.
Institutions – $50.00 per year.

The views expressed in essays and reviews are the responsibility of individual authors.

Our thanks to Ashley Shannon for her help in preparing this issue.

ISSN NO: 1353-1913

Composition by The Book Page, Inc.

Cover Design by Smith & Sawkins

Printed by Edwards Brothers, Inc.

Published by the University of Notre Dame Press

Contents

Essays

Review Article

Reviews

Ulster 1600-2000: Posing the Question?

Thomas Bartlett[*]

I

It may be worthwhile to begin with a short summary – hopefully non-contentious – of the history of the Ulster question. Leaving aside the wilder and more fanciful contentions of Mr. Ian Adamson and the Ulster Society, who would situate the origins of the Ulster problem in pre-history with the Cruthin,[1] it is generally accepted that its beginnings can be located in the early seventeenth century with the arrival into the province of Ulster of large numbers of English and Scottish settlers. Antrim and Down received most of the Scottish settlers, but they were plentiful in the area of the official plantation, especially along the Bann Valley. There were important differences between these Scottish and English settlers in social origins, cultural outlook, and political attitudes, but especially in religion, for while the English belonged to the Established Church, the Scots were Presbyterian, Calvinist theologically, and with no time for bishops or church hierarchy. Despite these differences, there was a strong bond in a common Britishness between them. This word 'British' was a new, inclusive term for English and Scottish people abroad, and one especially applied to those engaged in colonial endeavours. It was one much favoured, indeed it may even have been invented by the newly-crowned King of Britain, James I.[2] When added to the resident native Irish population – still Catholic in religion – the effect of these Scottish migrants was to complicate an already complex situation. Some of the native Irish welcomed the new arrivals, for they hoped, correctly, that they would benefit from the breakup of 'O'Neilldom'; others feared them, correctly, for they foresaw the collapse of the Gaelic order and Catholicism and the reduction of Gaeldom and Catholicism to vassal status, or worse.

Initially, relations between English, Scottish and Irish – between Established Church, Presbyterian, and Catholic – appear to have been relatively harmonious, and those historians who have investigated the development of the plantation in the years up to 1640 have concluded that the key themes were integration, accommodation, assimilation, and fusion.[3] Such notions of harmony were, however, shattered by the outbreak of the 1641 rebellion in Ulster and

---

[*] As this essay was written in 1996, the editors of *Bullán* very kindly asked me if I wished to revise it in the light of the Good Friday Agreement and the subsequent election and referendum. I have declined to do so.

the near-overwhelming with much bloodshed of the plantation. For the next ten years, Ireland found herself a theatre of war in the War of the Three Kingdoms; and for the ten years after that she found herself a laboratory for Cromwellian experiments. The Restoration period saw the renewal of the Catholic threat, for Catholic hopes rested on the accession to the throne of their co-religionist, James, Duke of York; but these hopes were ultimately dashed at the battles of the Boyne and of Aughrim. The ebb and flow of events in the seventeenth century had concluded resoundingly in smashing military victories: the Protestants of Ireland had their faith that they were under a special Providence confirmed; they were now indisputably the People of Ireland. The Catholics, who had shown terrifying powers of recovery after the devastations of the 1640s and 1650s, had been laid low and the Catholic threat had been seen surely off.

It may be noted at this stage that Protestant victory was not for all Protestants. At the height of the crisis in 1688, members of the Church of Ireland and members of the Presbyterian church had indeed not scrupled to worship together, but victory brought a return to exclusivist ways. The Presbyterians were excluded from the fruits of victory, subjected to a series of petty and not so petty slights and legal restrictions, while the members of the Established Church luxuriated in the glow of that self-satisfaction and self-confidence which comes from apparently unimpeded (and unrivalled) access to the loaves and fishes of office, pension, and place. As for the Catholics, their armies were scattered and their leadership cadre exiled; their swordsmen plied their trade abroad, their estates either having been confiscated or being broken up piecemeal. The Penal Laws, in effect, denied them ambition; they appeared to be doomed forever to a subordinate role, an inferior position, a subaltern rank.

In any event, while the early years of the eighteenth century witnessed relative stability in Irish politics, by the 1760s all that had changed. The Seven Years War (1756-63) saw Britain acquire by conquest an enormous swathe of territory in North America, India, and elsewhere. The impact of this new empire (on which the sun, famously, never set) on Ireland and on Anglo-Irish relations was profound. A new, far-flung empire, religiously and ethnically mixed, called into question cherished notions of exclusion and exclusivity. This new empire required soldiers to garrison it, and the idle masses of Catholic Ireland appeared willing to undertake this chore, though to admit Catholics to the armed forces of the Crown meant overturning a century of prohibition. Moreover, it was evident that the old ways of governing this new empire would no longer suffice and that new ways had to be found. In America, this search for new ways led ultimately to the American Revolution, the secession of the thirteen colonies, and the creation of the American Republic. These events had a direct impact on Ireland, where a nationwide defence force, the Volunteers, formed in response to a perceived French threat during the American War, moved rapidly into the political arena, and demanded the redress of grievances. In 1782, this armed body helped bring about the 'Revolution' of that year, in which a form of legislative independence was conceded by Britain to Ireland. Thereinafter, until the Act of Union ended both the century and the Irish Parliament, matters proceeded downhill at an alarming pace. The Catholic Question, supposedly moribund, became terrifyingly alive, not just constitutionally or in a parliamentary way, but on the ground, in the contested shatter zones of South Ulster, where Catholics, Presbyterians, and members of the Established Church patrolled a shifting ethnic and religious frontier. The formation of the United Irishmen in Belfast (in October 1791), with its insistence on substituting 'the common name of Irishman' for the sectarian label of Protestant, Catholic or Dissenter, seemed to represent a new era of accommodation; but as we know, the United Irishmen were confronted by 'Disunited Irishmen' and the former's injunction to forget the past was easily set aside by those who were determined, indeed were encouraged, to live by the lessons of 1641, the Boyne, and Aughrim. A rebellion in 1798, largely confined to the east coast, Antrim and Down, and Wexford and Wicklow cost much loss of life, reawakened sectarian hatreds that many had thought banished decades earlier, and only served to provide the moment, the motive, and the opportunity for the passing of the Act of Union. The quasi-independent kingdom with its quasi-independent parliament would now become a province of the newly-constituted United Kingdom of Great Britain and Ireland, and the decade that had seen the birth of the republican project closed, ironically, with Britain and Ireland bound ever more closely together.

Union proved the gateway to the British empire, and imperial opportunities at home and abroad helped reconcile those who had been neutral or hostile when the measure was passed, but integration into the British state proved impossible to achieve and the nineteenth century witnessed a series of movements which in their various ways sought to test the Union, to mend the Union, and ultimately to end the Union. In all of these, Ireland's different status was revealed. By the 1840s – perhaps before then, but from that time on – the term 'the Irish people' was taken to mean the Catholics, and conversely to be Catholic meant to be Irish. Protestants – members of the Established Church or Dissenters – were welcome to the club but they were not to be allowed to direct its affairs. A turning-point came in 1886, when W.E. Gladstone, driven by both Irish and British motives, decided that Home Rule for Ireland was to be the preferred option of the Liberal Party which he led. At a stroke, an aspiration which had hitherto been regarded as utterly illegitimate and wholly impossible received the imprimatur of a great British political party; and Protestant Ireland (and within Protestant Ireland, evangelical Ulster) took fright and determined to resist in defence of the Empire, the 'British way of Life' and the Union. Yet another turning point came in 1912: Faced with the likelihood that some form of Home Rule would in fact pass, a rebellion took place in Ulster (bloodless no doubt but a rebellion for all that). The Ulster Volunteer Force was formed in order to defeat Home Rule by seizing control of strong points in Ulster, setting up a Provisional government, and bidding Westminster and the world defiance.

By now, we have moved onto very familiar ground: how the outbreak of the Great War intervened to prevent a clash in Ireland; how the 1916 Easter Week insurrection rewrote the script of Irish nationalist politics; how matters moved seemingly ineluctably to war in the years after 1918, with partition as the outcome – an outcome which, it should be stressed, no one had forecast in 1900 and few had foretold as recently as 1914. From the 1920s, the two states of Ireland have gone their own ways, the social, economic, and political distance between them becoming ever more pronounced even if the physical distance has remained the same or, if measured by time, has in fact shrunk; and these divergent paths were confirmed by conflicting experiences of the Second World War – or the 'Emergency' – and by the impact of British Welfare legislation in the late 1940s and 1950s on Northern Ireland.

The two countries were, however, thrown together in the late 1960s by the outbreak of communal disorder in Northern Ireland, and the descent into violence in the 1970s and 1980s has been matched by an increasing, though resented, southern stewardship of the Catholic or nationalist position in Northern Ireland. In this endeavour, successive governments of the Irish Republic have worked with a series of British governments or British leaders over the last twenty years and the fruits of this joint approach have been revealed in various Anglo-Irish agreements, Downing Street Declarations, and Framework Documents. By the early 1990s, a certain war-weariness in Northern Ireland allied with some very adept diplomatic footwork on both sides of the Irish Sea, and indeed across the Atlantic Ocean, produced the first realistic hope of a ceasefire; and in October 1994 this was duly announced by the Irish Republican Army and a little later by the Combined Loyalist Military Command. That IRA ceasefire did not hold, though it was reinstated in August 1997; that of the Loyalists has held, more or less, for the past three years. Meanwhile a 'Peace Process' involving talks between most of the leading interests (including Sinn Féin but not the large Democratic Unionist Party of the Reverend Ian Paisley) has been conducted in conditions of strict secrecy. Joint talks have produced concrete results – and this is encouraging – but I don't think I am being unduly pessimistic when I state that few informed commentators feel they have any reason for optimism about the eventual outcome. The integrity of the conflict – the irreconcilable nature of the respective demands, the zero-sum aspects of the quarrel, put pithily in the late seventeenth century by Archbishop William King: 'in truth, there was no medium but that either we or they must be undone', but echoed daily today – all seem to point inexorably towards a

continuation of an uncivil society in which smothered war, repressive legislation, unrepresentative institutions, and social anomie prevail. How have we
gotten to such a pass? And can we find any way out?

II

One thing that must strike even the casual observer is the fact that the Ulster
Question (or the Irish Question) seems to be intimately bound up with the
period of the rise, decline, and latterly, fall of the British Empire. If we take the
late sixteenth century and later as the beginnings of empire both in Ireland and
in the New World, if we accept the nineteenth century as the heyday of empire
and if we regard the twentieth century as the period of its decline and fall –
a period which in my opinion has still many years to run – then we can situate the Ulster question at the heart of Britain's imperial centuries and perhaps gain an insight into its persistence, its perniciousness, and its recalcitrant
qualities. Moreover, as so much of the rhetoric, argument, and political vocabulary within which the Ulster Question was discussed had an imperial
flavour – involving questions of racial superiority, Christianity, and imperial
economics – then this should further direct our attention to the imperial dimension. In addition, issues of identity have ever been central to the Ulster
Question, and where once English, Scottish, and Irish jostled Anglican, Presbyterian, and Catholic, this has at least in this century crystallised into the pithy
slogan: Ulster is British.

Ulster was of course never wholly 'British', but the word 'British' had been
invented specifically to describe those subjects of James I, the King of Britain or
Great Britain, who had taken themselves off to Ulster in the early seventeenth
century. James was concerned lest the Scots and the English might come into
conflict with one another and the creation of the common name of British or
even 'Britaines' was, he felt, one way to avoid contest and ensure harmony.
But the word had a rather uneven circulation and its currency was by no means
widespread. The American colonists preferred to call themselves English or
Scottish, or whatever, and the colonies themselves were described as English, as was the empire throughout the seventeenth century; for example, the
well-known book by the pseudonymous R.B. (published in 1685) addressed
the prospects of *The English Empire in America*. However, there was a change in
the early eighteenth century with the Union of the Scottish and English par-
liaments in 1707. At that point, the words British and Britain really came into
fashion to describe both the empire and the home country: thus we had, in
1708, the publication of Oldmixon's *The British Empire in America, containing the
history of the discovery, settlement, progress and present state of all the British colonies
on the continent and islands of America*. But neither British nor Britain was used
to describe Ireland or the Irish. Ireland was not invited into the cosy arrange-

ment consequent on the Scottish Act of Union: Ireland, dubbed variously teague-land or bogg-land, was considered unworthy of incorporation. Scotland may have become for a time North Britain and the Scots (or some of them) may have referred to themselves as North Britons, but Ireland – exotic, barbarous, papist and *Irish* – was, as yet, spared the appellation West Britain. And as Linda Colley has shown in her fine study of the development of British national consciousness, the Irish – Protestant, Dissenter, or Catholic – were not part of the process of the invention of Britishness: 'I have not written about Ireland itself' explains Colley:

> The invention of Britishness was so closely bound up with Protestantism, with war with France, and with the acquisition of Empire that Ireland was never able or willing to play a satisfactory part in it.... Ireland was cut off from Great Britain by sea but it was cut off still more effectively by the prejudices of the English, Welsh and Scots and by the self-image of the bulk of the Irish themselves, both Protestants and Catholics.[4]

Colley places particular stress on what she calls Ireland's 'deeply ambiguous' position within the empire, but this ambiguity ceased with the Act of Union (1801) and from then on Irish Protestants and Catholics were happy to play their part in the British Empire. The Empire was not denominationally exclusive: Catholic missionaries and Catholic soldiers were as keen to take up the White Man's Burden as Protestant engineers and administrators. This point is well illustrated by Rudyard Kipling in his novel *Kim* and also in the *Soldiers Three* stories, where the empire is portrayed as a sort of melting pot in which the white races of the home countries, whatever their national origins, blend together to promote the imperial project. But Kipling, for all his apparent brash self-confidence, was deeply troubled by his fears for the future of the empire; and as we know, these fears were not groundless. The twentieth century, beginning with the assault by the Boers and followed soon after by the Ulster Rebellion of 1912 – both in their different ways attacks on imperial sovereignty – has witnessed the decline and fall of the British Empire. Two world wars, the second one only recently finished in 'Yugoslavia', were nothing more than Wars of Imperial Succession, or at least that is how they look to an eighteenth-century historian. And in this process of decline, the term British, a word which at one time encapsulated a whole matrix of shared references and common concepts, most of which had to do with matters imperial, has slipped its moorings and now floats like a giant and unanchored dirigible, the prey of every zephyr and every thermal. No wonder the Protestants of Ulster feel cast adrift, for that which had given them sustenance and identity has now gone. The Scots at least retained separate educational, legal, and ecclesiastical institutions, and the Welsh held onto their language; but Protestant Ulster was a creation of the seventeenth century and the erosion of Britishness has induced a particularly virulent form of disorientation.[5] British and Britishness were concepts coterminous with, inseparable from, Empire. Without Empire they are utterly meaningless: 'I am Kim, I am Kim... And what is Kim?' Kipling's eponymous hero wailed. We may now ask: Ulster is British, Ulster is British... and what is British?

III

If the Ulster Question in one form or another has been with us for four hundred years or more, the Union between Great Britain and Ireland, and latterly between Great Britain and Northern Ireland, has been a reality for almost half that time. So much so that Union is sometimes taken as a 'given' in Anglo-Irish relations, the nearest thing to fundamental law that the British Constitution allows. To question its validity might be seen as impertinent. And yet, surely after nearly two hundred years of Union, the purpose and perhaps the point of union can now be assessed afresh?

At one time, in the early eighteenth century, there had been some Irish interest in Union. There was a feeling that the Scots, by the Union of 1707, had gained what might be called today most favoured nation status – especially where access to the trade of the British Empire was concerned – and some elements in Ireland wanted the same. This Irish ambition could not, however, be entertained because Ireland was not at all regarded by Britain as a suitable country with which to unite. Ireland, as noted above, was not British, indeed may even have lacked the potential to be British; worse, she was an economic rival. By the end of the eighteenth century, however, all this had changed. Since about 1780, union with Ireland had been seen in British government circles as the preferred long-term solution to the Irish question; but equally it was recognised that major obstacles lay in the way of the achievement of this objective. In contrast to the early eighteenth century, there appeared now to be little Irish support for Union and since the Irish parliament would have to vote itself out of existence, this seemed to be an insuperable obstacle. The rebellion of 1798 changed all that, for it offered the British Prime Minister, William Pitt, both the moment and the opportunity he had sought: Union was to follow hard on the heels of Rebellion and the members of the Irish Parliament were bribed, bullied, and cajoled into voting themselves out of existence.

The arguments in favour of Union make interesting reading two hundred years on. William Pitt, as might be expected, gave the keynote speech. The Union, argued Pitt, gave the perfect riposte to those who had, in the rebellion, sought separation, and to that extent Union could be promoted as a key instrument of counter-insurgency, a vital strategic initiative drawing England

and Ireland closer and closer so as to frustrate those Irish Jacobins and their French allies who had sought to pry them apart. In any case, it was evident from the very fact of the 1798 rebellion that the Irish Parliament was bankrupt, and that the Irish political class had failed. There could be, therefore, no going back. Not for the last time in Irish history – as the fall of Stormont in 1972 revealed – large-scale disorder would lead swiftly to the scrapping of the institution held to be primarily responsible, or conveniently available as scapegoat. Looking to the future, Pitt claimed that it would only be in a United Parliament that the Catholic Question could be solved with benefit to Irish Catholics and without danger to Irish Protestants. Moreover, he argued that a union would bring tangible material benefits to Ireland: 'English manners and English industry' would infuse the country and there would be a huge inflow of capital. Especially, the new united parliament would be both an imperial institution *and* an impartial legislature, not only one capable of deliberating on knotty problems, far removed from the clamour and prejudices of local factions, but also of calmly and dispassionately adjudicating in the interests of all on the various problems that might arise within the entire empire.

But if Pitt stressed dispassion, impartiality, and deliberation, his Irish supporters – or some of them – looked forward unashamedly to the Act of Union as a sort of new Penal Law which would block the way forward for Irish Catholics forever. John Fitzgibbon, Earl of Clare, was perhaps the most outspoken in this regard. The events of the 1790s had convinced him that the existence of an Irish Parliament was a standing threat to the Protestant Ascendancy and that only in a union could the Protestants of Ireland find security. So long as an Irish Parliament existed, it would ever be an object of Irish Catholic ambition, and the Irish Parliament was – in his eyes – such a 'giddy' institution that he had no confidence that it could hold the line against Irish Catholic claims for admission. It was therefore vital for Irish Protestants to jettison their pretensions to a separate, sister-parliament and throw in their lot with the Protestants of Great Britain: why be a member of the minority in Ireland when you can face the world with confidence as a member of the majority of the United Kingdom?

Perhaps the most effective answer to Fitzgibbon came from the Speaker of the Irish House of Commons, John Foster. Foster opposed Union on economic grounds, perhaps on personal grounds too (he did not like Pitt), but he also condemned Union on the grounds that it would surely and ultimately mean the end of the Protestant Ascendancy. Fitzgibbon had forecast that only Union could save the Ascendancy; Foster countered that Union would encompass its downfall. Foster's reasoning is instructive. He was persuaded of the general unwisdom of Irish Protestants placing their future in the hands of British ministers and British political parties because he believed that no British government could be trusted. The fickleness of Pitt's government had already revealed itself when it had built up Catholic hopes only to dash them when it suited. Such recklessness was sure to continue into the post-Union period. Irish Protestants would, in the future, count themselves amongst the majority of the United Kingdom, but they would ever constitute a tiny minority of the United Parliament and therefore they would always have to rely on others to look out for their interests. In that vulnerability, thought Foster, lay the seeds of disaster.[6]

An extended treatment of the performance of the Union lies beyond the scope of this paper. What may be said is that Union did not release that cornucopia of benefits which Pitt had claimed for it. Even Catholic Emancipation, a relatively insignificant concession, was only prised out of the British Parliament at the threat of civil war in Ireland, and that modest concession, now imbued with utopian, even apocalyptic significance, came some thirty years after Union had held out the prospect of an impartial legislature to adjudicate dispassionately on such knotty problems. Nor can the land legislation be laid at the door of a responsive and caring institution; as before, it took disturbances in Ireland before the 'impartial' legislature intervened; and as for the famine of the 1840s, the general consensus from recent writings – to put it no stronger – is that the British government could have done better in its relief efforts.[7] Certainly an argument could be made that an Irish Parliament would have been less ideologically restrained in its response to the Great Famine. In the end, however, it is the bleak forecast held out by Foster that seems best to fit the facts. He had forecast that the Ascendancy would be betrayed by British politicians and by British governments, and so it proved. Betrayal over Emancipation was followed by betrayal of the Established Church, then by betrayal of the landlord class and finally by the betrayal of twenty-six counties to those who had ever been the enemies of both Union and Empire. And in the eyes of many Unionists, betrayal has not ended there, for what else but successive betrayals were the Anglo-Irish agreement, the Downing Street accord, the Framework document, and indeed the whole Peace Process?

What purpose does Union now serve? Or rather to what does Ulster owe union? Is the Union still possible? At the moment, in receipt of a hefty multi-billion annual subsidy, the benefits of Union seem clear; but what if this should cease? As Foster pointed out two hundred years ago, British politicians cannot be relied upon to fulfill their promises for all time. It is in the nature of the British parliamentary and party political structure that this should be so, for there is no such thing as fundamental law, and the vicissitudes of party life make policy shifts routine. Moreover, the recent pro-devolution votes in both Scotland and Wales are clearly ominous for the maintenance of the status quo. Martin McGuinness has vowed to smash the Union; David Trimble is pledged to defend it. In the light of the Scottish and Welsh referenda, the onlooker may well ask, 'What Union?' In addition, the implications for the Union of European Monetary Union or the proposed Federal Europe have still to be faced. Union, always problematic, seems to be almost an impossibility now and for the future. A sea of incomprehension separates Ulster Unionists from British unionists (if any exist); and given that the only link now is to England, it cannot be long before the strains in that connection become apparent. Sooner rather than later the folly of a mono-cultural society, strongly Christian, strongly monarchist, and strongly wedded to notions of private and personal morality, desperately seeking to maintain union with a multi-ethnic, pluralist, barely Christian, and increasingly republican society must be revealed. Surely the lovelessness of the current embrace will induce sooner rather than later a one-sided separation. Moreover, just as Union is no longer possible, so Unionism as a political creed is on the road to nowhere, despite the valiant efforts of fellow academics to hold out the prospect of a vibrant future for it.[8] The Unionist parties of Ulster are in terminal decline, collapsed stars, black holes emitting no light, incapable of development, unable to move beyond their nineteenth-century origins and ultimately powerless to deliver anything other than further meaningless constitutional re-assurances.[9] In reality, the Union and Unionism, like British and Britishness, were bound up with the rise of the British Empire. Once that Empire ceased to be, the vital current of electricity that illuminated and animated unionism was switched off, and what we were left with was a mixture of a sleepy patronage arrangement, a petty system of petty oppression, and a gimcrack constitutional settlement that is looking increasingly past its sell-by date.

IV

What of Irish Catholics or Ulster Catholics? So far we have considered Ulster Protestants and Ulster Unionists, even British Protestants, but where do Ulster Catholics fit into the Ulster Question? They are, of course, central to it, and the history of Catholic-Protestant relations in Ulster from the time of the plantation on seems to provide much evidence for the more pessimistic commentators on Irish affairs. Seventeenth-century Ulster society was formed by colonial settlement, and because the dispossessed natives remained a presence of some magnitude in the region it was inevitable that that relationship between settler and native should be governed primarily by fear. Equally inevitably, religious identities became the labels by which the descendants of settlers and descendants of natives came to identify each other in the north of Ireland, but these religious identities were not, as it were, born in a state of nature. Each was defined by the other, and the circularity and reciprocity of Catholic-Protestant identities must be understood: to be Protestant was *not* to be Catholic and vice versa. Indeed, by the mid-nineteenth century a considerable proportion of Protestant or evangelical theology seemed to be focused more on the perceived

Catholic threat than on mediating between God and man. But this is to antici-pate. In the eighteenth century, there was perhaps more room for flexibility and manoeuvre. By the 1780s, Catholic-Protestant relationships in the area of settle-ment appear to have been relatively stable. The Catholic military threat had been crushed at the Boyne and Aughrim, the Catholic leadership cadre had disintegrated in Ulster, and the Penal Laws were in place as a useful instrument of social control. Paternalism by Protestant elite figures towards poorer Catho-lics had succeeded the sharper and more oppressive settler-native relationship. However, appearances were deceptive for, as the late Frank Wright reminds us: 'Although the withering away of the Penal Law regime might seem to have heralded a better state of Protestant-Catholic relations, it was never a proba-bility that it would wither away without a major crisis'.[10] Quite what prompted the crisis of the late eighteenth century in Ulster is a matter of some debate amongst historians: possibly the movement of Catholics into contested areas or into disputed occupations, perhaps Catholic agitation for relaxation of the Penal Laws, but most likely, it was the spectacle of Catholics bearing arms (and thus claiming full citizenship) that set alarm bells ringing amongst Protestants and fuelled a demand for a return to traditional settler-native relationships. What is interesting about this crisis, however, is that the response to it did not follow entirely traditional lines.

On October 18, 1791, the Belfast Society of United Irishmen was set up. The Dublin barrister and pamphleteer, Theobald Wolfe Tone, was in atten-dance, and he was joined by his friend Thomas Russell, a former army officer, and by some of the leading luminaries of Belfast, most of them active in the city's commerce, among them Samuel Neilson, Samuel McTier, and Dr James McDonnell. Their resolutions ran along the following lines: that the weight of English influence in Irish affairs was intolerable; that only a thorough-going reform of the Irish Parliament could counteract this influence; and that no reform of the Irish Parliament could be 'practicable, efficacious or just' which did not include the Catholics.

The significance of this last resolution cannot be overstated, for what the United Irishmen were in fact doing was giving their reply to a question that has run like a thread through Irish history. The central question posed of Prot-estant Ireland then (and now) was 'How will you live with Irish Catholics?'; and the United Irishmen were attempting to answer: with respect, in peace and justice. This question has retained its validity in the two hundred years since that fateful meeting in Belfast, but it has not yet received a similar answer. It would have been natural for the United Irishmen to abandon the Catholics, to rule them out as being incapable of either enjoying or extending liberty, and certainly there were always some among them who had their doubts on that score. It would have been acceptable for them to abandon the Catholics, for to adopt their cause meant to incur unrelenting hostility from Dublin Castle and the British government. It would have been easy to abandon the Catholics, abide by the lessons of history, and retreat to the bulwarks of the Plantation. However, the United Irishmen were aware that unless the Protestants of Ulster could come to terms with the Catholics of Ulster, there would be no civil living for anyone in Ulster, only a precarious existence in an unquiet society riven with fear and distrust.

Ulster was the cock-pit of sectarianism. Hence the United Irishmen directed their attentions especially to that quarter, and because legal matters, trials and prosecutions loomed large, the United Irishmen were prepared to fee counsel and brief them to fight the cases of poor Catholics who found themselves victims of a partial justice. Again, it is difficult to overstate the importance of this initiative in the fraught state of Catholic-Protestant relations in the Ulster of the 1790s. Of course, there were practical, political reasons for the United Irish strategy, and the United Irishmen themselves exhibited on occasion an infuriating naiveté for which they have been much criticised, but they made an effort to move beyond the bloody battlefield of Irish history, and to display empathy and sympathy with those from whom they had been separated by tradition, religion, and upbringing. Nor would it be true to say that they failed. It is simply too soon to make a definitive announcement.

The United Irishmen had posed the key question of Irish Protestants: how will you live with Catholics? Various answers have been given since the 1790s. The Orange Order was one answer, so too was the Union, and the Second Reformation of the 1820s, and sectarian rioting in Belfast in the nineteenth century; and I suppose armed rebellion, partition, repressive legislation, and discrimination were answers this century; and latterly the Downing Street accord and the Framework documents have been further responses; but none of these has produced a civil society in Ulster, and in terms of community relations, the 1990s bear more than a passing resemblance to the 1790s. The question implicit in Irish history since the seventeenth century, and first posed explicitly by the United Irishmen, remains apposite, but still remains unanswered, and while that is so neither Ireland nor Ulster can know real peace.

V

Where do we go from here? If a shared Britishness is no longer possible; if a common British identity between the people of Ulster and Great Britain is forlorn (for the concept of Britishness was so bound up with empire that with its demise, the core element of Britishness went with it); if the Union itself is, in the opinion of many commentators, already gone, given that Northern Ireland and the rest of the United Kingdom are hurtling apart; if Unionism is little more than a habit, a sentiment, a piece of nostalgia, and has nothing left within it of the vibrant movement of the early twentieth century: then truly, where do we go from here? Where we do not go is to London for solutions to the Ulster Question. One hundred and fifty years ago, Charles Greville, the diarist, put his finger on the nub of Britain's Irish problem. The difficulty, he wrote, in devising a solution, 'lay in the difference of opinion... as to... what the people of England could be brought to consent and what the people of Ireland would be content to receive'.[11] Solutions devised in London are devised with English objectives in view, latterly the protection of bi-partisanship and, until recently, the conservation of a parliamentary minority. Such 'solutions' were always arrived at with a view to what 'the people of England could be brought to consent'. Nor are 'solutions' devised in Dublin any better. Ulster Catholics have little in common with their co-religionists in the Republic; intense mutual irritation might best describe their relationship. The thrust of recent work has been to suggest the emergence of a distinctive Northern Irish identity.[12] It remains to be seen if the election of Professor Mary MacAleese will in fact bridge that gulf of incomprehension between the Catholics in both parts of the island. Moreover, it is by now self-evident that if Britain has no selfish, strategic or economic aim in holding on to Northern Ireland, then Dublin has likewise no selfish, strategic or economic ambition to take it over. Margaret Thatcher allegedly dismissed German unification as West Germany acquiring twenty-five Liverpools. A similar condescending remark might be made about the 'Celtic Tiger's' interest in the unification of the island of Ireland.

What is needed is for both Britain and the Republic to pull back from Northern Ireland affairs, and there are signs that this withdrawal is already beginning. There is a reluctance in both Britain and the Republic to be seen to be holding the ring in Northern Ireland. So long as that was the case, there was no incentive to address seriously the question posed long ago by the United Irishmen: How will you live with Catholics? Britain and the Republic can set the context within which a settlement can be reached but for them to nudge the people of Northern Ireland along the road to peace means that they cannot remain involved as players. What might be suggested is that a Northern Ireland, separate from England – 'Britain' will soon disintegrate – and from the Irish Republic but with sentimental and economic links to both, might yet qualify for membership of the European Union and find her future within a European federal structure. Twenty years ago such a solution would have looked bizarre; can I conclude by forecasting that twenty years from now it will be accepted as the only way forward?

Notes

[1] Ian Adamson, *The Cruthin: A History of the Ulster Land and People* (Belfast, 1974).

2   My thanks to Nicholas Canny, University College Galway, and to John MacCafferty of UCD for discussing this point with me. I also had the benefit of reading in typescript N.P. Canny's 'The Origins of Empire' in N.P. Canny (ed.), *The Oxford History of the British Empire* Volume 1 (Oxford, 1998).

3   Raymond Gillespie, *Colonial Ulster: The Settlement of East Ulster, 1600-1641* (Cork, 1985); P.S. Robinson, *The Plantation of Ulster: British Settlement in an Irish Landscape, 1600-1670* (Dublin, 1984).

4   Linda Colley, *Britons: Forging the Nation: 1707-1837* (Yale, 1992), p. 8.

5   See Ian McBride, 'Ulster and the British Problem' in Richard English and Graham Walker (eds.), *Unionism in Modern Ireland: New Perspectives on Politics and Cultures* (Dublin, 1996), esp. pp. 13-4.

6   For an authoritative listing of the various publications for and against Union, see W.J. McCormack, *The Pamphlet Debate on the Union between Britain and Ireland 1797-1800* (Dublin, 1996).

7   See the useful review article by Cormac Ó Gráda, 'Making Irish Famine History in 1995', *History Workshop Journal,* Issue 42 (1996), pp. 87-104.

8   See the essays in J. Wilson Foster, *The Idea of the Union: Statements and Critiques in Support of the Union of Great Britain and Northern Ireland* (Harmondsworth, 1996), and in Patrick Roche and Brian Barton (eds.), *The Northern Ireland Question: Myth and Reality* (Aldershot, 1996).

9   For an equally bleak analysis but one that is considerably more upbeat in its conclusions, see Norman Porter, R*ethinking Unionism: An Alternative Vision for Northern Ireland* (Belfast, 1996).

10   Frank Wright, *Two Lands on One Soil: Ulster Politics before Home Rule* (Dublin, 1996), p. 24. My thinking on the Ulster Problem has been much influenced by this book.

11   Cited in D.G. Boyce, *The Irish Question in British Politics, 1868-1996* (London, 1996), p. 1.

12   See Fionnuala O'Connor, *In Search of a State: Catholics in Northern Ireland* (Belfast, 1993).

John Toland's Druids:
A Mythopoeia of Celtic Identity

ROBERT SULLIVAN

M odern Ireland, and especially modern Ireland's Christianity, scared John Toland into evoking a more congenial and reasonable world from various remains of ancient paganism. In 1687, before he was seventeen, he left his obscure Catholic origins in the remoteness of County Donegal and voyaged to Glasgow as the client of Protestant divines. The college there became his entryway into the republic of letters. Three years later, proudly enrolled as a Master of Arts, he defied the plan of his patrons that he become a missionary to his fellow Irish-speakers. He saw a nobler prospect for himself and moved south, first to London and then to the University of Leiden. Yet the Catholicism of his youth and the priesthood of his putative but nameless father always scared him. In *Christianity Not Mysterious* (1696), the book that made his reputation, he described himself as 'educated, from my Cradle, in the grossest Superstition and Idolatry', to be liberated by 'my own Reason, and such as made use of theirs'.[1]

With a consistency sustained by wrath, Toland thereafter represented 'Popery... [as] an extract of whatever is Ridiculous, Knavish, or Impious in all Religions; [as]... Priestcraft arriv'd at the highest Perfection... and [as]... the most insolent imposition that ever was made on the Credulity of Mankind'.[2] There was a tale about his christening that suggests that the break with his 'Cradle' haunted him. In improbable defiance of the strictures of Roman Catholic canon law, he supposedly received 'at the font' the heathen name of Janus Junius, but years later to foil classroom mockery a protective, English-speaking schoolmaster 'order'd him to be call'd John for the future; which name he kept for ever'.[3]

The Protestant Church of Ireland also scared John Toland, for it supported its own menacing priestcraft. In 1697, hope of political advancement brought him to Dublin. There some of the local oligarchs seized on Toland, now a notorious heretic, to embarrass their enemies, his patrons in the dominant Whig clique.[4] Facing prosecution, he fled Dublin and from the safety of London published *An Apology for Mr. Toland, In a Letter from Himself to a Member of the House of Commons* in Ireland; *written the day before his Book was resolv'd to be burnt by the Committee of Religion*. As if to objectify and so distance himself from Ireland, he wrote throughout in the third person. He expressed outrage that 'being an Inhabitant of England... he should be molested in *Ireland* (where he was only fortuitously born)'.[5] He brooded over the *auto-da-fé* urged in the parliamentary committee of religion: burning him along with a copy of his volume.[6] Months later, he publicly reprimanded himself in the second person, as if he were no longer the author of *Christianity Not Mysterious*, but another. 'You', he wrote, are 'a little too much concerned for the treatment you have met with in *Ireland*, and too apprehensive of the consequences of it'.[7] Never again was he in Ireland, though his memory, fearful and longing, often returned there. Alarm shadowed him for life.

Toland once quoted Cicero's precept that 'it is a wise Man's Business to uphold the Institutions of his Ancestors, and retain their Rites and Ceremonies'.[8] Following Cicero, Toland depicted inherited religion and language as the sinews of a *res publica*. But where did he, illegitimate and itinerant, find his own spiritual ancestors?[9] His three major representations of his own identity are difficult to reconcile. They suggest something of his complexity. They suggest as well that he was one of those fluent, uprooted persons who, by refashioning themselves to address different audiences in different circumstances, evade self-disclosure and perhaps self-discovery. In one voice, Toland represented himself as a cosmopolitan ultimately belonging to 'Mother Earth', because 'the World's my Country, and all Men are my Relations'.[10] In his political writings, however, he usually represented himself as an aggressive Englishman. Using that voice, Toland championed an English national religion that included all Protestants and opposed the otherness of Catholics, whether the tyrannical French or the grossly superstitious native Irish, among whom he was fortuitously born but from whom reason separated him, so that he became one of their English conquerors.[11]

Never quite persuasive as either a cosmopolitan or an Englishman, Toland sometimes wrote as an Irishman.[12] Along with his fear of modern Ireland's Christianity and his insecurity about his own origins, he longed, particularly during his later years, for the disappearing culture of Celtic Ireland. Both his cosmopolitan and English voices depended on the kind of conventional vocabulary he usually found deadening.[13] Like many of his Irish-born Anglican and Presbyterian contemporaries, however, he lacked easy words to express a distinctive sense of his Irishness. The Anglophone and Protestant thought of themselves as essentially English, and one of them supposedly gave John, originally Janus Junius, his identifying English name. To speak as an Irishman, therefore, Toland was drawn to create a virtual community of his own within the realm of memory. Already in 1694, he was reportedly working on an 'Irish dictionary and a dissertation to prove ye Irish a colony of ye Gauls'.[14] He may have toyed with that project for the rest of his life.

In 1718, he sketched an Irish civil religion that he asserted was virtually Protestant a millennium before Luther.[15] Toland followed the lead of the staunchly Protestant Archbishop James Ussher, whom he acclaimed as 'the glory of Ireland', and recommended to 'the posterity of the aboriginal Proprietors [of Ireland]... my countrymen and fellow-subjects' the ancient and reasonable faith of their fathers.[16] The simple Christianity of the early-medieval Irish 'consisted in a right notion of God, and the constant practice of virtue'.[17] Although they 'preserv'd their Faith unpolluted against the corruptions of Rome [longer]... than any other nation', they finally succumbed at the hands of the Romanising English and were rendered 'afterwards infamous if not literally barbarous... upon their changeing the purity and simplicity of their faith into gross Idolatry and endless Superstitions'.[18] While describing that precipitous fall, Toland hinted at the vision that animated the history of ancient Ireland that he was projecting: '[A]ccording to the best *Chronicles* of the Iland, the state of the country was infinitely better under Heathenism, than under their degenerate Christianity'.[19] Between June 1718 and April 1719, he produced 'A Specimen of the Critical History of the Celtic Religion and Learning'. Solidly grounded in comparative Celtic philology, it was a two hundred twenty-eight-page extract of an unwritten and unwritable history of the druids, which appeared only posthumously.[20] Perhaps more than anything else he wrote, it reflected the range of his life.

Toland's conflicted emotions about his own sense of Irishness charged the project. In 1708, when a French bishop publicly derogated him as illegitimate, he traveled to Prague to charm a pedigree from some exiled Irish friars. They showed him 'the most zealous affection of Country-men' and without naming his father or any other relation certified that his was an Irish ancestry not merely ancient and honourable but noble.[21] Six words that he wrote in the margin of a volume in 1720 offered an even more poignant glint of the injured sense of Irishness that underlay his obscuring and insecure self-fashionings. He scrutinised *A Description of the Western Islands of Scotland* because the ruins, language, and ethnography of the Hebrides, like those of Ireland, were a palimpsest of the world of the heathen Celts.[22] Where the book mentioned an islander who went to Glasgow but 'long'd to see his Native Country', Toland, a generation away from a similar voyage, wrote, 'I love him dearly for this'.[23] Toland never surrendered either his cosmopolitan or his English self, but he seemed late in life to desire to find in Celtic Ireland ancestors whose rites and ceremonies a reasonable man like himself could retain.

In 1720, he was also eyeing contemporary Irish politics. Robert Viscount Molesworth, the adult Toland's one stable connection to Ireland, approached William King, the Protestant archbishop of Dublin. Molesworth urged King to employ Toland to write against an English statute denying the Irish House of Lords appellate jurisdiction. A few months earlier, Toland conceded that until recently among 'our Countrymen... I was a greater stranger... than to most Nations of Europe'.[24] Although he then denied 'that Philosophy has eradicated all prejudices in favour of my native soil', he attributed 'the small efforts whereby

I have endeavored to serve Ireland... rather... [to] those principles which teach me what is due to all mankind, than... [to] any byas to that Kingdom, in which I have spent so little of my time'. Among his cosmopolitan principles was a conventional justification of English domination. As much as some of the oligarchs, Toland was indignant that at Westminster Ireland's Protestant 'conquerors should be as ill treated, if not worse, than the conquer'd' Irish Catholics.

Toland's assertion of his previous 'small efforts' in service to the Irish political nation was in any case inflationary. For decades, he slighted the affairs of the island. In 1701, it was probably he, writing anonymously in an English voice, who urged the union of England and Scotland.[25] The parliamentary system he proposed made it 'requisite that the Names of *English*, *Scots* and *Irish* should be disus'd' and replaced with 'Britains', the self-description then favoured by the Scots: '[T]he distinction should be *South*, *North*, and *West-Britains*'.[26] Nearly five of the twenty-three pages of the pamphlet dealt with Scotland, but just a single paragraph glanced at Ireland. Toland, still writing in his English voice, objected 'that our own Offspring who conquer'd that Country... should be look'd upon to be in the same condition with the native *Irish* whom they conquer'd and lose the Birthright of *Englishmen*'. Sixteen years later, he offered 'a particular account' of Great Britain that in the course of over one hundred pages barely alluded to Ireland.[27]

Archbishop King recalled Toland from 1697 as hostile to the oligarchy, ignorant of Ireland, and prone to mix 'wickednesse and thoughtlessnesse'.[28] By 1720, Toland seemed far more louche. King nonetheless indulged Molesworth and acquiesced in Toland's ghostwriting on behalf of those who anachronistically but plausibly can be termed Anglo-Irish.[29] The anonymous tract produced by Toland suggested his distance from present-day Ireland. He was fresh from constructing the identity once shared by all the heathen Celtic-speaking peoples of Europe. He also remembered too well the early 1690s, when alarmed by the spectre of papist hordes rallying to restore James II, the English oligarchs muted their aversion to the Scots Ulstermen and trumpeted Protestant unity. And so he warned that the offensive statute might yield a perverse result. If Irish Protestants lost their traditional rights, they could discover a community of interests with the subjugated natives. In Toland's imagination, a terrible Irish identity threatened to be born.[30]

In Dublin, however, a papist revanche seemed increasingly improbable. The oligarchy, secure as the political nation, reverted to their wonted disdain for the Ulster Scots. Safer political boundaries between the Anglo-Irish and the Catholics moved some oligarchs to redefine the terms of their relationship with the subject majority and therefore to redefine their own identity. Justifications of their ascendancy based on the contingent fact of conquest appeared insubstantial. Rather, many of them began to view the natives, particularly the barbarous and anachronistic Gaelic-speakers, as incapable of achieving their own empowering and essentially English civility.[31] In 1718, Toland retained enough of the cosmopolitan's – or conqueror's – air of cultural superiority to look down on the majority of Ireland as 'the present ignorant vulgar' or 'the common people'.[32] But he also felt some of the sting of the English condescension he sought to imitate.[33] In the 'Specimen' he subverted it by depicting Celtic Ireland's living memories as a fair reflection of the ancient past common to all the British isles.[34] He thereby both exploited and fostered the emerging English vogue of the earlier Gaelic cultures.[35]

In Ireland during Toland's lifetime, Protestant English-speakers, the Anglicans and Presbyterians with whom he sometimes identified himself, were unsure of their own Irishness. Each group possessed its own cultural dialect, but apart from the tropes of anti-popery they lacked a cultural language to unite them as the Protestant people of Ireland. They addressed the other living people of Ireland as their hereditary subalterns and were generally mute or contemptuous before Ireland's ancient Celtic people. English-speaking Protestants lacked a standard account of the Irish past either to inform or to inhibit Toland's historical imagination. Knowledge of the ancient Celtic culture was rudimentary. Even the fundamental concept of the prehistoric was wanting. Representing the alien world of the druids invited Toland's artifices of theory, erudition, and memory.

Hence he freely asserted his 'monological authority' over that world and described it in his own terms.[36] He was neither the first to interpret the druids as profound sages nor the last to interpret much of Irish history as a profound stasis.[37] For innumerable centuries the druids' heathen empire extended from the Mediterranean northward across Ireland, Scotland, Wales, and England, and Toland found its memory and authority still lambent along the insular fringes, including his native Donegal.[38] Leaving there, he acquired the classical learning and perspective he needed to construct a universally and eternally valid theory of religious experience. By imposing it on selected Greek and Roman references to the druids of ancient Gaul (nowhere did those sources mention Irish druids), snatches from medieval Irish manuscripts and from seventeenth-century histories, his knowledge of the several Celtic 'dialects' and oral literatures, travelers' accounts of living peoples and surviving monuments, as well as his own memories of Ireland, Toland willed to life British prehistory.[39] Propelling his effort was his masterful imagination, which earlier enabled him to transform a millenarian regicide into a sententious Augustan gentleman, to refine a seventeenth-century writer's 'peculiarly rebarbative' prose, to efface the Catholicism of a general history of the Irish people when it was translated into English, and to invent for himself both a heathen baptismal name and an aristocratic ancestry.[40]

Toland's work was 'intended for modern instances', among which was evoking the heathenism of the primordial Irish identity captured in the aboriginal language and customs of the people he sometimes chose to call his 'Country-men'.[41] His 'critical history' of the mores of the ancient Celts exposed the lost cosmopolitanism of the heathen peoples of the Atlantic archipelago, thus not only indicting Christians' sanguinary factiousness but also vindicating his own diverse life and perhaps easing his sense of alienation. In antiquity, no boundaries of religion and language separated the people of Ireland, Scotland, and England from one another or, indeed, from their fellow Celts on the Continent, any more than bastardy and a papist and Gaelic-speaking rearing bounded Toland's own identity. From Donegal, he advanced by way of Scotland to the republic of letters and a career championing English liberties and encouraging the better, reasonable capabilities of English Protestants. Janus Junius (later John) Toland's life seemed to recapitulate the world of the pagan Celts, free of any pales that defined transgressions and stigmatised transgressors.

Basic to Toland's monological authority over the druids was the long-developing universal theory of religious experience that he constructed from classical sources. His theory suggests that none of the schools claiming descent from Leo Strauss need exist. Toland could have invented them all. His reading of the ancients and his experience of modern Ireland left him as certain as that masterful savant that, since the death of Socrates, many philosophers defended themselves against persecution by using indirect expression, or 'secret writing'.[42] In the last book Toland published on religion, he related a story that captured his point:

> I have more than once hinted, that the External and Internal Doctrine, are as much now in use as ever; tho the distinction is not so openly and professedly approv'd, as among the Ancients. This puts me in mind of what I was told by a near relation to the old Lord Shaftesbury. The latter conferring one day with Major Wildman about the many sects of Religion in the world, they came to this conclusion at last; that notwithstanding those infinite divisions caus'd by the interest of the Priests and the ignorance of the People, All Wise Men Are of the Same Religion: whereupon a Lady in the room... demanded with some concern what that Religion was? to whom the Lord Shaftesbury strait reply'd, Madam, wise men never tell. And indeed, considering how dangerous it is made to tell the truth, 'tis difficult to know when any man declares his real sentiments of things.[43]

Toland's conviction of his own metaphysical identity with the wise ancients precluded a sense of either the pathos of their historical distance from himself or the jaggedness of historical development.[44]

It was perhaps inevitable that a conflicted Irish flamboyant became the most articulate early-modern theorist of philosophical discretion. Toland's libertinism was precocious and alienating. Just out of university, he was reportedly 'arraigned and convicted' by other revelers in an Oxford coffee house for burning a copy of the Book of Common Prayer.[45] The explicit radicalness of his early free-thought remains arguable. Within a few months of arriving in Oxford, he was considered a man of 'little religion', which he took to mean either 'an Atheist or Deist'.[46] Toland apparently succeeded in persuading an intrusive well-wisher that he was 'an Orthodox believer'.[47] Then he was perhaps readying an anonymous tract that insinuated both the rejection of the supernatural as superstition, reminiscent of the Epicurean Lucretius, and the vision of an all-informing and unifying deity like that portrayed by the Stoic Manilius, ancient poets whose works were on his mind.[48] Toland kept a copy of *De rerum natura* in the room where he died.[49] His mature cosmology, derived from various ancient sources that he interpreted with the aid of texts of Giordano Bruno and perhaps Thomas Hobbes and Baruch Spinoza, was naturalist and materialist. Its rational principle, known to an elite of sages and legislators throughout history, was that the universe, visible, tangible, and eternally self-moving, was the one god.[50]

In the beginning, Toland sought to disseminate that principle indirectly by establishing that the human ability to form and express clear and distinct ideas defined reality. It followed that true ideas of God must be as limpid as those of material objects. While finishing *Christianity Not Mysterious*, he was cautioned to expect trouble for laying 'all the deep and hidden things of God... open to the meanest capacities'.[51] He ignored the warning. *Christianity Not Mysterious* essayed completing the correlative accommodation of Anglicanism and rationalism so attractively advanced by some recent Latitudinarian divines. Extrapolating from both their hermeneutics and the monist implications of contemporary Unitarian tracts, Toland privileged a single method for reading every kind of text. He offered a single-minded interpretation of some elements of that epistemology but carefully avoided specifying its implications for metaphysics. It was enough to insist on the insupportableness of the paradox attending every effort to use ordinary human language to know the transcendent. Epistemological naturalism both enabled Toland and other members of the elite to be publicly tenacious of the English establishment and brought 'Advantage to the Vulgar' literate by disabusing them.[52]

Toland asserted that it was 'evident to any that can read, that *Mystery* in the whole *New Testament* is never put for *any thing inconceivable in it self, or not to be judg'd of by our ordinary Notions and Faculties, however clearly reveal'd*'; instead, mystery always signified '*some things naturally intelligible enough*'.[53] He also scorned the ancients, who 'all made high Pretences to some rare and wonderful

Secrets not communicable to every one of the Learned, and never to any of the Vulgar'.[54] The binary implications of his primary concept of reason were clear. Revelation confirmed only what was always and everywhere naturally intelligible, and natural intelligibility was the norm for determining the truth of the allegedly supernatural.[55] Because *'Religion is always the same, like God its Author*, with whom there is no Variableness, nor Shadow of changing', any purportedly new revelation was unnatural, mere nescience and superstition.[56]

Toland fled Dublin with his hope of disabusing 'the Vulgar' permanently abridged. Modern Christian Ireland once again demonstrated that there was a permanent division between masters and subalterns paralleling that between reason and superstition. He dropped as impossible his plan for two sequels to *Christianity Not Mysterious,* in which he proposed first to explain and then to vindicate what he knew to be the rational content of the Gospel.[57] Instead he concentrated on political writing. He edited, or reshaped, the works of many of the seventeenth-century English commonwealthmen and wrote biographies of a few of them. Those works provided the core of 'the republican canon of the eighteenth century'.[58] Central to Toland's project was the conviction that social hierarchy was inevitable and ramifying in its consequences. He boxed in the democratic aspirations of his chosen authors to make their ideas more respectable. Unlike them, he urged achieving a wider diffusion of power within the restricted English political nation more than expanding its ranks.[59]

Without abandoning radical Whiggery, he came to embrace an ancient theory with direct implications for contemporary politics and religion. In every society there were a few reasonable guardians and the unreasonable many whom they must guard. Like all who ever embraced that bifurcating distinction, Toland was impervious to any temptation to identify either himself with the majority or his ideas with theirs. Possessing 'at the font' a noble ancestry and an impeccably classical and pagan name, schooled in the classics and liberated by reason, Toland was one of the privileged cognoscenti.[60] By right, he belonged to the reasonable, learned, and free elite who, throughout history, were at once threatened by and responsible for 'the Vulgar': irrational, ignorant, and potentially lethal in their credulity.[61]

Even when writing in Latin for other 'Wise Men', Toland usually evaded fully and unambiguously owning his cosmology. A veil of intertextuality protected it. For example, in a pamphlet ostensibly defending the accuracy of the classical geographer Strabo, he wrote, 'Mosem enimvero suisse Pantheistam, sive, ut cum recentioribus loquar, Spinosistam' ('Moses himself was in truth a pantheist, or to speak according to more recent usage, a Spinozist').[62] In the same paragraph, Toland quoted from Cicero's *De natura deorum* to imply that Moses' religion was shared by all wise but discreet ancients. Interpreting their esoteric belief and specifying its 'more recent usage' enabled Toland to instruct and to encourage other wise moderns competent to grasp the 'Internal Doctrine'. To see how he read Cicero and the Roman Stoic Varro is to penetrate the intertextuality with which he covered the modern intentions of his classicism.

After over 1700 years, Cicero was for Toland still 'the greatest Philosopher' and more erudite than anyone except Varro, 'that prodigy of knowledge and *perpetual opposer of superstition*'.[63] Toland aspired to edit 'the divine volumes of Cicero' and reverently cited them, including *De natura deorum*, which he came to read as confirming his own interpretation of the surviving fragments of Varro's *Antiquitates rerum divinarum*.[64] During the late Republic, the clash between the moral and intellectual gaucheries of the inherited Roman religion and the polite and skeptical qualities of Greek philosophy challenged patriotic philhellenists like Cicero and Varro to achieve a reconciliation. Cicero therefore hailed Varro for leading the wandering citizens of Rome 'right home' by establishing 'the laws of its religion and its priesthoods... the terminology, classifications and moral and rational basis of all our religious and secular institutions'.[65]

Varro assumed both that politics legitimated religion and that an official religion imaging the cosmic order legitimated the *res publica*. There were potentially three levels of religion: the hopelessly mythical invented by the poets; the politically functional created by the state, which preserved enough poetic residues to appease the incorrigible irrationality of the many; and the objectively true discovered by the philosophers, for whom the cosmos was a vast, unified organism that could be seen as both material and spiritual. Scouting the inherited poetic religion, Varro considered it possible in the abstract to make civil religion virtually identical with the truth known to the few. In practice, however, the best that could be done to refine the Roman cult was to increase its philosophical credibility by reducing its quantity of myth. The result would be truthful, though not completely true, and required that the wise elite use doses of allegory as an intellectual analgesic.

Despite considerable equivocation and seeming hesitation, Toland eventually accepted that Varro's layered theology captured the permanent differentiation of humanity's religious experience.[66] After 1700, Toland made explicit the metaphysical implications of his naturalist epistemology. He also looked to circumstances to determine how far the 'external' religious doctrine of the English commonwealth was adaptable to the 'internal' doctrine of the perennial philosophy. The menacing outrage evoked by *Christianity Not Mysterious* proved that wisdom was fragile, priestcraft recrudescent, and credulity enthralling.[67] His initial optimism about uprooting popular superstition gave way to pessimism, only to stir again, though with reduced fervor. Even when his disdain for 'the Vulgar' grew vehement, he remained a civil theologian, more ambitious than a self-protective theological liar.[68]

During the years after he fled Dublin, he remained alert to questions of divinity. In 1698, he acquired a copy of Bruno's *The Expulsion of the Triumphant*

Beast, which mingled plaints for the true religious insight of ancient heathens, including the druids, with excoriation of Christian outrages.[69] Toland cherished and perhaps translated the book and mechanised its cosmology into his own pantheism: 'there is in it a complete system of natural law' ('il y a un systeme complet de la loi naturelle').[70] By 1700, he enjoyed occasional literary contact with Pierre Bayle, who once admitted him to the sanctuary of a footnote in the great *Dictionnaire* to assert that matter could think.[71] Some of Bayle's paradoxical texts helped to define the context of Toland's mature discourse about religion. In 1704, Bayle published a book describing what he imagined to be 'the omnipresence of Spinozism in the history of philosophy'.[72] Against Jean LeClerc, Bayle was then vigorously defending the thesis that immanentist cosmologies, including all forms of paganism, were effectively materialist.[73] In response to Bayle and with rash disregard for the burden of the weightiest contemporary scholarship, LeClerc retrieved and serialised excerpts from Ralph Cudworth's *True Intellectual System of the Universe* (1678). The book was the swan song of efforts to vindicate the truth of Christianity by demonstrating that it commanded virtually universal consent. With imperious erudition, Cudworth labored to prove that classical polytheism both derived from and led to monotheism and that even ancient speculative atheists effectively presumed the one true God worshipped by Christians and, before them, Jews.[74]

Toland's intervention in the controversy was the *Letters to Serena.* Using an epigraph from Cicero's *De natura deorum* as an imprimatur, he inverted Cudworth's interpretation and sketched a metanarrative of the fall from the primordial light of reason into the chiaroscuro of superstition.[75] Toland also insinuated the perennially true religion of the elite, the ancient rational theology universally known to pantheists. In Egypt, when civilisation dawned, priests, always sinuous and often sinister, exploited the blinding force of prejudice to invent the 'Doctrin of Spirits' and to foster the illusion that the soul is immortal.[76] Prejudice, moreover, undergirded every other manifestation of idolatry. Professing to confute Spinozism while in fact improving on it, Toland insisted that motion was essential to matter.[77] The wise ancients knew as much. It was the 'Discovery of the same perpetual and universal Action, that gave a Being to the Systems of the Stoics, Plastics, Hylozoics, and others'.[78] And an immanentist, materialist religion still prevailed nearly everywhere: 'The present Heathens, who inhabit the greatest part of Africa, vast Tracts of Asia, almost all America, and some few corners of Europe, agree with the Antients in their Opinions'.[79]

Thereafter, Toland continued his project of insinuating a British civil religion relieved of superstition, even as he revealed more and more of his own construction of the perennially true religion of the wise.[80] In *Adeisidaemon* (1709), for example, he maintained against Bayle that a few widespread but harmless superstitions were tolerable in a commonwealth, unlike open 'atheism, which pertains to a few individuals' ('denique ad paucos').[81] Paradoxically, *Adeisidae-mon* means 'without superstition'. Continuously paginated with that text is *Origines Judaicae*, where Toland represented Moses as an adept of the esoteric pantheism of the Egyptian hierophants. One learned contemporary read Toland's argument as 'capable of overturning religion' ('capables de bouleverser la Religion').[82]

Pantheisticon, Toland's penultimate discourse about religion, included the Latin 'philosophical canon' of a modern Socratic Society. It evoked litanies as old as Egypt and linked the modern Socratics with the ancient druids in the communion of reason.

> The Pantheists can deservedly be stiled the 'Mysts' and 'Hierophants' of Nature; for as formerly the 'Druids, Men of an elevated Genius, kept up to the Strictness of their brotherly Union, (as the Authority of Pythagoras has decreed) so also they are versed in the Knowledge of the most abstruse Things, and their Minds are lifted up by the Contemplation of the Sublimest Mysteries.' The *Socratic Companions* strenuously ruminate upon the same Studies, for which the *Druids* and *Pythagorics* made themselves so illustrious, both instituted Societies, yet the *Pantheists* allow not all their Words and Deeds; for where they depart from Truth, there we also depart from them, praising voluntarily what we approve of, and giving Thanks to those, by whose Labour we have in any Share benefited ourselves.[83]

Toland was, however, more than Sarastro with a brogue. The double implication of the name 'Socratic' remained serious and apposite. A martyr to popular superstition, Socrates taught by evoking the permanent truths that reasonable beings everywhere implicitly knew. An essentially static theory about religion (which was also an educational agenda coloured by Toland's conflicted sense of Irishness), aversion to Christianity, restrictive Whiggery, and identification with the reasonable world of classical paganism informed his 'critical history' of the druids.

The text of the 'Specimen of the Critical History of the Celtic Religion and Learning' included three sections of approximately equal length, framed as letters to the Viscount Molesworth. Three basically philological appendices completed the work. In the first and most complex section, Toland set forth his general interpretation of the druids' role in the ancient Celtic culture and sought to establish the importance of his subject, as well as his own unique competence to study it. Although he deprecated the learned ancients' reliance on 'emblems and allegories' when writing about religion and eschewed 'deviating ever so little from plain truth', he himself used allegory to read double truths into some primary myths.[84] Any straightforward reading of mythology would defeat his effort to establish that there existed a perennial, essentially rational philosophy whose adepts included the druids. Hence he relied on 'that most judicious writer about the nature of the gods', Cornutus (fl. 60 C.E.), a major Stoic allegoriser.[85] Ruins dominated the second section, where Toland cataloged many of the druidical 'carns', still visible throughout the British isles and on the Continent. Primary among them was Stonehenge, 'according to me one of the Druid cathedrals'.[86] The third section drew heavily on his own memories, observations, and often strikingly original interpretations of ancient myths. Digressions punctuated the 'Specimen', but his rhetorical flair, single-mindedness, and nerve sustained the flow of his basic arguments. The combative style Toland learned as a theological student and mastered during a career of religious polemics suited his quick intelligence and rich inventiveness.

The earliest recorded reading of the 'Specimen' was alert. A manuscript of the first section came into the hands of the Lord Chancellor of England, who said that it was something 'he did not understand, but wch he suspected to be level'd against Christian Priests, &c'.[87] Near the end of the section Toland paid tribute to the druids as 'men thus sacred in their function, illustrious in their alliances, eminent for their learning, and honour'd for their valor, as well as dreaded for their power and influence'.[88] That artfully balanced eulogy exemplified his technique of offsetting condemnation of the druids' enormities with praise for their achievements. Toland knew that despite their sometimes nasty 'priestcraft', they possessed the 'internal', philosophical religion that distinguished 'All Wise Men' throughout the ages.

He was thus able to read the classical accounts of the druids selectively enough to advert with bare disapproval to their ritual sacrifice and burning of 'criminals and victims'.[89] Whatever the druids' priestly enormities, they were essentially rational. They held the 'two grand doctrines of the eternity and incorruptibility of the universe, and the incessant revolution of all beings and forms', the timeless, reasonable pantheism that was 'very figuratively expressed' in their civil theology as *allanimation* and *transmigration*'.[90] The Gallic proto-druids' knowledge was so precocious and formidable that even 'the ancient Greecs' learned philosophy from them.[91] Toland began the first section by indicting the druids for their virtual popery, as a 'heathen priestcraft... [in] perfection', unrivaled in antiquity in 'the art of managing the mob, which is vulgarly called *leading the people by the nose*', but he closed it by paying tribute to the druids as a group and especially praising as 'a great man' an Irish 'chief druid' whom he called 'Bacrach'.[92] Toland went on to present a roll of Irish druids.[93] Even today, all druids remain buried in the namelessness of prehistory.

In contrast, he was steadily cool toward known Irish 'Christian Priests' of every historical period and denomination. He dropped his recent distinction between early-medieval Ireland's reasonable pre-Roman and superstitious Romanising Christians, as well as the parallel distinction between modern Ireland's Protestant conquerors and their Catholic subalterns. Absent were the expressions of respect for 'Holy men' that marked his recent evocation of early Irish Christianity, and Archbishop Ussher was demoted from scholarly 'glory' and given short correction.[94] Mimicking Ussher's favorable estimate of the fundamental reasonableness of the ancient Irish, Toland insinuated that there was a stark, primeval, and enduring contrast between ancient heathen Irish learning and subsequent Christian Irish ignorance: 'there florish'd a great number of Druids, Bards, Vaids, and other authors, in Ireland, long before Patric's arrival; whose learning was not only more extensive, but also much more useful than that of their christian posterity'.[95]

It was 'Patric', moreover, who first inflicted on Ireland the Christian ritual of book-burning by firing numerous 'volumes, relating to the affairs of the Druids'. A report of that primal conflagration roused in Toland memories of alarm.

> What an irreparable destruction of history, what a deplorable extinction of arts and inventions, what an unspeakable detriment to learning, what a dishonor upon human understanding, has the cowardly proceeding of the ignorant, or rather of the interested, against unarm'd monuments at all times occasion'd! And yet this book-burning and letter-murdring humor, tho far from being commanded by Christ, has prevail'd in christianity from the beginning.[96]

Toland's eloquence was riveting, but here as elsewhere in the 'Specimen' his history was imaginative, even mythopoeic.[97] Notoriously, the ancient Irish language was completely unwritten until very late, and the druids jealously protected that illiteracy. Christian scribes, moreover, were apparently uninhibited about writing down what before them was pagan oral literature.[98] Toland ingeniously labored to prove that the druids possessed 'the secret of writing', and even asserted that with the triumph of Christianity the ancient script became generally unintelligible and 'the *secret of writing*, came to signify *secret writing*'.[99] Despite all that, there existed no volumes relating to the affairs of the druids for 'Patric' or any other 'book-burning and letter-murdring' Christian priest to burn.

The 'Specimen' was 'intended for modern instances', but its rich mythopoeia recalls the ancient genre of *gēographia*. Classical writers like Strabo, whom Toland praised as 'one of the foremost authors in my esteem', rummaged for stories 'they thought credible enough to claim a reader's attention', and they therefore not only tried 'to separate fact from fiction' but also 'often retold even those [tales] they deemed incredible'.[100] Profoundly alienated from Christian modernity and searching for congenial intellectual roots, Toland, for his part, aimed to write a 'history... which, tho' a piece of general learning and great curiosity' was also 'no less entertaining than instructive to all sorts of readers'.[101] Long before the nineteenth-century Romantics, countercultural thinkers in search of a congenial and usable past innocent of Christianity were inventing traditions.

Toland saved his most arcane myth for last. He concluded the 'Specimen' with a twenty-eight page essay associating the Hebrides with the mythical land of the fortunate Hyperboreans, and identifying Abaris, a mysterious shaman and savior figure of Greek myth, as a druid.[102] Possibly the essay was a satiric allegory on modern English pretensions to cultural superiority over the aboriginal Celtic-speaking peoples of the British isles, for Toland eulogised the supposed druid Abaris 'as a philosopher of the Brittish world'.[103] Perhaps Toland also satirised Christian pretensions to superiority over the pagans. He quoted from Horace's sixteenth Epode, long associated with Virgil's fourth Eclogue, which Alexander Pope and Samuel Johnson still treated as a pagan oracle of the birth of the Messiah.[104] In the 'Specimen', Horace's poem became as much a plaint for the 'barbarous' world of the heathen druids (perhaps superior in virtue and wisdom 'to our modern ideas' and still discoverable in the Celtic-speaking corners of modern Europe) as it was an escapist fantasy about the eighteenth-century Hebrides.[105] An irony thus animated Toland's effort to 'revive and illustrate the memory of the Druids'.[106] By insisting on obtaining clarity where clarity was unobtainable, he who once proposed to evacuate all mystery from Christianity became the mythologist of a fundamentally reasonable Celtic paganism.

Toland thus helped to complete a protracted intellectual reversal that, as I hope to show elsewhere, shaped the metanarrative of European history that was dominant until the day before yesterday. By 1719, when he finished the 'Specimen', the researches of generations of learned Christians, mostly philologists, had subverted imperious assumptions that there existed a seamless metaphysical continuity between classical paganism and modern Christianity. Among those scholars were Toland's contemporaries Richard Bentley, Jean Mabillon, Pierre Bayle, and Bernard de Montfaucon. Slowly and cumulatively, but also uneasily and inconsistently, they and their predecessors and successors first questioned and then yielded the longstanding Christian mastery over the interpretation of the texts of classical paganism.[107] By 1700, it was incredible to the most acute Christian *érudits* that everything instructive in pagan thought once prefigured Christianity, now belonged to Christianity, and thus deserved to be remembered primarily in Christian terms.

A coincidence epitomised that reversal. Several months after Toland, in suburban London, confidently finished recreating the druids' religion and learning in the image and likeness of his own concept of timeless reason, in faraway Naples a more devout reader of Varro arrived at a jarring conclusion about the ancients' asserted rationality. With incredulity, Giambattista Vico discovered that facing the most remote past required him 'to descend from our own humane and cultivated natures to those quite wild and savage natures that we cannot at all imagine and can understand only with great effort'.[108] Vico's sense of dissilience partook of historical understanding. Toland for his part exploited such dissilience to invert Cudworth's encompassing and ahistorical Christian reading of ancient thought and to fashion from Varro and Cicero an equally seamless genealogy that made all the wise ancients, including the druids, his philosophical ancestors.

For nearly three centuries thereafter, the antithesis between classical pagan reason and subsequent Christian superstition informed more learned, subtle and credible histories of the intellectual descent and progress of Europe and its cultural provinces. With greater or lesser confidence and clarity, all those stories about what by 1800 was identified as civilisation asserted that a modern European elite had recovered and improved the essential rationality which the wisest ancient heathens possessed but Christians later repudiated.[109] The historical vision that animated John Toland's deeply personal evocation of the druids' world proved to be curiously attractive, powerful, and tenacious.

Notes

1   John Toland, *Christianity Not Mysterious* (1696) (Reprint, Stuttgart, 1964), p. ix. The account of Toland's biography draws on Robert E. Sullivan, *John Toland and the Deist Controversy: A Study in Adaptations* (Cambridge, MA, 1982), pp. 1-50.

2   John Toland, *The Art of Governing by Partys* (London, 1701), pp. 145-6.

3   Pierre Des Maizeaux (ed.), 'Some Memoirs of the Life and Writings of Mr. John Toland', *A Collection of Several Pieces of Mr. John Toland* 2 vols. (London, 1726), I: v.

4   King to Tenison (13 October 1697), King Papers, Trinity College Dublin, N.3.1, f. 86.

5   John Toland, *An Apology for Mr. Toland* (London, 1697), p. 35.

6   Toland, *Apology*, pp. 25-6.

7   John Toland, *A Defense of Mr. Toland in a Letter to Himself* (London, 1697), p. 14.

8   John Toland, *Pantheisticon: or, the Form of Celebrating the Socratic Society* (1720), trans. anonymous, (London, 1751), p. 87, paraphrasing Cicero, *De divinatione* 2.148.

9   Compare Stephen H. Daniel, 'The Subversive Philosophy of John Toland' in Paul Hyland and Neil Sammells (eds.), *Irish Writing: Exile and Subversion* (New York, 1991), pp. 8-11; Richard Kearney, *Postnationalist Ireland: Politics, Culture, Philosophy* (London, 1997), pp. 93-4, 157-68; Pierre Lurbe, 'John

Toland, Cosmopolitanism, and the Concept of Nation' in Michael O'Dea and Kevin Whelan (eds.), *Nations and Nationalisms: France, Britain, Ireland and the Eighteenth-Century Context* (Oxford, 1995), pp. 251-9; Philip McGuinness, 'Looking for a Mainland: John Toland and Irish Politics' in Philip McGuinness, Alan Harrison, Richard Kearney (eds.), *John Toland's Christianity Not Mysterious: Text, Associated Works and Critical Essays* (Dublin, 1997), pp. 261-92.

10   Toland, *Pantheisticon*, p. 33. The title page of the original Latin edition (*Pantheisticon, sive formula celebrande sodalitatis Socraticae*), which was printed in London, bears the imprint 'Cosmopoli, 1720'. Here, as in so many other places, Toland is cryptic. Is 'Cosmopoli' equivalent to London, or an aspect of London, or a London that might be or might have been, or just no place? In contrast, his description in the preface of 1720 as 'Anno aerae vulgaris' is transparent.

11   Cf. Toland, *Art of Governing*, pp. 34, 48-9, 54; *Limitations for the Next Foreign Successor, or New Saxon Race. Debated in a Conference betwixt Two Gentlemen. Sent in a Letter to a Member of Parliament* (London, 1701), p. 18; *The Grand Mystery Laid Open* (London, 1714), pp. 5-6; *The State-Anatomy of Great Britain* (London, 1717), pp. 19, 22, 49, 50, 58, 80, 93.

12   Compare Anne Goldgar, *Impolite Learning: Conduct and Community in the Republic of Letters, 1680-1750* (New Haven, 1995), p. 158, and, more generally, pp. 150-73, with Thomas Hearne, *Remarks and Collections of Thomas Hearne*, ed. C.E. Doble, 11 vols. (Oxford, 1885-1921), XI: 395.

13   Compare John Barrell, *Poetry, Language, and Politics* (Manchester, 1988), and Linda Colley, 'Britishness and Otherness: An Argument', *Journal of British Studies* Vol. 31 (1992), pp. 309-29.

14   Lhwyd to Aubrey (9 January 1693/4), *Life and Letters of Edward Lhwyd* in R.W.T. Gunther (gen. ed.), *Early Science in Oxford*, 15 vols. (Oxford, 1923-1945), XIV: 217.

15   Toland, *Nazarenus: or, Jewish, Gentile, and Mahometan Christianity.... With An Account of an Irish Manuscript of the Four Gospels; with A Summary of the ancient IRISH CHRISTIANITY, before the Papal Corruptions and Usurpations* in Gesine Palmer, *Ein Freispruch für Paulus: John Tolands Theorie des Judenchristums mit einer Neuausgabe von Tolands 'Nazarenus' von Claus-Michael Palmer* (Berlin, 1996), pp. 15-6, 101-31. Dr. Justin Champion of the Royal Holloway College, University of London, is preparing what promises to be the definitive critical edition of the work.

16   Toland draws on Ussher's *Veterum epistolarum Hibernicarum sylloge* (Dublin, 1632), for which see 'Books in My Room...October 1720', British Library, Add. MS. 4295, f. 41; for praise of Ussher's scholarship see *Nazarenus*, pp. 102, 109, and for the recommendation see p. 16.

17   Toland, *Nazarenus*, p. 109; on pp. 111-121 he set forth under seventeen headings, 'A SUMMARY OF THE ANCIENT IRISH CHRISTIANITY'.

18   Toland, *Nazarenus*, pp. 16, 110.

19   Toland, *Nazarenus*, p. 110.

20   It was first printed in *A Collection of Several Pieces of Mr. John Toland*, I: 1-228. Citations are to Robert Huddleston (ed.), *A new edition of Toland's History of the Druids* (Montrose, 1814), which reproduces the 1726 text with supplementary material. For the genesis of the work, compare *History of the Druids*, pp. 51-2, and Alan Harrison, 'John Toland and Celtic Studies' in C.J. Byrne, M. Harry and P. O'Siadhail (eds.), *Celtic Languages and Celtic Peoples: Proceedings of the Second North American Congress of Celtic Studies* (Halifax, NS, 1992), p. 564.

21   The certificate appears in Des Maizeaux, 'Some Memoirs', *A Collection*, I: v-vi; for the visit to Prague, see Toland to *** (January 1708), in *A Collection*, II: 381-2.

22   Martin Martin, *A Description of the Western Islands of Scotland*, (2nd ed., London, 1716). Toland's copy is in the British Library C.45.c.1; see the comment at pp. 159-60.

23   Martin, *Description*, p. 288, with marginal comment.

24   The paragraph quotes and summarises Toland to Southwell (27 April 1720), in *A Collection*, II: 458-60.

25   Toland, *Limitations*, p. 18.

26   Toland, *Limitations*, p. 18; c.f. David Hayton, 'Anglo-Irish Attitudes: Changing Perceptions of National Identity among the Protestant Ascendancy in Ireland, ca. 1690-1750', *Studies in Eighteenth-Century Culture* Vol. 17 (1987), pp. 151-2.

27   Toland, *State-Anatomy*, pp. 49-51.

28   Patrick Kelly, 'A Pamphlet Attributed to John Toland and an Unpublished Reply by Archbishop William King', *Topoi* Vol. 4 (1985), pp. 81-90.

29   King to Molesworth (10 and 29 September 1720), King Papers, Trinity College Dublin, N.3.6, ff. 117-9, 124-5.

30   John Toland, *Reasons Most humbly offer'd to the Honble House of Commons* (London, 1720), pp. 5, 8-10, 23.

31   Nicholas Canny, 'Identity Formation in Ireland: The Emergence of the Anglo-Irish' in Nicholas Canny and Anthony Pagden (eds.), *Colonial Identity in the Atlantic World, 1500-1800* (Princeton, 1987), pp. 159-212; David Hayton, 'From Barbarian to Burlesque: English Images of the Irish, c. 1660-1750', *Irish Economic and Social History* Vol. 15 (1988), pp. 5-31; Jacqueline R. Hill, 'Popery and Protestantism, Civil and Religious Liberty: The Disputed Lessons of Irish History', *Past & Present* No. 118 (1988), pp. 96-129; Thomas Bartlett, 'Protestant Nationalism in Eighteenth-Century Ireland' in

Nations and Nationalisms, pp. 79-88; Patrick Kelly, 'Nationalism and the Contemporary Historians of the Jacobite War in Ireland' in *Nations and Nationalisms*, pp. 89-102; Joseph McMinn, 'Hottentots and Teagues: Swift and Barbarous Nations' in *Nations and Nationalisms*, pp. 297-305; T.C. Barnard, 'Protestants and the Irish Language, c. 1675-1725,' *Journal of Ecclesiastical History* Vol. 44 (1993), pp. 243-272; Jim Smyth, '"Like Amphibious Animals": Irish Protestants, Ancient Britons, 1691-1707', *Historical Journal* Vol. 36 (1993), pp. 785-97.

32   Toland, *History of the Druids*, pp. 70, 130-1.

33   Toland, *History of the Druids*, pp. 52-55, 60-1, 93, 134-6, 147-9.

34   Toland, *History of the Druids*, pp. 176-82.

35   A.L. Owen, *The Famous Druids: A Survey of Three Centuries of English Literature on the Druids* (Oxford, 1962), pp. 27-154, and Stuart Piggott, *The Druids* (New York, 1968), 131-81.

36   Toland, *History of the Druids*, pp. 57, 72, 79-80, 111-2, 135-6, 141, 158-9; cf. p. 161; the phrase comes from James Clifford, 'On Ethnographic Authority', *Representations* Vol. 1, No. 2 (1983), p. 141.

37   For an example of earlier idealisation of the druids, see R.E. Asher, *National Myths in Renaissance France: Francus, Samothes and the Druids* (Edinburgh, 1993), pp. 88-107.

38   Toland, *History of the Druids*, p. 65; compare pp. 52n., 68, 70-1, 75, 93, 113, 120-31, 134, 137, 147, 155, 187-90.

39   Toland, *History of the Druids*, pp. 63-5, 94-5. J.J. Tierney, 'The Celtic Ethnography of Posidonius', *Proceedings of the Royal Irish Academy*, Sec. C, Vol. 60 (1960), pp. 189-275, and Nora K. Chadwick, *The Druids* (Cardiff, 1966), offer competing interpretations of the Greek and Roman sources, with Tierney emphasising the theme of the druids as sanguinary priests and Chadwick the theme of the druids as sages by osmosis with Greek civilisation.

40   A.B. Worden (ed.), *Edmund Ludlow, A Voyce from the Watch Tower: Part Five, 1660-1662*, Camden ser. 4 Vol. 21 (London, 1978), pp. 4, 21-34, 51; David Wootton (ed.), 'Introduction', *Republicanism, Liberty, and Commercial Society, 1649-1776* (Stanford, 1994), p. 31; David Berman and Alan Harrison, 'John Toland and Keating's History of Ireland (1723)', *Donegal Annual*, No. 36 (1984), pp. 25-9, and Hill, 'Popery and Protestantism', pp. 102-3 n.34.

41   Toland, *History of the Druids*, p. 62n.

42   Compare John Toland, *Letters to Serena* (London, 1704), p. 114, and Leo Strauss, *Persecution and the Art of Writing* (Glencoe, IL, 1952), pp. 22-37.

43   'Clidophorus; or of the Exoteric and Esoteric Philosophy, that is, of the External and Internal Doctrine of the Ancients: the one open and public, accommodated to popular Prejudices and the establish'd Religions;

the other private and secret, wherein, to the few capable and discrete, was taught the real TRUTH stript of all disguises' (*Tetradymus* [London, 1720], pp. 94-5). Pierre Lurbe, '*Clidophorus* et la question de la double philosophie', *Revue de synthèse* Vol. 116 (1995), pp. 379-98, is a sophisticated reading of the various messages of the tract.

44 C.f. Toland, *Nazarenus*, p. 131.

45 Gibson to Charlett (9 April 1694), Ballard MSS., Bodleian Library, Oxford, V, f. 27.

46 —— to Toland (4 May 1694), *A Collection*, II: 295, and 'Mr. Toland's Answer', n.d., II: 302.

47 —— to Toland (30 May 1694), *A Collection*, II: 310.

48 Rhoda Rappaport, 'Questions of Evidence: An Anonymous Tract Attributed to John Toland', *Journal of the History of Ideas* Vol. 58 (1997), pp. 339-48, vigorously pummeled my unqualified assertion (*John Toland*, pp. 6, 174-6) that Toland wrote 'L.P., Master of Arts', *Two Essays sent in a Letter from Oxford* (London, 1695). Professor Rappaport properly insisted that there exists no certain external evidence that Toland was the author and that the internal evidence for his authorship is, like all such evidence, necessarily inconclusive. She was, however, unable to identify a more plausible author. Attributing the *Two Essays* to Toland requires no Byzantine strategy of reading. Everything contained there was accessible to Toland in 1694-95. The tract is, moreover, compatible with both the constricting naturalism of *Christianity Not Mysterious* and the essentials of his mature pantheism. For Toland and Lucretius and Manilius, see Toland to —— (Jan. 1694), *A Collection*, II: 294.

49 Toland, 'Books in My Room... October 1720', British Library, Add. MS. 4295, f. 41.

50 Jean Seidengart, 'L'infinitisme panthéiste de Jean Toland et ses relations avec la pensée de Giordano Bruno', *Revue de synthèse* Vol. 116 (1995), pp. 315-43, offers a careful analysis of development of Toland's cosmology from 1704 to 1720.

51 —— to Toland (30 May 1694), *A Collection*, II: 312.

52 Toland, *Christianity Not Mysterious*, pp. xviii-xix. Terry Eagleton, 'Crazy John and the Bishop', *Crazy John and the Bishop and Other Essays on Irish Culture* (Notre Dame, 1998), pp. 46-67, provides a theoretically informed discussion of the politics and aporia of Toland on Language.

53 Toland, *Christianity Not Mysterious*, pp. 111-2 (italics in original).

54 Toland, *Christianity Not Mysterious*, p. 99.

55 Compare Sullivan, *John Toland* pp. 121-4; Stephen H. Daniel, *John Toland: His Method, Manners, and Mind* (Kingston, 1984), pp. 42-57; Joel C. Weinsheimer, *Eighteenth-Century Hermeneutics: Philosophy of Interpretation in England from Locke to Burke* (New Haven, 1993), pp. 46-71; and Frederick C.

Beiser, *The Sovereignty of Reason: The Defense of Rationality in the Early English Enlightenment* (Princeton, 1996), pp. 220-65.

56 Toland, *Christianity Not Mysterious*, p. xiii (italics in the original).

57 Compare Toland, *Christianity Not Mysterious*, pp. xxvi-xxvii, and Toland, *A Defense*, p. 3.

58 Blair Worden, 'Republicanism and the Restoration, 1660-1683', in *Republicanism, Liberty, and Commercial Society*, pp. 177-8, 192-3.

59 Worden, 'Republicanism and the Restoration', pp. 182-3, 185, 443n.133.

60 The classic analysis of secret-keeping as a means of self-inflation is Georg Simmel, 'Secrecy', in Kurt H. Wolff (trans. and ed.), *The Sociology of Georg Simmel* (New York, 1964), pp. 332-3.

61 Compare 'A Letter Concerning the Roman Education' in *A Collection*, II: 4-5, and 'A Memorial Presented to a Minister of State' in *A Collection*, II: 250-1.

62 John Toland, *Adeisidaemon, sive Titus Livius a Superstitione vindicatus.... Annexe sunt ejusdem Origine Judaicae* (1709) (Reprint, Amsterdam, 1970), pp. 117-8.

63 John Toland, *The Life of John Milton* (1698) in Helen Darbishire (ed.), *The Early Lives of Milton* (London, 1932), p. 192; for Cicero and Varro, see 'Cicero Illustratus, Dissertatio Philologica-Critica' in Toland, *A Collection*, I: 241, and Toland, *History of the Druids*, p. 130 (italics in the original).

64 Toland to Clayton (7 December 1698), *A Collection*, II: 325; 'Cicero Illustratus', I: 262-3, 284-5, and Toland, *State-Anatomy*, p. 80. Most of the surviving fragments are preserved by Augustine in *De civitate Dei*, bks. 4 and 6-7. My presentation of Varro's tripartite theology conflates Jean Pepin, *Mythe et allégorie: les orgines grecques et les contestations judéo-chrétiennes* (Paris, 1958), pp. 276-314; R.A. Markus, 'Saint Augustine and *theologia naturalis*', *Studia Patristica, Texte und Untersuchungen* Vol. VI (1962), pp. 476-9; Godo Lieberg, 'Die "theologia tripartita" in Forschung und Bezeugung' in Hildegard Temporini (ed.), *Aufstieg und Niedergang der Romischen Welt: Geschichte und Kultur Roms im Spiegel der Neurer Forschung* Vol. 1: 4 (Berlin, 1973), pp. 63-115; J.H.W.G. Liebeschuetz, *Continuity and Change in Roman Religion* (Oxford, 1979); H.D. Jocelyn, 'Varro's *Antiquitates Rerum Diuinarum* and Religious Affairs in the Late Roman Republic', *Bulletin of the John Rylands University Library of Manchester* Vol. 65 (1982), pp. 148-205.

65 Cicero, *Academica* 1. 9, trans. H. Rackham (Cambridge, MA, 1939), p. 419.

66 Compare Toland, *Letters to Serena*, 'Preface', paragraphs 11-12 and 15, and pp. 120-27; *History of the Druids*, pp. 130-6, 141-3; and *Tetradymus*, p. 91.

67 Toland, *Letters to Serena*, No. 1, 'The Origin and Force of Prejudices', pp. 1-18, which amplifies Cicero, *Tusculanarum Disputationum* 3. 1-4, with help from Nicolas Malebranche's *Recherche de la vérite* (1674*)*; compare Toland, *History of the Druids*, p. 187.

68   Cf. David Berman, 'Deism, Immortality, and the Art of Theological Lying' in J.A. Leo Lemay (ed.), *Deism, Masonry, and the Enlightenment: Essays Honoring Alfred Owen Aldridge* (Newark DE, 1987), pp. 61-78; and Justin A.I. Champion, 'Legislators, Impostors, and the Politic Origins of Religion: English Theories of "Imposture" from Stubbe to Toland' in Silvia Berti, Françoise Charles-Daubert and Richard H. Popkin (eds.), *Heterodoxy, Spinozism, and Free-Thought in Early-Eighteenth-Century Europe: Studies on the 'Traité des Trois Imposteurs'* (Dordrecht, 1996), pp. 333-56.

69   *Spaccio della Bestia Trionfante. Or the Expulsion of the Triumphant Beast*, 'Translated from the Italian of Jordano Bruno' (London, 1713), pp. 223-4, 228-9, 231, 245, 232-3.

70   Toland to Hohendorff (19 November 1709), Cod. Vind. Lat., Oesterreichische Nationalbibliothek, 10390, ff. 396v-397v, as cited in Pagnoni Sturlese, 'Postille autografe di John Toland allo *Spaccio* del Bruno', *Giornale critico della filosofia italiana* Vol. 65 (1986) p. 30; that meticulous essay, along with Saverio Ricci, *La fortuna del pensiero di Giordano Bruno 1600-1750* (Florence, 1990), pp. 131-6, 239-330, a richly learned book, are indispensable.

71   *A General Dictionary Historical and Critical* 10 vols. (London, 1734-41), IV: 592-3, note L (s.v. 'Dicearchus').

72   Elisabeth Labrousse, *Pierre Bayle* 2 vols. (The Hague, 1963-64), II: 199; compare Giovanni Bonacina, *Filosofia ellenistica e cultura moderna: epicureismo, stoicismo e scetticismo da Bayle a Hegel* (Florence, 1996), pp. 17-41, and Ruth Whelan, 'La religion à l'envers: Bayle et l'histoire du paganisme antique', in *Les religions du paganisme antique dans l'Europe chrétienne XVI-XVIIIe siècles* (Paris, 1987), pp. 115-28.

73   Rosalie L. Colie, *Light and Enlightenment: A Study of the Cambridge Platonists and the Dutch Arminians* (Cambridge, 1957), pp. 117-44; Pierre Rétat, *Le 'Dictionnaire' de Bayle et la lutte philosophique au XVIIIe siècle* (Paris, 1971), pp. 35-7, 225-7.

74   Richard H. Popkin, 'The Crisis of Polytheism and the Answers of Vossius, Cudworth and Newton' in James E. Force and Richard H. Popkin (eds.), *Essays on the Context, Nature and Influence of Isaac Newton's Theology* (Dodrecht 1990), pp. 9-26.

75   Compare, for example, Ralph Cudworth, *The True Intellectual System of the Universe* 2 vols. (1678) (Reprint, New York, 1978), 1: 525-7 and 434-40, and Toland, *Letters to Serena*, pp. 22-4.

76   Toland, *Letters to Serena*, pp. 32-3.

77   Rienk Vermij, 'Matter and Motion: Toland and Spinoza' in Wiep van Bunge and Wim Klever (eds.), *Disguised and Overt Spinozism around 1700: Papers Presented at the International Colloquium Held at Rotterdam, 5-8 October 1994* (Leiden, 1996), pp. 275-88.

78   Toland, *Letters to Serena*, p. 237.

79 Toland, *Letters to Serena*, p. 124.

80 Laurent Jaffro, 'L'art de lire Toland', *Revue de synthèse* Vol. 116 (1995), pp. 399-420, is persuasive on the play of intersection and divergence between civil and philosophical theology in Toland's mature writings.

81 Toland, *Adeisidaemon*, p. 78.

82 Cuper to LeClerc (15 November 1709), in Mario Sina and Maria Grazia (eds.), *Epistolario / Jean Le Clerc* 4 vols. (Florence, 1987-97), III: 228.

83 Toland, *Pantheisticon*, pp. 95-6; Toland quotes from Ammianus Marcellinus, *Rerum gestarum* 15. 9. For resonances of Egypt, see *Pantheisticon*, pp. 34 and 47.

84 Toland, *History of the Druids*, pp. 87-92.

85 Toland, *History of the Druids*, p. 89.

86 Toland, *History of the Druids*, p. 135.

87 John Chamberlayne to Toland (21 June 1718), British Library, Add. MS. 4295, ff. 27-8.

88 Toland, *History of the Druids*, p. 104.

89 Toland, *History of the Druids*, pp. 138-9; compare pp. 99-100, 142-3, 172-6.

90 Toland, *History of the Druids*, p. 94; compare pp. 209-210.

91 Toland, *History of the Druids*, pp. 122-3.

92 Toland, *History of the Druids*, pp. 56, 59, 104.

93 Toland, *History of the Druids*, pp. 102-4.

94 Cf. Toland, *Nazarenus*, pp. 111-21, 102, 109, and *History of the Druids*, p. 52n.

95 Toland, *History of the Druids*, p. 96.

96 Toland, *History of the Druids*, p. 105.

97 For the ancient literary convention of the burned library, see Luciano Canfora, *The Vanished Library*, trans. Martin Ryle (London, 1989), p. 191.

98 Compare Anthony Harvey, 'Early Literacy in Ireland: The Evidence from Ogam', *Cambridge Medieval Celtic Studies* Vol. 14 (1987), pp. 1-15.

99 Toland, *History of the Druids*, pp. 81-7, 91, 95-6, 99-100, 168-71; the quotation appears on p. 84.

100 Toland, *History of the Druids*, p. 194; James S. Romm, *The Edges of the Earth in Ancient Thought: Geography, Exploration, and Fiction* (Princeton, 1992), p. 5.

101 Toland, *History of the Druids*, p. 78.

102 Toland, *History of the Druids*, pp. 201-28; for the Hyperboreans, see Romm, *Edges of the Earth*, pp. 60-7, and for Abaris, see Albin Lesky, *A History of Greek Literature*, trans. James Willis and Cornelis de Heer (New York, 1966), pp. 158-161.

103 Toland, *History of the Druids*, pp. 222-3, 208-9.

[104] Toland, *History of the Druids,* p. 220; compare Eduard Fraenkel, *Horace* (Oxford, 1957), pp. 42-55, and Wendell Clausen, *A Commentary on Virgil, Eclogues* (Oxford, 1994), pp. 126-9.

[105] Toland, *History of the Druids*, pp. 96, 219, 224-5.

[106] Toland, *History of the Druids*, p. 106.

[107] Catherine M. Northeast, *The Parisian Jesuits and the Enlightenment 1700-1762* (Oxford, 1991), and Gianni Paganini, 'Tra Epicuro e Stratone: Bayle e l'immagine di Epicuro dal Sei al Settecento', *Rivista critica di storia della filosofia* Vol. 33 (1978), pp. 72-115, offer windows onto that involved and anxious history; Anthony Grafton, *Defenders of the Text: The Traditions of Scholarship in an Age of Science, 1450-1800* (Cambridge, MA, 1991), and Joseph M. Levine, *The Battle of the Books: History and Literature in the Augustan Age* (Ithaca, NY, 1991), learnedly survey some of its chief monuments.

[108] Giambattista Vico, *Scienza Nuova* (1725), in Benedetto Croce and Fausto Nicolini (eds.), *Opere* 7 vols. (Bari, 1911-42), IV: 1-2.

[109] Cf. J.B. Bury, *A History of Freedom of Thought* (New York, 1913), pp. 50-1; Peter Gay, *The Enlightenment: An Interpretation* 2 vols. (New York, 1966-69), I: 326-7, 423-5 and II: 124-5; and E.R. Dodds, *The Greeks and the Irrational* (Berkeley & Los Angeles, 1951), p. 254.

Subscribe to Ireland's Illustrated History Magazine

SUBSCRIPTION RATES
(including post & packing)

	I YEAR	2 YEAR	3 YEAR
IRELAND	£14	£28	£42
UK	£14	£28	£42
EUROPE	£20	£40	£60
USA & REST OF WORLD	US$35	US$70	US$105

SUBSCRIPTION FOR   1 year (4 issues) ☐

2 years (8 issues) ☐   3 years (12 issues) ☐

Cheques/postal orders payable to
History Ireland and send to :

Tommy Graham
Dept. of Modern History
Trinity College Dublin
Ireland

Phone: 01-4535730 Fax: 01-4533234

History **IRELAND**

Brendan Bradshaw *Interview*

Alvin Jackson *on Larne Gunrunners*

Kevin Whelan *on Hurling*

The Crosshill Railway Murders

• REVIEWS • NEWS • EVENTS • CURRICULUM • SOURCES •

Name ....

Address ....

....

....Phone No ....

PLEASE CHARGE TO MY CREDIT CARD ACCOUNT:

Master Card / Access / Visa / American Express / Diners Club / Eurocard

TOTAL sum of .... My card number is:

For gift subscription fill out the name & address of recipient on a separate piece of paper

CARD EXPIRY DATE.....................**Signature** ....

Gender and Self-Representation in Irish Poetry: The Critical Debate

Catriona Clutterbuck

This paper focuses on self-representation, not because it is concerned with the particular portrayals of the self in the work of poets in Ireland, but because it is concerned with the idea and function *of* that representation in their writing. The theorist Judith Butler warns us of the significance of this distinction:

> Language is not an *exterior medium or instrument* into which I pour a self and from which I glean a reflection of that self... presuppos[ing] a potential adequation between the 'I' that confronts the world, including its language, as an object, and the 'I' that finds itself as an object in that world... the subject / object dichotomy, which here belongs to the tradition of Western epistemology, conditions the very problematic of identity that it seeks to solve.[1]

Critical insight is called for here into 'the necessary limits of identity politics'.[2] Such insight is precisely what is offered through that concentrated focus on textual self-representation which is a crucial, though still largely uninvestigated, aspect of Irish poetry. The purpose of this paper is to examine the basis in cultural criticism for such an investigation. In doing so, it suggests that the neglect of self-representation in poetry may be related to a more general under-reading of the significance of gender in cultural discourse in Ireland.

Critical recognition of self-representation in Irish poetry is adversely affected by doubt about the status of biographical and psychological approaches to texts as a means of measuring standards of excellence. This anxiety is itself a symptom of unease among literary scholars about a perceived appropriation of literature by the amorphous, newly-institutionalised phenomenon of Cultural Studies. The situation of the author within contemporary Irish poetry criticism, as a result of these old and new kinds of bias, tends to be shackled ever more firmly within the significant but *essentially contained* realm that is variously defined as 'background information', 'cultural context', or 'intended political message'. Thus, one kind of exegesis attends to the issue of self-representation in terms of direct biography in order to discuss the inspiration for the poem, the origin of specific cultural references in the text, and to speculate about the kind of 'personal' resolution the poet has arrived at through the poem as well as the public implications of any such resolution. Little sustained attention is paid to the poet's consciousness of this specific represented self as an element of theme. More 'serious' literary critics, insofar as they attend to self-consciousness, consider it in terms of the text's exploration of its own processes of communication, not in terms of the authorial position. For them (taking their cue from Joyce studies), the poem signals the only valuable kind of 'self-consciousness' to be the thematisation of poetic form as part of the public function of the artist in interrogating culture.

I would like to illustrate the foregoing discussion by examining Seamus Heaney's early, and by now canonical poem, 'Digging'.[3] In the conclusion of the poem, ('Between my finger and my thumb / The squat pen rests. / I'll dig with it'), the valorisation of the artist is generally read as an innocent by-product of the valorisation of the artistic process. However, the fact that this text's attention to form-as-theme naturalises the status of the speaker as artist is only the first part of its process. Although a sleight of hand is going on, whereby self-projection into the status of artist is disguised as mere self-representation in an already achieved position of authority, the poem at a deeper level wants its bluff to be called. What becomes apparent in 'Digging', if one looks at it closely, is an inversion of the vocational heritage it proclaims. Far from the speaker's father and grandfather inaugurating a tradition of 'digging' into the depths which the poet can follow, it is the speaker who has retrospectively created that 'tradition': he continues to 'look down' from his airy vantage point '[un]till' he can imaginatively see his father in the past. He creates the memory to suit his purpose. Such a sleight of hand can only succeed if the author of the poem (the biographical Heaney) is taken by the reader to be precisely coterminous with the speaker of the poem (the 'writing self'), *and* if this speaker is, in turn, taken to be exactly equivalent to the represented 'I' in the text (the 'written self', the poet-figure). By fusing these three distinct identity functions and by ignoring the distance between them, the speaker writes himself, apparently conclusively, into the vocation of artist: 'snug as a gun'. However, an 'innocence' of his self-appointment as bard on the part of Heaney could only ever sustain itself through an equivalently dangerous innocence on the part of his audience. In fact, we and Heaney operate together as readers of the projection of identity on the screen of the text, and if we read what is two-dimensional as though it were full-blown three-dimensional reality after the show has ended, then that is at least as much our responsibility as Heaney's. The poem suggests as its underlying deepest theme, I think, that the creation of an individual's public authority is a communal phenomenon which carries dangers with it for everyone if this factor of collusion is unrecognised.

My larger argument has been that the two types of attention to 'self' in the literary text – self-as-formal-methodology and self-as-author – nearly always proceed within criticism as though they were only incidentally linked.

Heaney's 'Digging' helps illustrate, however, that this is not the case. Only when criticism recognises that author-as-theme and form-as-theme cannot exist independently but are unavoidably linked in a radically complementary relationship in the action of the effective poem will poetry start to reach its potential level of impact upon the development of consciousness within the larger Irish cultural sphere. In short, only through critical recognition and exploration of a poem's formative condition of double self-reflexivity can its importance be accurately measured and realised.

This problem, of course, is not an Irish phenomenon. The association between the two modes of self-consciousness under discussion, authorial and formal, has been rendered obscure throughout the Western world as a result of the fiercely contested swings in literary commentary over the past half century between new criticism's perceived exclusive and excluding concern with literary form and post-structuralism's fascination with public ideologies traceable to the individual who has authored the text. While each of these two approaches promotes the occasional borrowing of the other's tools, the primary understanding of their relation still assumes that emphasis on one requires attack of the other's position – a concern with poems as poems, with form, and with the autonomy of the text invariably demands (it seems) rejection of the critical position advocating a reading of literature for the presence within texts, and subversion through them, of political hegemonies, and *vice versa*. I argue, in contrast, that both main approaches – textual form and authorial presence – should be attended to as equally significant because they operate co-dependently, rather than independently, to effect the action and value of the poem.

The separation of these approaches is further ratified by debates beyond the confines of strict literary criticism. To summarise the philosophical pitch on which artists and critics alike play with the concept of 'self', since the Enlightenment, discourse on subjectivity has been conducted along a spectrum established between two contrary, though linked, theoretical positions. The first is that 'self' is determined by forces beyond personal agency (broadly generalisable as class, position, and heredity in the nineteenth century; language in the twentieth century); the second, that 'self' is natural, given, deriving from an autonomous base and individual responsibility: primarily acting rather than acted upon, self-created rather than externally constructed. Applied to the self in writing, the former position, carried to its extreme, would advocate that the voice of the writer be understood as equivalent to that of a ventriloquist's dummy, where all formulations of truth – ironic and sincere, dramatic and lyrical – are ultimately diagnosable as rhetoric, historically deployed by those forces seeking absolute and global economic power and designed to ameliorate the powerless masses with delusions of subjectivity, agency, and 'control' over their own decisions. In the opposed tradition, the voice of the writer would be regarded as transparently that of the self, engaged in exploring and formulating its own truth through the interaction of that 'self' with society. In the first extreme, the authority of the 'author' becomes a deliberately cultivated illusion of which the writer is naively unaware since his or her writings function to obscure rather than (as he or she thinks) reveal reality; in the latter, though the authority of the artist is allowed to need to develop – for example, he may have to suffer at certain stages from Bloomian anxiety of influence – that authority is never actually questioned as the birthright of the 'true' artist. In practice over the last three hundred years, enquiry into the position of the self, in writing as in culture in general, has situated itself at many and varying points between these two poles, borrowing and seaming together declarative banners from each extreme in the process.

The question of whether the individual's condition demonstrates a clear recognition or a blurring of the boundaries between the constructed and given status of the self is fundamentally linked to the politics of the state and to the particular economic system it sanctions and protects. This fact is peculiarly pertinent to countries which have been colonised, where the familiar 'for your own good' rationalisation for external control is exactly coterminous with the shifting boundary between a constructed and a given self. The old antagonistic combination of the ideal of autonomy and the reality of state control is more visible in the colonial than in any other system of government. Among European nations and the territories they affected through colonialism, this fact is peculiarly relevant in Ireland. Here, the unavoidable blurring of boundaries between native and coloniser through longevity of association, territorial proximity, the absence of a colour bar, and the (systematically stimulated) absence of a language bar only accelerated the need to blur the boundaries between a constructed and a given identity if external control was to be maintained,[4] or, ironically, to be resisted. The latter situation is well illustrated by characters as various as those of Somerville and Ross and J.M. Synge or by the speakers of James Clarence Mangan's verse, all of whom participate in a cycle of constructing and de-constructing the self in order to present the 'truth' of their own identity. In such texts, a very thin, indeed, a porous line exists between self-representation and self-projection. As a result of such complex interaction between 'true' and 'false' selves on and between both sides of the colonial divide, the issue of identity in Ireland slips with discomforting ease from a private to a public (most often a national) context and *vice versa*. It is the reality of this slippage, displacing as it does the traditionally antithetical poles of private and public realms, that renders the question of the given or constructed status of the self indispensable to a study of Irish culture. I would argue that this slippage is interrogated most accurately and comprehensively not through political or cultural discourse *per se,* but through the fiction, drama and poetry produced in Ireland or by Irishmen and women. The public response to that literature is accordingly significant.

Two contemporary poets have become peculiarly associated with the tension generated by this question: Eavan Boland and Medbh McGuckian. The canonical tension linked with their output (proclaimed through the anthology wars and contradictory stances on their reputations in critical debate)[5] is less a sign of uncertainty about where to place two individual Irish poets than it is a sign of a rapidly-surfacing crisis in contemporary criticism about how to *read* Irish poetry. Irish women poets, and Boland and McGuckian in particular, have come to represent a pervasive conflict in the state of Irish criticism sourced in its condition of profound uncertainty regarding the shifting relationship between the public and private zones in Irish culture. Boland and McGuckian are at the eye of a gathering storm of reaction to two perceived agendas which are mutually opposed: first, that poetry should be read exclusively for its public content; second, that it should be read exclusively for its private import.

Boland, the longer-established of the two writers, is the focus of the former complaint. Peter Sirr's plaintive comment, for example, illustrates resistance to understandings of Irish poetry which seem to assume that art succeeds only as a function of popular political agendas – a practice for him exemplified in the Boland critical industry: 'It shouldn't be necessary to praise everything simply because the work fits into a particular political perspective, or to create the kind of critical atmosphere around the work where to question any aspect of it is to be consigned to a doghouse for the unreconstructed'.[6] McGuckian, at the other extreme, is the focus of an increasingly audible reaction to the pressure to suspend public criteria, including basic semantic comprehensibility, in favour of the exclusively private criterion of reader-dependent 'intuition'.[7] The result is criticism which 'dares' to take McGuckian to task for what is judged to be her solipsism, most infamously exemplified by Patrick Williams' attack on what he perceived to be McGuckian's self-reflexive irrelevance: 'McGuckian's concoctions of endless poeticisms are non-visionary, and the funny sealed little worlds where harmless cranks parley with themselves in gobbledygook won't impinge on the real world of loot and dragons'.[8]

Critical disapproval of both Boland and McGuckian as representatives, respectively, of an exclusively public-focused and an exclusively private-focused criterion for value in poetry is fundamentally based upon a misreading of the element of self-reflexivity in their work. Whether the poet is judged to 'parley with herself' in 'Medbh-speak'[9] (demanding reader-acquiescence with the author's arrogant dismissal of the communicative function), or live 'in a constant state of nervous self-definition'[10] via Eavan-speak (demanding reader-acquiescence with a 'universal' politics of identity which has been formulated through middle-class, female, suburban experience alone), matters little. In each case almost no attention is paid to the actual complex 'self' which features in the poetry text.

The reason for this in the larger Irish critical context is that the very intensity of disputes on the political nature of the issue of identity (exemplified in the well-documented Field Day/Revisionism antagonism) has ironically functioned to render ever more obscure the basis of the question of 'self' and its construction in cultural representation, and while arguments *about* identity fiercely rage, there exists a curious dearth of critical focus *on* identity as a specific thematic tool in the products of culture. Nowhere is that necessary focus applied with more clarity than through the close readings of the nature and function of 'self' which are produced by poets themselves in their own texts. Criticism of these poets which does attend to the issue of identity fails in so far as it reads 'self', and not 'self-consciousness and self', as the true concern of these artists. When a poet, particularly a woman poet, produces a sufficient quantity of the pronoun 'I' in combination with domestic backdrops throughout his or her corpus, he or she will be accused of running the risk of privatising art, of validating the immunisation of the individual from the historical process.[11] But privatisation is simultaneously enacted and interrogated in the work of the most significant of Irish poets: privatisation is itself politicised through the interrogation of representation it calls in its wake.

However, the potential for calling that critical consciousness into being can only be realised when the axis of debate on the relationship between the private and public realms is recognised to intersect with that of gender. The debate on the nature and function of the self in Irish poetry can be regarded as attaining its primary effect at the co-ordinate of gender-concern. This is equally true of male and female authored texts, but is brought to light in contemporary Ireland because of the increasing prominence of poetry by women. Gender attains its significance in Irish poetry not so much as an issue in itself (where it can be side-lined as a 'woman's concern'), but as the unknown quotient, the unacknowledged eye through which debate on the role of the poet in Ireland is drawn backwards and forwards, as, in Anne Tannahill's words, it 'underpins and overshadows the other categories of religion, class and politics'.[12]

This larger significance of the issue of gender in Irish poetry, however, remains mostly invisible because gender has become, within Irish criticism, an important means not of making possible but rather *avoiding* recognition of the congruence of the personal and the aesthetic as the basis of public political literature. Criticism has effected this by associating the concept 'personal' in aesthetic terms with 'female' and, tautologically, with 'private', taking permission from the fact that historically, the public representation of Irish women has been predominantly understood and accepted as being associable with their domestic capacity as wives and mothers. But women are simultaneously required to function as test-grounds or enablers of the public realm, without being themselves granted agency in that arena. This combination produces a hegemonic cocktail whereby Irishwomen are kept 'symbolically central and materially peripheral'.[13] That cocktail provides the underlying rationale for Irish writing's vision of public agency as resulting from the *defeat* of the private zone (as classically exemplified in Yeats's *Cathleen Ni Houlihan*), rather than the recognition of the fact that the private zone is intimately related to the public zone as its realised, concrete form.

The increasing evidence of Irish women's historical and contemporary participation in public life on their own terms[14] has surprisingly little impact on this pattern of sanctioned public self/vaunted-but-essentially-unwanted private self. This may be because current interpretations of these women consider their new-found visibility to be more proof of their individual success in gaining access to the public realm (which can remain essentially unchanged) than of their fundamental alteration of the status of the private zone. In other words, the dichotomy between private and public may actually be reinforced rather than undermined by the manner in which Irish women's voices are being retrieved.

This is demonstrated particularly by the manner in which idealisations of the kind of subversion which the female voice can offer within literature have become a feature of the work of several prominent critics of Irish cultural affairs. For example, Edna Longley approvingly remarks that Paul Durcan's poem 'The Mayo Accent' 'symbolizes and idealizes an originary speech which the state or Nation has forgotten, but poetry, women and the father's better self remember'.[15] On the evidence of this statement, poetry is linked to women in a totalising gesture traceable to Longley's larger critical project of proving aesthetics as embodying an ideal of cultural self-sufficiency. Longley, in the above comment, partakes in a version of that process of de-historicising Irishwomen for which she, along with many others, have rebuked *The Field Day Anthology*.[16] However, Seamus Deane, in a statement closely related to that quoted from Longley above, also associates the potential of aesthetics with the figure of woman, using Joyce as his chosen exemplar: 'Joyce's writing is founded on the belief in the capacity of art to restore a lost vitality. So the figures we remember are embodiments of this "vitalism", particularly Molly Bloom and Anna Livia Plurabelle. The fact that they were women is important too, since it clearly indicates some sort of resolution, on the level of femaleness, of what had remained implacably unresolvable on the male level'.[17]

Ironically, in the attempt to oppose such idealisations of aesthetics, women are equally de-historicised. For David Lloyd, women function as agents, not of an aesthetic utopia but of the utopia of what he terms 'adulteration'. Here, the figure of promiscuous female sexuality operates as the medium for Lloyd's rejection of bourgeois subjectivity, including its embodiment in nationalism.[18] In adulteration, he says, 'The uncertainty that attaches to the paternal origin... threatens always to undermine the integrity of the name, of the determination of paternal property and of identity itself.... Hence... the reason that any nationalism must police the desire of women'.[19] In Lloyd's ideal, unbounded female sexuality undermines and supplants male subjectivity, the collective supplants the idea of the individual, metonymy supplants metaphor.[20] Lloyd's analysis, however, neglects *woman's* historicisation in its social, economic and political dimensions,[21] instead suggesting this is realised sufficiently through the medium of her free sexual function. This solution, only one element in Lloyd's larger critique involving an outright rejection of constructs of subjectivity in Irish texts as in politics, bears an uncomfortable resemblance to his diagnosis of the original problem: the female body underwriting re-writings of Irish political identity.

Working in tandem with these two factors – critics' elision of the significance of the private zone in their recovery of Irish women's voices, and the idealisation of the subversion of the public realm offered by those women – is a third consideration which threatens to render ineffective current efforts to establish and develop the agency of women in Irish culture. This is the consistent register of threat in male responses to the female who is still within the *private*, not the public, realm. Declan Kiberd notes in much literature of colonial contexts, for example, the association of women with the private zone from which they effect the emasculation of the male.[22] The menacing aspect of women sited in hidden, therefore private, locations is one of the most consistent threads running through contemporary Irish poetry by men. In male poets' representations of these figures, voyeurism is inverted and leads to an encounter with an absent, hidden, or false woman in which power is transferred to the female and threatens the male. Take, for example, the figure of Thomas Kinsella's grandmother in her darkened shop (in the sequence 'Notes from the Land of the Dead') who threatens to devour the male, or the visual caricatures of the female, placed in locations easily missed or inaccessible, in Seamus Heaney's poem 'Sheelagh na Gig', or Richard Murphy's anatomisations of carved and painted female figures in his volume *The Mirror Wall*.[23] This recurrent trope suggests that, rather than any inherently menacing attribute in herself, it may be the female's association with the private zone which makes her dangerous. On this point, note how writers such as Austin Clarke and Brian Moore, in their portraiture of the Irish female, associate concern with 'the self' simultaneously with women and ill-health: the woman figure's lack of self-realisation is diagnosed to be a result of these women's 'narcissistic absorption with the self'.[24]

The underlying conditions for denigration of the private zone in Irish cultural discourse are established, then, along gender lines. The division between 'serious' and 'amateur' artist, for example, emerges through the over-frequent assumption by male critics that work by women artists can be read as personal autobiography.[25] We must remember here that the value of *autobiography* is not at issue, but rather, the value of where the autobiography is located. In the Irish tradition, autobiography understood as the narrative of personal and communal agency is sited *on* the female body, not where the female body is sited. In Ireland, as in other nations, women are traditionally situated at, and thus render visible, the shifting border between the dual ideals of national and personal self-determination. The congruence between 'self', women, and national aspiration is readily recognisable in the eighteenth-century Aisling tradition of poetry, wherein 'intense personal feeling, combined with the trope of female sorrow, made a considerable impact on the development of national political attitudes expressed in Irish poetry for the next two hundred years'.[26] In this tradition, 'Woman was central to [the] site of the tussle for the artistic license to portray a validated community'.[27] Although attempts by women poets to relocate autobiography to where the female body is sited have met with severe criticism (see William Logan's review of Eavan Boland's *Outside History*, where he states: 'Poems of quiet desperation in the kitchen do not form an original aesthetic'[28]), Clair Wills has shown that it is that physical re-location, rather than any attempted erasure of the representative function of the female body, which enables the development of the Irish woman poet: 'To take her place in an Irish poetic tradition in some senses "enabled" by the troping of motherhood as a public image, [she] must "divert" the tradition through the "domestic", since the discourse of sexuality is the only "public" language to which, as a woman writer, she has legitimate access'.[29] Aesthetic realisation, however, remains tautologically associated with the male gender as an underlying structuring principle in a surprising number of contemporary Irish literary commentaries. Denis Devlin's poetry, for example, is praised as having a 'fresh, worldly, masculine seriousness about it';[30] elsewhere a commentary on Joyce genders the concept of 'intellectual vocation' by contrasting the continental tradition Joyce drew from with the 'evangelical, female puritan spirit which so dominated the sentimental English novel'.[31]

How, then, can gender become truly operative in the quest for 'self' to realise its potential as the construct which enables art to break down the given barrier between private and public realms in Irish life? How can gender-awareness be considered 'an appeal to the history of the possible',[32] rather than a marker for immutably carved-out boundaries of consciousness? It can be so considered by focusing on the potential of gender-play, not gender-defence (by masculinists or feminists) in arriving at understandings of identity. That gender-play is discussed by Judith Butler:

> As the effects of a subtle and politically enforced performativity, gender is an 'act', as it were, that is open to splittings, self-parody, self-criticism, and those hyperbolic exhibitions of the 'natural' that, in their very exaggeration, reveal its fundamentally phantasmatic status.... Paradoxically, the reconceptualization of identity as an *effect,* that is, as *produced* or *generated*, opens up possibilities of 'agency' that are

insidiously foreclosed by positions that take identity categories as foundational and fixed.[33]

In the Irish poetic tradition, ironically, the gender-play necessary to enable these developments has long played a significant role. In the bardic tradition, while women were actively excluded from the role of 'poet', gender role-play – the easy alteration between male and female as one's public 'identity' – was integral to the position of the poet. As Nuala Ní Dhomhnaill describes it, 'one of the commonest tropes for the relationship of the poet to his chief was that of a woman to her lover'.[34] According to Máire Cruise O'Brien, such gender inversion on the part of the poet had a powerful political motivation – an essential part of establishing the rule of his patron was the poet's transformation into not only lover but sovereign goddess.[35] The male poet playing with being a woman has its echoes in contemporary Irish poetry, from Yeats's Crazy Jane through Heaney, Durcan, and several others.[36] However, a careful distinction must be made between a literary tradition which appropriates the female, including acts of gender-play, purely to *legitimise* itself, and one which allows gender to become the instrument of its serious self-examination. In considering the bardic tradition we must remember that the poet was not the woman he played. It is this exclusion of women from the role of poet (or the subsequent silencing of their actual inclusion[37]) up to and including the present period,[38] and, specifically, contemporary women poets' reaction to that, which must be addressed in the context of any debate on the larger potential of gender in reconstituting the question of identity in Irish writing.

Women poets within a tradition in which female precursors are scarce, absent, or invisible[39] demonstrate a particular concentration on self-image. Peculiarly recognising the effect of what Eavan Boland calls 'the elusive distance between writing a poem and being a poet',[40] women writers, through their consciousness of the bases of gender politics, are open in a particular way to the issue of 'self' in poetry.[41] Gerardine Meaney persuasively argues that: 'The ability to be both subject and object, writer and written, is necessary to any writer who wishes to use the first person singular. But that perspective poses particular problems for the woman poet who is more "properly" the object or inspiration of poetry.'[42] I suggest, however, that the peculiar attentiveness to the hyphenated, self-conscious self that is required of women writers is in the end more an advantage than a problem. Irish women poets' defence of subjectivity, unless it leads towards the issue of representation as a political concern *through* an investigation of self-representation as a textual concern, will limit rather than expand their writings' challenge to calcified concepts of the identity and role of the poet.

The most effective means by which identity politics in Ireland can broaden into realising the actual capacity for new understandings of 'self' through women's writing may be by means of the debate on self-marginalisation in Irish women's writing. The action of women in colluding with their own loss of 'self' has generally been regarded as a form of disease of the confidence which is to be eliminated.[43] However, it can, in fact, operate as an enabling condition in so far as collusion with images of the self can also indicate a powerful capacity for self-construction, for the theatricalisation of identity. The choice between these interpretations is based upon the difference between the slavish and subversive mimeses of hegemonic subjectivity that is influentially debated by the theorist Luce Irigaray, among others.[44] Accounts of the marginalisation of women writers which are driven from a political standpoint that avoids a full consideration of the agency of language lead, as has been suggested, to simplistic readings of the self. These readings involve the assumption that the self is a hidden nugget awaiting intact excavation from beneath layers of stereotype imposed, for their own masculinist purposes, by men. The debate on self-marginalisation,[45] in contrast, opens wide a gap between the original 'self' that is unknowable and approximations of it as personae in texts; a serious consideration of the construction of the self is unavoidable once that gap opens, and the debate on the 'self' of poetry as one about the *self in process* becomes properly audible. I again cite Judith Butler in support of this alternative:

> For an identity to be an effect means that it is neither fatally determined nor fully artificial and arbitrary. That the constituted status of identity is misconstrued along these two conflicting lines suggests the ways in which the feminist discourse on cultural construction remains trapped within the unnecessary binarism of free will and determinism. Construction is not opposed to agency; it is the necessary scene of agency, the very terms in which agency is articulated and becomes culturally intelligible.[46]

My argument in this paper has been for an authorial and readership position of active negotiation in the texts of Irish poetry, *between* the 'self' as given and the 'self' as arbitrary. Such negotiation is vital because it is this agency of the constructed self which underwrites the major acts of subversion that Irish poets are offering today – their revision, in Eavan Boland's words, of 'the old conservative stance of the poet within the poem'.[47] Only by attending to the issue of self-representation in all its shifting conditions can such a revision, such a renewal, take place:

> An object of the images we make is
> what we are and how we lean out and
> over the perfect surface where
> our features in water greet and save us.
> Eavan Boland, 'The Art of Grief'[48]

Notes

1   Judith Butler, *Gender Trouble: Feminism and the Subversion of Identity* (London, 1990), p. 143-4.

2   Butler, *Gender Trouble*, p. 4.

3   Seamus Heaney, *New Selected Poems 1966-1987* (London, 1990), p. 1.

4   The rule of law must constantly attempt to render obscure the overt mechanisms of control within the colonised territory to those people who both mediate and are victims of that control.

5   For example, in recent years the Irish critic Rory Brennan can declare Boland to be one of four Irish poets who will be 'regarded as touchstones... well into the new millennium', but Deborah Consalvo can firmly state that though Boland is 'an established transnational voice... her work is marginalized within the patriarchally determined Irish canon'. Rory Brennan, 'Contemporary Irish Poetry: An Overview' in Michael Kenneally (ed.), *Poetry in Contemporary Irish Literature* (Gerrards Cross, 1995), p. 27; Deborah McWilliams Consalvo, 'In Common Usage: Eavan Boland's Poetic Voice', *Éire-Ireland* Vol. 28, No. 2 (1993), p. 100.

6   Peter Sirr, 'The Figures in the Tablecloth', Review of *Irish University Review, Vol. 23, No. 1 – Special Issue – Eavan Boland*, *The Irish Times* (26 June 1993), p. 8.

7   Kimberly Bohman's critique of McGuckian, completely displacing as it does responsibility for individual texts' meaning from poet to reader, exemplifies the form of commentary that will catalyse such negative reaction: '[T]he coherence of [McGuckian's] poetry is relative to the reader's awareness of her own conscious forces which inhibit the intuitive connection Medbh-speak facilitates'. Kimberly Bohman, 'Borders or Frontiers?: Gender Roles and Gender Politics in McGuckian's Unconscious Realm', *Irish Journal of Feminist Studies* Vol. 1, No. 1 (March 1996), p. 130. Clair Wills similarly gives priority to the role of the reader: '[T]he meaning of her work depends entirely on how people are prepared to read her'. Clair Wills, *Improprieties: Politics and Sexuality in Northern Irish Poetry* (Oxford, 1993), p. 169. Martin Mooney focuses on text rather than reader to make the same point: '[T]he criticism [the poetry] deserves may exist only as a loose network of unstated assumptions buried within the techniques of the work itself'. Martin Mooney, 'Body Logic: Some Notes on the Poetry of Medbh McGuckian', *Gown Literary Supplement* (Queen's University Belfast, 1988), p. 16. The premise by all three critics of the necessity for an ideal, or in different terms, elitist reader, gives rise to the anxiety to which I refer here.

8   Patrick Williams, 'Spare that Tree', Review of Medbh McGuckian's *On Ballycastle Beach, The Honest Ulsterman* No. 86 (Spring / Summer 1989), p. 51.

9   Bohman, 'Borders or Frontiers?', p. 120.

10 Peter Sirr, 'The Figures in the Tablecloth', p. 8.

[11] Seamus Deane exemplifies critics' legitimate concern with the ill-effects of privatisation, asserting that liberalism's 'idea of the best of all possible worlds is based on the hope of depoliticizing the society to the point where it is essentially a consumerist organism.... The full realization of the individual self is regarded as an ambition that institutions exist to serve'. Seamus Deane, 'Wherever Green is Read' in Máirín Ní Dhonnchadha and Theo Dorgan (eds.), *Revising the Rising* (Derry, 1991), p. 97.

[12] Anne Tannahill, 'Ingredients of Regional Identities (Northern Ireland)' in Proinsias O Drisceoil (ed.), *Regions: Identity and Power* (Belfast, 1993), p. 121.

[13] Sabina Sharkey, 'Frontier Issues: Irish Women's Texts and Contexts', *Women: A Cultural Review* Vol. 4, No. 2 (Autumn 1993), p. 130.

[14] See, for example, Margaret Ward, *Unmanageable Revolutionaries: Women and Irish Nationalism* (London, 1989).

[15] Edna Longley, *The Living Stream: Literature and Revisionism in Ireland* (Newcastle-Upon-Tyne, 1994), p. 66.

[16] Longley, *The Living Stream*, p. 34.

[17] Seamus Deane, 'Heroic Styles: The Tradition of an Idea' (Field Day Pamphlet No. 4) in *Ireland's Field Day* (London, 1985), p. 51.

[18] See Clair Wills for a related critique (*Improprieties*, p. 53).

[19] David Lloyd, 'Writing in the Shit', *Anomalous States: Irish Writing and the Post-Colonial Moment* (Dublin, 1993), p. 53.

[20] Lloyd, *Anomalous States*, pp. 80, 146-7.

[21] Lloyd deflects this issue in *Anomalous States*, stating that 'A full consideration of the antagonisms between certain feminisms and the nationalism of the state would require at least another essay' (p. 81).

[22] Declan Kiberd, 'The War Against the Past' in Audrey S. Eyler and Robert F. Garrett (eds.), *The Uses of the Past: Essays on Irish Culture* (Cranbury, NY, 1988), pp. 45, 50. See also Sean Ryder, 'Male Autobiography and Irish Cultural Nationalism: John Mitchel and James Clarence Mangan', *Irish Review* 13 (Winter 1992/93), pp. 70-7.

[23] Thomas Kinsella, *Poems 1956-1973* (Mountrath, Portlaoise, 1980), pp. 139-40, 144-8; Seamus Heaney, *Station Island* (London, 1984), p. 49; Richard Murphy, *The Mirror Wall* (Newcastle-upon-Tyne, 1989), especially pp. 16, 20, 22, 27, and 41.

[24] Patricia Bourden, 'No Answer from Limbo: An Aspect of Female Portraiture', *The Crane Bag* Vol. 4, No. 1 (1980), pp. 97, 98, 99, 95.

[25] As noted by Máirín Nic Eoin, 'Gender's Agendas', *Graph* 12 (1992), p. 6. Sidonie Smith, in her investigation into the absence of women's texts from the texts of autobiographical criticism, notes this 'pervasive decoding', and elaborates: 'When applied to texts by men "autobiographical" signals the positively valued side of binary opposition – the self-consciously "crafted and aesthetic". When applied to texts by women, it announces the nega-

tively valued side of opposition – the "spontaneous, natural"'. Sidonie Smith, *A Poetics of Women's Autobiography: Marginality and the Fictions of Self-Representation* (Bloomington and Indianapolis, 1987), p. 16. John Wilson Foster gives grounds for Smith's analysis through a comment in his introduction to the contemporary fiction section of *The Field Day Anthology*, which suggests that 'love' can be read as 'the feminine version of male subjectivity'. John Wilson Foster, 'Introduction', 'Irish Fiction 1965-1990' in Seamus Deane (gen. ed.), *The Field Day Anthology of Irish Writing* 3 vols. (Derry, 1991), III: 940.

26 Alan Harrison, 'Introduction', 'Literature in Irish 1600-1800' in *The Field Day Anthology of Irish Writing*, I: 274-5.

27 Elin Ap Hywel, 'Elise and the Great Queens of Ireland: "Femininity" as constructed by Sinn Féin and the Abbey Theatre, 1901-1907' in Toni O'Brien Johnson and David Cairns (eds.), *Gender in Irish Writing* (Buckingham, 1991), p. 36.

28 William Logan, 'Animal Instincts and Natural Powers', review of Eavan Boland's *Outside History*, *The New York Times Book Review* (21 April 1991), p. 22.

29 Clair Wills (speaking of Medbh McGuckian), 'Voices from the Nursery: Medbh McGuckian's Plantation' in Michael Kenneally, *Poetry in Contemporary Irish Literature* (Gerrards Cross, 1995), p. 375.

30 Gerald Dawe, 'An Absence of Influence: Three Modernist Poets', *Against Piety: Essays in Irish Poetry* (Belfast, 1995), p. 54.

31 Seamus Deane, *Celtic Revivals* (London & Boston, 1985), p. 76.

32 Lloyd, *Anomalous States*, p. 80.

33 Butler, *Gender Trouble,* pp. 146, 147. If a consideration of gender (as Butler and this essay suggest) has the potential to free up constructs of identity, then the resulting pliable, multiple 'self' may in turn act as the most appropriate lever to loosen the deadlock on the issue of gender in Irish writing which has been articulated most clearly in the debate surrounding the forthcoming fourth volume of the *Field Day Anthology* concerning anthologising Irish women's writing and writing about Irish women.

34 Nuala Ní Dhomhnaill, 'What Foremothers?', *Poetry Ireland Review* No. 36 (Autumn 1992), p. 20. Also see Bernadette Cunningham, 'Women and Gaelic Literature, 1500-1800' in Margaret McCurtain and Mary O'Dowd (eds.), *Women in Early Modern Ireland* (Edinburgh, 1991), p. 155.

35 Máire Cruise O'Brien, 'The Female Principle in Gaelic Poetry' in S.F. Gallagher (ed.), *Women in Irish Legend, Life and Literature* (Gerrards Cross, 1983), p. 29.

36 The idea of merging with the female is substantiated in the significant tropes of feminised males and gender inversion that surface repeatedly in the texts of contemporary Irish male poets. In Seamus Heaney, for example,

the possibilities of joining with an unacknowledged female self are found in 'Sweeney's Returns' (Heaney, *Station Island*, p. 114), where Sweeney searches for his wife's face in her bedroom and finds, to his shock, only himself in her mirror. Poems based apparently on the sexual act demanding man and woman as opposites emphasise getting inside the female to the extent that the two identities are merged. In 'Sheelagh na Gig' (Heaney, *Station Island*, p. 49), Heaney images himself as 'wearing the bag [womb] like a caul'; in 'On the Road' (Heaney, *Station Island*, p. 119), the Sweeney / Heaney protagonist takes up the typical location of the female Sheelagh na Gig: He would 'hide in the cleft / of that churchyard wall'. The 'cleft' in the wall may be the open cleft in the Sheelagh's body; Sweeney / Heaney's seeking to enter here is a journey 'to the deepest chamber'. The imagery of entry into the female body is unmistakably linked to the idea of entry into the innermost room of the self.

37   See Ann Owens Weekes, *Unveiling Treasures: The Attic Guide to the Published Works of Irish Women Literary Writers* (Dublin: Attic Press, 1993), for an introductory bibliography of Irish women's writing since 1700 (including eighty-five poets).

38   For contemporary debate on the marginalisation of Irish women poets, see Patricia Boyle Haberstroh, *Women Creating Women: Contemporary Irish Women Poets* (Dublin, 1996); see also Eavan Boland, *Object Lessons*, and Nuala Ní Dhomhnaill's 'What Foremothers?'; also Katie Donovan's 'Irish Women Writers - Marginalized by Whom?' in Dermot Bolger (ed.), *Letters From the New Island* (Dublin, 1991), pp. 105-147.

39   This is argued by Eavan Boland in 'Outside History', *Object Lessons*, pp. 123-153, and Nuala Ní Dhomhnaill in 'What Foremothers?'; also see Denis J. Hannon and Nancy Means Wright, 'Irish Women Poets: Breaking the Silence', *The Canadian Journal of Irish Studies* Vol. 16, No. 2 (December 1990), pp. 57-65.

40   Eavan Boland, 'An Argument in Defence of Workshops', *Poetry Ireland Review* No. 31 (Winter / Spring 1991), p. 42. This may take the shape of the woman poet effecting a form of collusion with loss of self, as described by Ruth Hooley in relation to her experience of women reading their work publicly: '[S]he [would be] fairly apologetic, and then it was a real inverted ego trip of a performance'. 'Ruth Hooley' in Gillean Somerville-Arjat and Rebecca E. Wilson (eds.), *Sleeping with Monsters: Conversations with Scottish and Irish Women Poets* (Dublin, 1990), p. 166.

41   For example, Nuala Ní Dhomhnaill's placing of self at centre stage (conducted through an exploration of Irish mythology and folklore) is dependent on her investigation of gender. Ní Dhomhnaill deals with the female psyche, not only because she thus explores herself, but because she believes that 'there is a huge, enormous, psychic jump going on in this generation

in women' and therefore that women in particular exemplify the integral connection between unconscious and historically recognisable change (Michael Cronin, 'Making the Millennium: Interview with Nuala Ní Dhomhnaill', *Graph* No. 1 [1986], p. 8).

42 Gerardine Meaney, 'History Gasps: Myth in Contemporary Irish Women's Poetry' in *Poetry in Contemporary Irish Literature*, p. 103.

43 See, for example, Nuala O'Faoláin's medicinal admonishing of women writers, where she traces women's collusion in their own oppression to the real strength and power of the images of women that are created in the Irish male literary tradition: 'the self-respect of Irish women is radically and paradoxically checkmated by respect for an Irish national achievement'. Nuala O'Faoláin, 'Irish Women and Writing in Modern Ireland' in Eiléan Ní Chuilleanáin (ed.), *Irish Women: Image and Achievement* (Dublin, 1985), p. 129.

44 Luce Irigaray, *This Sex Which Is Not One* (1977), Trans. Catherine Porter with Carolyn Burke (Ithaca, NY, 1985), especially p. 76.

45 Gerardine Meaney suggests the lineaments of the self-marginalisation debate with her comment: 'If patriarchal history has portrayed us as bystanders to the political process, it has lied. We have always been implicated, even in our own oppression'. Meaney, *Sex and Nation: Women in Irish Culture and Politics*, (Dublin, 1991), p. 15.

46 Butler, *Gender Trouble*, p. 147.

47 Jody Allen-Randolph, 'An Interview with Eavan Boland', *IUR* Vol. 23, No. 1 (1993), p. 128.

48 Eavan Boland, 'The Art of Grief', *Collected Poems* (Manchester, 1995), p. 208.

In the Fenians' Wake:
Ireland's Nineteenth-Century Crises and Their Representation in the Sentimental Rhetoric of William O'Brien MP and Canon Sheehan

Patrick Maume

Many of the central questions of nineteenth- and twentieth-century Irish cultural history are involved in the careers of William O'Brien (1852-1928) – journalist, land agitator, MP – and the Catholic novelist, Canon P.A. Sheehan (1852-1913). Each attempted to articulate the ambiguous relationships between parliamentary and physical-force nationalism, the Land War, and the decline of aristocratic power; the challenge posed to the Catholic Church by the growth of a Catholic lay professional class; the tension between Catholic belief in the interchangeability of Faith and Fatherland, and the need to incorporate the powerful Protestant minority in the anticipated political settlement. Their writings are smothered in the sentimental idiom of nineteenth-century popular religious and political oratory, and cannot be fully understood outside a context which vanished with the Union; yet their immense contemporary popularity, their extensive and easily-accessible writings, and their attempts to confront their own shifting identities and the tensions in Irish society as it moved towards self-government have attracted scholarly attention of a very high standard in recent years, though definitive studies have yet to appear.[1] This paper discusses their attempts to assuage the conflicts of nineteenth-century Ireland by articulating anti-utilitarian discourses of Irishness based on Catholicism and nationalism, and the extent to which this reflected the tensions and crises of their personal belief-systems, with particular reference to two related novels about the Fenian movement: *When We Were Boys* (1890) by O'Brien and *The Graves at Kilmorna* (1914) by Sheehan. These are not major works of literature; they are discussed as expressions of political ideas (though intellectual coherence – or incoherence – is relevant to any literary valuation).

O'Brien and Sheehan were contemporaries from similar Catholic middle-class backgrounds in Mallow, North Cork. (They attended the same elementary school.) Sheehan's father was a shopkeeper; O'Brien's was managing clerk to a prominent local attorney and owned house property in the town. O'Brien's mother was related to an old Catholic gentry family, the Nagles; he was proud of their relationship to Burke. O'Brien's elder brother, James Nagle O'Brien, was intended for the priesthood but expelled from the diocesan seminary for Fenianism (dismaying his parents, former Young Irelanders grown conservative with political defeat and family responsibilities).[2]

In adolescence, both Sheehan and O'Brien experienced deep bereavement through the loss of parents and siblings, exacerbated by what Tom Garvin describes as the formative experience of nationalist intellectuals of this period: the discovery that the new Catholic middle class could not guarantee their children a secure place in a world dominated intellectually, socially, and economically by Britons and Protestants.[3] Sheehan's parents died; he was entrusted to the guardianship of a priest relative, and became a priest himself despite early professional ambitions.[4] Geoffrey Austin, central character of Sheehan's first two novels (*Geoffrey Austin, Student* and *The Triumph of Failure*) represents the Canon's ideas of himself as he might have been if he had not become a priest. He wanders for years through dead-end jobs, retaining a nominal commitment to Catholicism but driven by intellectual pride to wrestle with modern thought like a timid Stephen Dedalus, until a child and a Catholic lay evangelist melt his heart by their simple faith and he finds refuge in religious life.[5] The early deaths of two sisters deepened Sheehan's introspective melancholy; while a clerical student he suffered a nervous breakdown (related to persistent feelings of unworthiness for the priesthood) and spent a year convalescing before proceeding to ordination.[6]

O'Brien's father suffered business failure, sold up and moved his family to Cork, where he died shortly afterwards. When James Nagle lost his job for taking part in a Fenian procession, the young William, now a journalist, became the sole support of his mother, sister, and two brothers. For a time he attended the local Queen's College, despite ecclesiastical restrictions, but left because of financial constraints. James Nagle continued to participate in Fenian raids under the famous Irish-American guerrilla, Captain Mackey-Lomasney (later killed planting a bomb in London). William was involved with the IRB for some years and was impressed by the integrity of its members, but left when he realised it had no chance of staging a successful rising, was infiltrated by informers, and that a few dishonest members used it as a cover for criminal activities. Over the next decade, while William became one of the most prominent reporters on *The Freeman's Journal*, his family succumbed to TB. His brothers and sister died within a few months in 1879-80; his mother followed in 1882. By the time of her death, O'Brien had made the acquaintance of Parnell, become editor of the new Parnellite paper *United Ireland*, and been imprisoned in Kilmainham. Soon after his release in 1882, he was elected MP for Mallow. Until marriage in 1890, O'Brien lived in a Dublin hotel, with all his possessions in two portmanteaus.[7] He claimed that until Parnell told him of Gladstone's conversion to Home Rule in 1886, he expected the Parnell movement to end in rebellion and the scaffold. He felt his political effectiveness was increased because he lacked dependents to suffer by his destruction.[8]

As a priest, Sheehan did not experience the same sort of social insecurity, but knew of it through his brother, D.B. Sheehan, whose experience of a college which 'crammed' pupils for Civil Service entrance examinations provided the basis for *Geoffrey Austin, Student*.[9] Some later novels mention discrimination against Catholic white-collar workers in Protestant-owned businesses and the Civil Service, though Sheehan never treats this subject in depth. One of his central concerns is that the rising Catholic professional classes, whose social mobility rendered them less amenable to traditional religious constraints, would look up to Protestants and imitate them.[10] A striking example of his view of the perils of social ambition occurs in *Geoffrey Austin, Student*, when ambitious parents who send their son to a Queen's College – then under ecclesiastical prohibition – cause his subsequent unbelief, debauchery, attempted priest-murder, death without repentance, and damnation. The anti-clerical Frank Hugh O'Donnell – graduate of Queen's College Galway, former nationalist MP, and *déraciné* with aristocratic fantasies – remarked that such attitudes would hardly promote Catholic lay education, and that the Catholic-run civil service college in the same novel was full of bullying and other misdemeanours.[11]

Sheehan's social insecurity, instead, reflected awareness that orthodox Christianity, and the Catholic priesthood, were becoming marginal to the concerns of the modern world and its professional culture. *Geoffrey Austin, Student* argues that Catholic schools should pay less attention to state examinations and more to Catholic thought and culture – in other words, they should resemble seminaries which, in the Middle Ages, trained their students to carry out clerical duties performed by civil servants under modern conditions of mass literacy.[12] Sheehan experienced further shocks when he went on the English mission for some years after ordination. He was already acquainted with English literature; now he saw London itself: its power, wealth, and confidence in its own beliefs (or lack of belief), its lack of interest in Catholicism, and its slow assimilation of the Irish who lived there. From 1881-89, he was a curate in Queenstown (Cobh), adjusting with difficulty to his parishioners' lifestyle. At this time Fr Keller, a close friend of Canon Sheehan, led the land agitation on the nearby Ponsonby estate, a crucial battleground for the Plan of Campaign led by William O'Brien.[13]

O'Brien had become one of Parnell's chief lieutenants and organisers, a powerful, emotional orator who could dominate a crowd better than any of his colleagues,[14] and a fierce publicist whose vituperative attacks on the Dublin Castle administration (including the exposure of a homosexual ring involving Dublin Castle officials) were compared by Unionists to the obscene demagogues of the French Revolution.[15] Separatists denounced him as a self-dramatising poseur who inflated every trivial clash with the administration into an epic battle while avoiding an actual appeal to arms,[16] and commentators then[17] and now[18] pour scorn on his hysterical populist sentimentalism in contrast with the reserved and incisive professionalism of Parnell or even the scabrous Mitchelian wit of Healy. O'Brien's endless flow of adjectives is quite frankly unreadable (and its sheer bulk poses tremendous difficulties for his biographers; he seems to have had a compulsion to speak and write lasting almost to the hour of his death). The disasters O'Brien periodically brought on himself (and many unfortunate followers) when he became intoxicated with his own rhetoric, the dictatorial behaviour produced by his obsession with his own projects, and the embarrassing U-turns which saw associates rhetorically transformed from demons to demigods as his political alliances shifted, certainly contributed to his eventual political marginalisation and to the demise of the Irish Party. But his critics often show the disdain of elites (parliamentary or revolutionary) for the methods needed to achieve mass mobilisation in support of what was, after all, a semi-revolutionary movement; they judge battlefield rhetoric as utterances in cold print and treat the self-dramatisation needed for mass leadership as a rule of everyday life (errors in which O'Brien unfortunately anticipated them). His theatre of defiance helped to undermine old methods of control through social elites and put pressure on the government to make concessions.[19] Unionist contempt and Nationalist admiration for O'Brien were at their height during the Plan of Campaign (1887-90), when he was imprisoned several times and engaged in a widely-publicised struggle during his first jail term over his refusal to wear prison clothing.

When We Were Boys was written during two subsequent (more tranquil) spells of imprisonment. Some shortcomings reflect the circumstances of its composition; O'Brien wrote the second half without access to the first, could not correct proofs because he had jumped bail on another charge, and refused to rewrite later editions in case changes might be interpreted as acceptance of claims by some critics that the book was anti-clerical.[20] O'Brien had meant to write it for years;[21] the hero is partly James Nagle O'Brien but as the novel progresses he increasingly resembles O'Brien himself. The book has a very complicated plot. It is best to give a brief summary and let further details emerge while discussing some central themes: Fenianism, religion, and reconciliation.

Ken Rohan is the son of a miller, Myles Rohan, a former Young Irelander with enough of his old spirit to stand up to the land agent on the Board of Guardians as no one has ever done before. The novel opens with Ken leaving home to attend the Diocesan Seminary, whose president, Dr O'Harte, is based on Archbishop Croke (an old friend of the O'Brien family).[22] Ken discovers he has no vocation and is introduced to Fenianism by Jack Harold, the flippant, French-educated nephew of the saintly curate Fr Phil. Ken returns home to become a local Fenian leader, despite denunciations by the parish priest, Monsignor McGrudder.

Meanwhile, the landlord, Lord Drumshaughlin, lives in seedy debauchery in London while his agent, Hans Harman, squeezes the tenants, embezzles the rents, and plots with a local gombeenman to get the estate. (Critics interested in the Irish antecedents of Dracula should note the vampiric subtext associated with Harman; he is always preternaturally cheerful and vigorous while those around him – the tenants, his invalid wife and spinster sisters – are drained of life, his teeth are 'as sharp-looking as fixed bayonets, as well as equally shining'; he excels at ensnaring vulnerable people and making them his creatures.) Lord Drumshaughlin's illegitimate son Harry, left to vegetate on the estate in drink and ignorance, drifts into the Fenian conspiracy.[23] His (legitimate) sister Mabel comes back from England to look after her brother and finds herself drawn in when she takes an interest in the tenants. Mabel meets Ken and they are increasingly attracted to one another. Business difficulties leave Myles Rohan at the mercy of the agent. Myles is saved from bankruptcy at the last time minute by Mabel's intervention, but his health is broken and he dies soon afterwards.[24]

The national Fenian leaders bungle their preparations for the Rising through dreamy inattention to practicalities.[25] Irish-American help arrives, but the Rising has to be called off. A drunken and desperate tailor leads the dregs of the movement in an orgy of destruction. In saving Mabel from the mob, Harry is killed; Ken is wounded and captured by the authorities.

Joshua Neville – a visiting English industrialist and friend of Ken and Mabel – discovers the agent's frauds and saves the estate. With Neville's help, Father Phil and local Fenian sympathisers nominate Ken at a by-election against the place-hunting Catholic Attorney-General and elect him, despite the opposition of landlords and Whig priests led by Monsignor McGrudder. The tailor turns Queen's Evidence and blames Ken, who is sentenced to death. His sentence is commuted to life imprisonment, and the novel ends with Ken boarding a prison transport for England. Joshua Neville assures the broken-hearted Mabel 'This is NOT THE END'. O'Brien adds a note telling his English readers that Ireland's fate still hangs in the balance; they will decide what shall be THE END.[26] O'Brien intended to write a sequel set after Home Rule dealing with the Land League and Home Rule movement, showing how Parnell and Croke together achieved the freedom the Fenians could not win.[27]

This schema and the title implicitly present Fenianism as the product of generous but immature youthful idealism. O'Brien notes in passing that the farmers kept aloof from the movement (a point also admitted by contemporary Fenians), because, unlike the Land League, it offered them no material advantage – though their unexpected support for Ken in the by-election reveals their hidden patriotism.[28] The only national Fenian leader introduced is a dreamy poet whose dreams will be harshly dispelled in Portland prison (a cruel reference to Kickham, who denounced the Land League as morally degrading).[29]

The rank and file are brave but naïve, with no idea of the odds against them.[30] Ken only realises the extent of British military power when he sees warships in Bantry Bay on the eve of the Rising.[31]

Several local Fenian leaders, including the tailor and an impecunious editor based on the Tipperary Fenian, Peter Gill, drink heavily.[32] (Surviving Fenians found this particularly offensive; O'Donovan Rossa predicted its author would eventually receive a British government pension.[33]) The drunken tailor who leads others to murder and then turns informer shows the dangers of revolutionary demagogues and secret societies. (He reappears in Sheehan's *My New Curate* as 'Hop-and-Go-One', an anti-clerical whose sinister activities are foiled by the curate.[34] 'Hop-and-Go-One' was criticised in Arthur Griffith's *United Irishman* by separatists who noted the anti-Fenian message and its source in O'Brien's novel.[35]) For a British audience, the tailor distances the nationalist mainstream from outrages, as the Parliamentary Party distanced itself from Captain Moonlight and the Invincibles.

Nevertheless, O'Brien presents the Irish-American Fenians as *deus ex machina*, and claims their experience and Irish enthusiasm would have helped produced a sweeping victory had the British not discovered the plans just before the Americans arrived in force.[36] In fact, Irish-American Fenians were as much beset by internal disputes and shortage of funds as those involved in the movement at home.[37] O'Brien was unwilling to accept that the Rising could not have succeeded; this would bring him too close to the cynicism of Jack Harold, so he escapes into fantasy. This also reflects his increasing identification with Ken as the novel progresses. Ken becomes famous in an implausibly short time as editor of a clandestine newspaper, based on O'Brien's own experiences with *United Ireland*.[38] He is tried in Dublin and is credited with what appear to be O'Brien's own reflections about standing in the dock where Emmet stood; a Fenian arrested in West Cork in 1867 would have been tried, however, in Cork City.[39] Ken's by-election conflates Rossa's election for Tipperary and O'Brien's election for Mallow, but the nationalist majority in the novel is far greater than was the case in either of these actual contests.[40]

In 1896, after the defeat of the Second Home Rule Bill, O'Brien used a similar portrayal of the Rising to threaten the Tory government with another incursion when diplomatic tension developed between Britain and America;[41] but in 1890, his primary concern was to 'place' Fenianism in international politics, reflecting the late nineteenth-century turning of Irish nationalist hopes for external aid from France to America. O'Brien was a Francophile; shortly after the publication of *When We Were Boys* he married a Frenchwoman of Jewish birth.[42] He thought the French Revolution, for all its horrors, more good than evil, and disagreed amicably with Sheehan over the priest's novel of the French Revolution, *The Queen's Fillet*.[43] (Sheehan admitted the horrors of the *ancien regime*, but disliked the Revolution and most aspects of nineteenth-century French culture.

He preferred the idealistic and monarchical Germans.)[44] Nevertheless, *When We Were Boys* presents the French revolutionary tradition represented by Jack Harold as morally unstable because pervaded by religious scepticism. Jack's dabbling in many subjects gives him a superficial brilliance which lacks substance (a classic British-Romantic stereotype of French metropolitan culture).[45] As Ken grows, Jack shrinks; the stolid Ken becomes the patriot hero while Jack turns unsuccessful place hunter, courts an old maid for her money, and nearly becomes an informer.[46] Jack is saved at the last minute by instinctive moral revulsion and is sent to America to make something of himself.[47]

O'Brien presents Irish-Americans as models for the future, reconciling enterprise and democracy with national and religious sentiment. The Irish-American officers (the most prominent is based on Captain Mackey-Lomasney) lament the dreamy, unenterprising nature of the Irish at home, yet, when challenged, they admit it is fidelity to a dream which brings them back to Ireland.[48] Elsewhere, O'Brien claimed that exposure to Irish-American ideas had dissolved the deference to the gentry he remembered from his youth in Mallow.[49] O'Brien described the theme of his novel as conflict between the new Irish-American democracy and Cardinal Cullen's attempt to yoke Catholicism to the Irish *ancien régime*.[50] This portrayal of the conflict between Church and Fenians, however, caused controversy. O'Brien complained that passages from the novel, taken out of context, gave him an anti-clerical reputation, a theme which is taken up by a recent critic who presents *When We Were Boys* as the first appearance of the anti-clerical literary intelligentsia so important in twentieth-century Irish cultural history.[51]

O'Brien's beliefs certainly contrasted acutely with those of Sheehan, who shared the contemporary upper-class Catholic tendency to regard the social hierarchy as divinely ordained and suggested – using religious sentiment to veil exploitative power relations – that all would be well if only the landlords were Catholics.[52] O'Brien conscientiously tried to be fair to Monsignor Mc-Grudder, but this reflects his sense of duty rather than any deep interest in the character. O'Brien is not interested in the Cullenite mindset. For him, Cullenite Bishops were simultaneously arrogant theocrats and timid survivors of pre-Emancipation days.[53] Monsignor McGrudder's pretensions are firmly deflated (he boasts of hobnobbing with the Roman aristocracy, but is regularly reminded he is the son of a petty publican). We are told that he is personally sincere, lives in uncomfortable splendour because he considers it due to his office, neglects his people's poverty only because he thinks it divinely ordained, is preoccupied with dreams of revived mediæval theocracy,[54] and keeps silent when threatened, not from cowardice but to preserve his assailant from the sin of murder. But these defences insinuate the charges ostensibly denied. His most memorable scenes involve Fenian defiance of his diatribes.[55] It is clear from these exchanges that O'Brien thought Papal resistance to Italian unity mistaken.[56] The parallels with the Irish *ancien regime* were too strong to ignore, and O'Brien's opinion of Vatican political wisdom cannot have been improved by its condemnation of the Plan of Campaign. In the Diocesan College of *When We Were Boys,* the Prefect of Studies is a bully who encourages sneaks and insincere flatterers;[57] the chief flatterer goes to Trinity (forbidden by the Bishops) as soon as his gombeenman father can send him,[58] becoming a budding member of the hypocritical 'electro-plated Catholic upper class' (represented by the loose-living, place-hunting Attorney-General),[59] whose advancement is promoted by the Church and identified with the Catholic faith.

A social role held in former centuries by a proletariat of unbeneficed clergy was shared in O'Brien's age by other nationalist intellectuals and literati like the scholastic Joyce, who lacked a fixed social position, and tried to secure one by the power of the word. Sheehan prescribed the traditional remedy for such wanderers – the cloister. O'Brien was attracted (he told his wife that before meeting her, he dreamt of becoming a monk when Home Rule was won).[60] This dream had an element of self-deception (his public life was punctuated by 'final' retirements and returns 'by popular demand') but its existence marks him out from later, more secular literati. O'Brien said Cullen's folly had set at odds what should be inseparable – Faith and Fatherland; but by the 1880s, they were reunited and Monsignor McGrudder represented an extinct species replaced by a new generation of patriot priests.[61] The Monsignor is contrasted with his humble, saintly (and patriotic) old curate, just as the College President offsets the bestial Prefect of Studies.[62]

O'Brien was an extremely pious Catholic with a fervent, emotional religious faith. He carried *The Imitation of Christ* everywhere.[63] O'Brien revered the fifteenth-century Rhineland mystics (from whom à Kempis sprang) as keepers of the faith in a corrupt world. Mysticism can encourage dismissal of abstract doctrine and church structures (the Rhineland mystics are often seen as precursors of the Reformation; some Catholic writers on mysticism came under suspicion in the modernist crisis of the early twentieth century), but O'Brien did not go so far. He was not particularly interested in theology, but never denied its importance. In 1914, he told an English reporter he was proud modernism made no impression on the people of Munster.[64] In *When We Were Boys*, Ken reads the mystics at Gougane Barra, dreaming of austere seventh-century Irish hermits.[65] Yet Ken explains to Dr O'Harte (who attributes his decision not to enter the priesthood to excessive scrupulosity) that he knows most people can never be mystics and Irish priests are no less holy because they mingle in everyday life.[66]

O'Brien admired the new church buildings rising across Ireland as the Catholic Church reasserted its place in Irish life. He thought it miraculous that when the yoke of persecution was removed 'the same faith that once inhabited the ruined shrines is rebuilding them',[67] even if the replacements were at present rather showy and vulgar, and their clerical occupants often more snobbish and ambitious than was good for them.[68] His indiscreet social observations on some of the incongruities attending the project of replacing the Protestant Ascendancy with a Catholic ruling class in alliance with the clergy does not mean, as Murphy suggests, that O'Brien had abandoned the project itself.

Jack Harold tells Ken that his exposure to modern thought left him without faith in anything; Ken replies that he is familiar with modern thought and present-day attacks on Christianity contain nothing not refuted centuries ago. Ken does not reject the nineteenth century – 'that glorious mother age' – which has brought political freedom and material progress ('Applied Christianity') to the human race; but its triumphs do not touch the ultimate questions of life, and when humanity has solved its earthly problems it will return to the faith of the seventh century in search of meaning.[69] (This is out of character for Ken, supposedly a naïve young provincial; O'Brien forgets himself and speaks with his own voice.) O'Brien (like Sheehan) wrote of Ireland's mission to rally the 'Celtic spirit' of faith and idealism against all-pervading scepticism; the besetting disorder of modernity, the 'Giant Despair' consuming the modern world.[70] O'Brien himself was not safe from Giant Despair, the sudden fear of futility. Jack Harold was as much part of him as Ken Rohan; O'Brien's insistence that Christianity must be true because without it life would be meaningless suggests a nagging awareness of the alternative possibility. O'Brien alternated bursts of feverish activity with depression and abrupt withdrawal from public life; he barely fought off drug addiction as a young man,[71] and contemplated suicide at one particularly black moment in the early 1880s.[72] Millenarianism was a remedy for despair. O'Brien belongs with those Catholic/nationalist intellectuals who combined criticism of the actual behaviour of the Church's representatives with hope for spiritual regeneration within the parameters of doctrinal orthodoxy: with Terence MacSwiney (another reader of the *Imitation* and critic of clerical reservations about nationalism as 'materialistic'),[73] Frank Duff (who also had disciplinary problems with bishops),[74] and Aodh de Blacam (who combined criticism of the behaviour of actual priests with millennial visions of an utopian Catholic-nationalist social order),[75] rather than Joyce and Ó Faoláin.

O'Brien later claimed that *When We Were Boys* prefigured the policy of conciliation between nationalists and unionists associated with his later career. He does not notice the incongruity of this claim with his emphasis on the inseparability of Faith and Fatherland. In fact, reconciliation between Anglo-Irish Protestants and Anglo-Irish nationalism is relatively underplayed in the novel. A conversation in one chapter between Catholic and Protestant, Irish, English, and Irish-American characters allegedly foreshadows the harmony of the future. Harmony is easily achieved, since the Ascendancy contingent consists of aristocratic Fenian sympathisers and a tame Protestant rector who disapproves of proselytisation and admits the Church of Ireland should be disestablished.[76] The Ascendancy is symbolised by the familial and financial chaos of the Drumshaughlins and by Mabel's lament as she asks the origins of a local place-name: 'I am an alien, and am not in the secret'.[77] Ken tells the story behind the placename; O'Brien implies that once England puts Irish affairs in order, the Ascendancy will shake off their sordid past and merge into a deeper, spiritually satisfying Irish identity (though O'Brien sees this taking place by natural attraction rather than force – hence the implied union between Ken and Mabel[78] – and his concept of Irish identity included an idealised picture of the Protestant patriot tradition as well as of the Catholic and Gaelic past).

Reconciliation is a major theme of *When We Were Boys*, but O'Brien has in mind the reconciliation of Great Britain and Ireland. The book reflects the 'Union of Hearts' of the late 1880s, when the Irish Party hoped Gladstone's last moral crusade would awaken the British public, bringing a Liberal landslide and Home Rule. Joshua Neville (based on the Gladstonian MP Jacob Bright) is a model for the English reader moving from fear and prejudice to support for Irish nationalism. English misrule of Ireland (at least in the nineteenth century) is blamed on misunderstandings. Economic development as a cure for Irish na-tionalism (expounded by a naively utilitarian Liberal Chief Secretary vaguely based on W.E. Foster) is doomed to failure;[79] but once Ireland's house is in order she will gladly employ hardheaded English expertise. The novel abounds with stereotypical Arnoldian stolid Saxons and dreamy Celts. O'Brien claims Home Rule will fulfil the Arnoldian project of blending the best qualities of both, and litters the text with symbols of this hope: a mixed fire of coal and turf, supposedly burning brighter than either separately;[80] the marriage of Joshua Neville's son Reggie to the tomboy Georgey O'Meagher, who instantly becomes dutiful and submissive.[81]

There is a certain tension between this and O'Brien's exaltation of the Celt as unassimilable. Were the Saxons really likely to be transformed so profoundly? Might not the spirituality O'Brien exalted be connected more intimately than he suspected to the poverty he hoped to abolish through a constitutional settlement? A separatist (or an intelligent Catholic Whig) might remark that whether or not O'Brien himself realised it, his millenarian dream amounted to a new settlement continuing the project of his despised Whig predecessors, with a larger and more powerful Catholic middle class as senior instead of junior partner in the Irish ruling elite, and a fuller measure of autonomy for Ireland within the United Kingdom.

Instead of a Union of Hearts, however, Ireland experienced the Parnell Split. O'Brien sided with the Anti-Parnellites, then supported John Dillon against the clericalist Healy and discovered that Monsignor McGrudder was not extinct.[82] After the failure of the Second Home Rule Bill, O'Brien retired to Mayo, re-emerging a few years later to lead a new land campaign to re-unite the factions. The land campaign ended in 1903 with the Wyndham Land Act, the terms of which were negotiated at a conference of landlord and tenant representatives. O'Brien combined his violent invectives against landlordism with predictions that if the land question were solved, the landlords could be converted to nationalism. This was an old hope hackneyed from long use; there was widespread surprise when it was discovered that O'Brien meant what he said and believed a national conference modelled on the Land Conference could bring about a Home Rule settlement by consent. This departure from the longstanding exclusionary rhetoric directed against landlords and all symbols of Britishness during two decades of land struggle was too great to be achieved by a leader as volatile as O'Brien; there was a new struggle within the Party, and O'Brien resigned.[83] For some years, he operated on the fringes of Irish politics, keeping in touch with sympathisers within the Party, allied with Healy and some Devolutionist landlords. In 1910, he led a breakaway Conciliationist party based in his native Cork. One of the few priests who supported this movement was Sheehan, who wrote editorials for the O'Brienite *Cork Free Press* before being warned off by his bishop. He also endorsed a local Protestant O'Brienite landlord, Langley Brazier Creagh, in the 1911 County Council elections.[84]

This alliance reflected personal friendship and Sheehan's conservatism rather than any deeper ideological affinity. Sheehan was basically an intelligent Catholic Whig. His attitude to his Doneraile parishioners was benevolent paternalism. He worked closely with the local landlord, Lord Castletown of Upper Ossory, for the welfare of the area.[85] (The eccentric Castletown, active in the Gaelic League and the Irish industrial movement, was a political ally of O'Brien after 1903.)[86] Sheehan's best-loved novel, *My New Curate* (about a tired old parish priest trying to cope with an enthusiastic new curate) may owe something to the strain placed on this arrangement when Sheehan's curate in 1900, Fr T. O'Callaghan, became one of the most active land campaigners in Munster.[87]

Both O'Brien and Sheehan dreamed of a Catholic Utopia, but where O'Brien dreamed of a mystical reconciliation between Catholicism and modernity in which neither would be sacrificed, Sheehan's ideal was a static hierarchical society of aristocrats, priests, and peasants united in piety. Sheehan saw this ideal as inseparable from Catholicism, and without faith his life – and the deaths of his parents and sisters – would become meaningless. He was uneasy at the growth of the Catholic middle class. Sheehan feared that the social prestige of the Anglo-Irish and the weight of English culture might lead Catholic professionals – and Ireland – away from the Faith; his pious, unmaterialistic peasants conformed to an origin-myth assimilating the new class to the old pattern.

Sheehan complained about Irish ignorance of European Catholic culture (he often refers to great Catholic theologians and continental writers and laments that their works are unknown in English-speaking countries) and called for Irish Catholicism to prepare itself intellectually for the challenges it faced. He predicted sanguinely that classicist neo-paganism, materialism, and utilitarianism were in decline, and the Idealist revival showed the world was returning to God.[88]

Some priests were suspicious of Sheehan: would discussion of the problems of the priesthood assist hostile critics?[89] Sheehan shared these fears and advised priests to assist economic development, but worried nonetheless that material progress might encourage illusions of self-sufficiency and forgetfulness of God. (Contemporary clerical writers such as Msgr Michael O'Riordan replied to charges of discouraging economic progress by simultaneously listing priests involved in local industries and arguing that urban industrialism was soul-destroying and the Irish were better – though poorer – without it.[90] Craft industries, as praised by O'Riordan, are founded by Fr Lethaby in *My New Curate* and by the Canon in *Luke Delmege*; in both cases the industry is wrecked by forces outside the priests' control and accepted as divine judgment.) The Faith must be defended against intellectual challenges, but could the most formidable apologetic replace simple faith? Might intellectualism bring scepticism, undermining the faith it meant to preserve? Sheehan brooded on nineteenth-century priest-intellectuals who abandoned the Church, like Renan and Lammenais; one poem describes attempting to say Mass in Hell.[91] The priest renouncing his books to avoid temptation recurs in his work.[92] Shortly before his death, Sheehan destroyed his manuscript memoirs to avoid provoking a scandal.[93]

O'Brien's All-for-Ireland League failed to expand outside Cork. Its election campaigns were marked by rioting between O'Brienites and Redmondites. As a Third Home Rule Bill approached, its support dwindled – assisted by Party patronage.[94] O'Brien and Sheehan thought the Redmondites sectarian place hunters dominated by the Ancient Order of Hibernians, and believed the terms of the Bill were disastrous.[95] Sheehan also feared that machining public opinion and discouraging dissent paved the way for what he believed had happened in France at the abrogation of the Concordat – a passive, demoralised populace allowing a ruthless anti-clerical elite to crush the Church. In his literary dialogue *The Intellectuals*, one character predicts that unless 'the great Protestant Conservative element' can be brought back into politics after Home Rule, the Bishops will one day go mitre in hand to the Imperial Parliament to save them from the Irish Government.[96]

As Sheehan worked on *The Graves at Kilmorna*, O'Brien's political fortunes were declining and Sheehan's health was breaking down. (He died before revising the novel.) Sheehan returned to memories of his boyhood, when he saw Fenians drilling, and looked over the seminary wall at the funeral of Peter O'Neill-Crowley (a Fenian guerrilla leader killed in a skirmish at Kilclooney

Wood)[97] to describe how Ken Rohan might have fared after emerging from prison.[98] *The Graves at Kilmorna* charts the spiritual growth of Miles Cogan, a miller's son disgusted by the drunken corruption of electoral politics in the 1860s. His Whig father disapproves of his Fenian activities and dies of a stroke partly caused by them.[99] The Anglo-Irish element is written out; perhaps Sheehan found it difficult to deal with its religious implications. The love interest in *The Graves at Kilmorna* derives from a minor subplot of *When We Were Boys*, Ken's calf-love for Lily Dargan, daughter of the local gombeenman. Her social-climbing parents make her marry a police inspector with gentry connections; she later uses information obtained from her husband to warn Ken of his impending arrest.[100] The equivalent character in *The Graves*, a friend of Miles's sister, loves Miles from a distance. She gets her police suitor to arrest Miles to save him from participation in the Rising, but Miles is rescued and only recaptured after a skirmish and the death of his friend Halpin (a poverty-stricken schoolmaster and local Fenian leader, in love with Miles's sister).[101] Miles is sentenced to death but his sentence is commuted to life imprisonment.

Ten years later, after suffering the cruelties endured by Rossa and Davitt in English jails, Miles is amnestied and returns to an Ireland which has forgotten him. His sister has kept the family business going despite an unscrupulous Northern competitor. Soon after Miles returns, she enters a convent. (The sister who has an admirer killed in the Rising and becomes a nun also derives from *When We Were Boys*.[102]) Miles finds himself out of sympathy with the trend of Irish life and politics; he places his chief clerk in charge of the business and devotes himself to prayer and study under the guidance of his friend Fr James. Miles sees the modern world – including Ireland – as hopelessly corrupt and materialistic, though a mystical monk at Mount Mellary assures him Ireland will repent and enjoy a great spiritual mission. When the son of his old admirer and the police inspector (an intelligent, honest young man) naïvely stands against the machine as an Independent Nationalist, Miles is persuaded to support him, despite threats that the Cogan business will be boycotted.[103] The old Fenian is killed by a drunken election mob; Father James buries him beside Halpin.[104]

O'Brien presented the Fenians as rash dreamers but could not bring himself to admit they had no chance of success. Sheehan explicitly states they had no chance of success – and glorifies them for it. The Irish-Americans whom O'Brien depicted as combining the best of tradition and modernity are presented less favorably by Sheehan, who denounced emigrants as betraying tradition for material gain, though his primary audience were Irish-Americans. His popularity reflected emigrant guilt.[105] Early in *The Graves*, an American emissary denounces Irish incompetence.[106] Miles seeks reassurance from Halpin and is told that while defeat is certain, their deaths will reawaken a people degraded to a drunken election mob: 'Ireland is sinking into the sleep of death, and nothing can rouse her but the crack of the rifle'.[107] During the Rising, Halpin dismisses his followers to avoid needless slaughter and fights alone (except for Miles and an American officer based on Mackey-Lomasney) until mortally wounded.[108] In the short term, Halpin is vindicated. Miles proclaims his blood sacrifice doctrine from the dock, and while the judge tries to refute it with utilitarianism, he breaks down in tears and leaves the Bench. Justice Murrurty, who tries O'Brien's Fenian, is a fictionalised William Keogh, who incited Whiteboys as a nationalist politician, then accepted government office and got a judgeship for his political services. O'Brien justifies Fenian dreams by contrasting them with those of Keogh and the place-hunting Attorney-General (based on the law officer and former Young Irelander, M.J. Barry). Sheehan's Attorney-General is also a corrupt place hunter, the employer of the drunken mob in the opening chapters, but his nameless Judge is an abstract embodiment of Justice, and the breakdown of this character illustrates Sheehan's theme of the insufficiency of materialist Reason before idealist Faith.[109]

Sheehan's portrayal of Fenianism as pure idealism plays down the actual content of Fenian ideology. Miles says in his speech from the dock that he has no particular vision of a free Ireland, and accepts after his release that 'the dream of independence was impracticable'.[110] The Church's ban on Fenianism is downplayed as much as possible; Sheehan says, as narrator and through Father James, that the Church was right, but does not argue a case.[111] Miles never doubts his Faith and feels agony at exclusion from the Sacraments; in prison, he repents his quarrel with the Church and becomes extremely devout.[112] After his release he is active in local Church affairs and brings back many old comrades to religious observance.[113] He leads the life of a monk: Sheehan hints that – like Peter O'Neill Crowley – he has taken a vow of celibacy.[114] Under Father James's guidance, he comes to see that the problems affecting Ireland, which he wrongly attributed to Britain alone, are pathologies of modernity spreading across the whole developed world. The local old Fenians associate together (they intimidate Cogan workmen who might go elsewhere for higher wages, and turn out en bloc for Miles's funeral; Sheehan is thinking of the Old Guard Union, a friendly society of old Fenians, organised openly in most Irish towns),[115] but the survival of the secret IRB after 1867 is ignored because it would imply continuing conflict with the Church. (This explains the apparent incongruity between this novel and Sheehan's hostile portrayal of post-1867 Fenians in *My New Curate*.)

Constitutional politics are portrayed in *The Graves* in the blackest terms. The Whig father in O'Brien's novel is brave and honest and opposes his son's Fenian activities from bitter experience and concern for his welfare. In desperation, he sinks so far as to beg a government job for him from his old enemy, Hans Harman.[116] In Sheehan's novel, the father is totally corrupt, wants his son to become a place-hunting lawyer, and hints that Miles should sow a few wild oats.[117] (O'Brien's father played the same role in the election of the crown prosecutor, Edward Sullivan, that Miles Rohan's father has in the novel, and entertained similar hopes for James Nagle.[118]) The portrayal of the election mobs at the beginning and end of the novel implies contemporary machine politics are indistinguishable from the Whiggery of the previous generation.

O'Brien would have agreed, but saw this as degeneration from the days of Parnell and the Land League. Sheehan, however, presents that tradition as corrupt from the beginning. Davitt ('McDermot') appears eaten up by hatred and desire for revenge, though he does possess a certain love for Ireland and a clearer realisation of the people's material suffering than Fenian idealists.[119] Where O'Brien intended to show the Land League fulfilling Fenian ideals through a firmer grasp on realities, Sheehan endorses the purist Fenian view that it was a betrayal of true nationalism; the League encouraged the farmers' basest material instincts and was directly responsible for agrarian atrocities.[120] Parnell ('Mr Fottrel') is an arrogant dictator subjecting public opinion to regimented unanimity, forcing strangers and anti-clericals on unwilling constituencies.[121] Sheehan shared the Healyite-clerical preference for a decentralised Party structure less able to challenge priests' local authority; his populism is really an objection to a secular political leadership disputing, as O'Brien had done, clerical claims to represent the people's best interests. The people's submission to politicians proves their degradation. The Catholic lay evangelist Charlie Travers in *The Triumph of Failure* is Sheehan's idea of what 'Charlie' Parnell *should* have been. He raises the people by appealing disinterestedly to their highest religious instincts and is *falsely* accused of embezzlement and sexual relations with an English prostitute. As he lies dying after his vindication, Charlie is saluted by a great procession of the Dublin trades – whose adhesion to Parnell and turn-out at his funeral fanned priestly fears of anti-clericalism.[122]

Where O'Brien is optimistic, Sheehan is pessimistic. Sheehan fears the 'Union of Hearts' is all too successful. He laments that England has finally learned that harshness breeds martyrs but that kindness is making Ireland 'West Anglia'. 'Modern business methods', practised by Miles's Northern rival, are intrinsically dishonest. Sheehan echoes a widespread nationalist belief that the economic success of Northern Protestants derived from fraud and unfair trading methods.[123] O'Brienite conciliation was directed towards the traditional landed elite, and ignored the new Ulster Unionism. Modern education is superficial and utilitarian. Even the physique of the Irish race has allegedly decayed since Sheehan's youth.[124] Miles meets a German aristocrat who laments that democracy is destroying the glorious symbols of Throne and Altar for monotonous egalitarianism. Sheehan can only hope a miracle may reverse the process.[125]

When Sheehan's novel appeared, shortly before the Easter Rising, some separatists hailed it;[126] and after 1916, many commentators (including O'Brien), noting the similarity between the blood sacrifice rhetoric of Halpin and Pearse, proclaimed Sheehan as a prophet.[127] (This was not the only political reading of the novel; just before the Rising a Redmondite priest cited it in a book of pro-recruitment essays.)[128] In fact, the novel ends despairingly; Fr James tells a little group of old Fenians that he has nothing to say beside the two graves containing the hopes of their generation.[129]

O'Brien eventually endorsed Sinn Féin (and supported the Republicans in the Civil War) while maintaining that his conciliationist policy had been correct and that he had always been consistent; when the channels of constitutional recourse were corrupted, violence was necessary to secure a hearing for moderation.

Sheehan and O'Brien both hoped to win mass support for an elite-led reconciliation between old and new regimes by presenting it, as they represented it to themselves, in terms of spiritual rebirth and national renewal. Neither had a clear understanding of the full difficulties involved; O'Brien saw the political aspect more clearly than Sheehan, while Sheehan saw intellectual consequences of modernity overlooked by the sanguine O'Brien. Their rhetoric was co-opted by a new, Catholic, middle-class generation which combined O'Brienlike millenarianism and Sheehan-style dreams of pious peasants ruled by a paternal elite in a self-image justifying the social arrangements of the independent Irish state in the decades after 1922. More recently, after this image broke down, attempts were made to enlist both men as voices of tolerance and liberalism.[130] Both these projects can find source-material in their writings, although neither can explain the existence of the other, for neither captures the full complexity of the personal griefs and social tensions which beset them in the final decades of the Irish *ancien regime*.

Notes

[1] Paul Bew, *Conflict and Conciliation in Ireland 1890-1910* (Oxford, 1987); Sally Warwick-Haller, *William O'Brien and the Irish Land War* (Dublin, 1990); Philip Bull, *Land, Politics and Nationalism: A Study of the Irish Land Question* (Dublin, 1996); James H. Murphy, *Catholic Fiction and Irish Social Reality, 1870-1922* (London, 1997); Catherine Candy, *Priestly Fictions* (Dublin, 1995); Ruth Fleischmann, *Catholic Nationalism in the Irish Revival: A Study of Canon Sheehan* (London & Dublin, 1997).

[2] William O'Brien, *Recollections* (London, 1905).

[3] Tom Garvin, *Nationalist Intellectuals in Ireland 1858-1928* (Oxford, 1987).

[4] Fleischmann, *Catholic Nationalism in the Irish Revival*, p. 20.

[5] Canon P.A. Sheehan, *Geoffrey Austin, Student* (Dublin, 1895); *The Triumph of Failure* (London, 1901).

[6] H.J. Heuser, *Canon Sheehan of Doneraile* (London & New York, 1917), p. 37; Fleischmann, *Catholic Nationalism in the Irish Revival*, p. 22.

7   O'Brien, *Recollections and Evening Memories* (Dublin & London, 1920), pp. 27-8.
8   O'Brien, *Evening Memories*, pp. 101-2.
9   Heuser, *Canon Sheehan*, p. 17.
10 Cf. the Wilson family in Sheehan, *Luke Delmege* (London, 1901). The father is a Catholic doctor who joins the Freemasons for professional advancement (pp. 123-4), the mother is a social climber and their son is an atheistic profligate who dies of debauchery and is only saved from Hell by the self-sacrifice of his pious sister.
11 Frank Hugh O'Donnell, *The Ruin of Education in Ireland, and the Irish Fanar* (London, 1902), pp. 167-70.
12 Sheehan, *The Graves at Kilmorna* (London, 1914; hereafter *Graves*), pp. 234-5, 237-8; Sheehan, *Geoffrey Austin*, p. 33. For the social processes behind these developments see Ernest Gellner, *Plough, Sword, and Book* (London, 1988).
13 Laurence Geary, *The Plan of Campaign* (Cork, 1986).
14 Michael MacDonagh, *The Home Rule Movement* (Dublin, 1919), p. 172.
15 'Parnellism and Crime', *The Times* (London, 1887), pp. 119-20.
16 P.J.P. Tynan, *The Irish National Invincibles and their Times* (London, 1894), pp. 248-9.
17 D.P. Moran, *Tom O'Kelly* (Dublin, 1905).
18 Frank Callanan, *The Parnell Split* (Cork, 1992).
19 Bull, *Land, Politics, and Nationalism*, pp. 120-3.
20 O'Brien, 'Introduction', *When We Were Boys* (reprint, Dublin, 1920, hereafter *WWWB*), p. xvii.
21 O'Brien, *Recollections*, pp. 206-8.
22 O'Brien, *WWWB*, pp. xi-xii.
23 Some aspects of Harry's character – his unintellectual nature and love of outdoor life – may be based on O'Brien's younger brother, Dick (*Recollections*, p. 169).
24 O'Brien, *Recollections*, p. 546.
25 O'Brien, *Recollections*, pp. 213, 285.
26 O'Brien, *Recollections*, pp. 549-50.
27 O'Brien, 'Introduction', *WWWB*, pp. vi-vii, xi.
28 O'Brien, *WWWB*, pp. 175, 511, 513, 545.
29 O'Brien, *WWWB*, pp. 393-4, 396, 548. For Kickham, see R.V. Comerford, *Charles J. Kickham* (Dublin, 1979).
30 O'Brien, *WWWB*, pp. 396-8.
31 O'Brien, *WWWB*, pp. 430-1.
32 O'Brien, *WWWB*. pp. 151-64, 437-8, 449-51. For Gill (uncle of T.P. Gill, MP), see O'Brien, *Recollections*, pp. 106-9.
33 Jeremiah O'Donovan Rossa, *Recollections* (New York, 1898; repr. Shannon, 1972), p. 129.

34 Sheehan, *My New Curate* (London, 1899), Chapter XI.

35 Review of *My New Curate* by 'Hop and Go One', *United Irishman* (15 September 1900), p. 3; see also defence of Sheehan by 'Maire' [Mary Butler], *United Irishman* (6 October 1900), p. 7, and renewed criticisms by 'Hop and Go One' and 'An Irishman', *United Irishman* (13 October 1900), p. 7.

36 O'Brien, *WWWB*, pp. 444-9.

37 Leon O. Broin, *Revolutionary Underground* (Dublin, 1976); R.V. Comerford, *The Fenians in Context* (Dublin, 1985).

38 O'Brien, *WWWB*, pp. 297-301, 394; compare O'Brien, *Recollections*, Chapter XIII.

39 For an account of the Cork Fenian trials, see A.M., T.D., & D.B. Sullivan, *Speeches from the Dock* (Dublin, 1968).

40 O'Brien, *WWWB*, p. 357.

41 O'Brien, 'Was Fenianism Ever Formidable?', *Contemporary Review* (May 1897), pp. 680-93; cf. also T.D. Sullivan's sarcastic comments on this essay in *Reminiscences of Troubled Times in Irish Politics* (Dublin, 1905).

42 Warwick-Haller, *William O'Brien and the Irish Land War*, pp. 144-7.

43 O'Brien to Sheehan (late 1911), quoted in Heuser, *Canon Sheehan*, pp. 257-8; see also *WWWB*, p. 76.

44 Heuser, *Canon Sheehan*, pp. 195-202.

45 O'Brien, *WWWB*, pp. 281-7.

46 A possible model is the relationship between Hardress Cregan and Kyrle Daly in Gerald Griffin's *The Collegians*.

47 O'Brien, *WWWB*, pp. 481-3, 583-9.

48 O'Brien, *WWWB*, pp. 248-9.

49 'The Lost Opportunities of the Irish Gentry' in O'Brien, *Irish Ideas*, pp. 16-24. This deference was not fully extinct, to judge from O'Brien's praise in *When We Were Boys* for the disdain of the established West Cork gentry at the introduction of a social-climbing gombeenman into their club, as well as for the lenient treatment of the absentee landlord by comparison with his agent; Captain O'Shea sarcastically commented on O'Brien's fondness for lords (F.S.L. Lyons, *Charles Stewart Parnell* [London, 1977], p. 304). O'Brien was later accused of expecting the same deference from his followers.

50 O'Brien, 'Introduction', *WWWB*, pp. v-vii.

51 James H. Murphy, 'William O'Brien's *When We Were Boys*: A New Voice from Old Conventions', *Irish University Review* (Autumn/Winter 1992), pp. 298-304; and *Catholic Fiction and Irish Social Reality 1870-1922* (London, 1997).

52 Fleischmann, *Catholic Nationalism in the Irish Revival*; for wider manifestations of this tendency see Murphy, *Catholic Fiction*.

53 O'Brien, *WWWB*, pp. 168, 514-5.

54 O'Brien, *WWWB*, pp. 169-71.

55 O'Brien, *WWWB*, Chapters XVII, XXXI, XXXVIII. Hence Griffith called Monsignor McGrudder the only good thing in this 'book of ten thousand adjectives' (*United Irishman*, [22 April 1899], p. 2).

56 O'Brien, *WWWB*, pp. 169-70, 469.

57 O'Brien, *WWWB*, pp. 21, 25, 29-31.

58 O'Brien, *WWWB*, pp. 23-4.

59 O'Brien, *WWWB*, pp. 171, 469-70.

60 O'Brien to Sophie in Sophie O'Brien (ed.), *Golden Memories: The Love Letters and the Prison Letters of William O'Brien* 2 vols. (Dublin, 1929) I: 35-6; see also p. 45.

61 O'Brien to Sophie, *Golden Memories*, I: vii, 168. This also acknowledges English fears of priestly power while assigning them to the past and showing lay nationalists prepared to defy illegitimate political claims.

62 O'Brien to Sophie, *Golden Memories*, I: 21, 129-33, 169. The curate was modelled on a curate at Mallow in O'Brien's childhood, but his patriot views are O'Brien's invention (O'Brien, *Recollections*, pp. 21-2).

63 Sophie O'Brien, *Golden Memories*, I: 35. Tim Healy said he knew that he had taken O'Brien's coat by mistake if he found *The Imitation* in the pocket.

64 Harold Begbie, *The Lady Next Door* (London, 1914), pp. 53-4. This interview praises priests as religious leaders while criticising them as politicians (i.e. for opposing his All-for-Ireland League) and combines exalted praise for their religious devotion with indiscreet remarks about the tendency for some priests to develop drink problems – all very reminiscent of *When We Were Boys*.

65 O'Brien, *WWWB*, pp. 124-5.

66 O'Brien, *WWWB*, p. 125.

67 O'Brien, 'The Irish National Idea', *Irish Ideas* (London, 1893), pp. 1-12.

68 O'Brien, 'The Irish National Idea', pp. 14-15.

69 O'Brien, 'The Irish National Idea', pp. 284-91.

70 O'Brien, 'The Influence of the Irish Language', *Irish Ideas*, pp. 47-77.

71 O'Brien, *Recollections*, pp. 172-5.

72 T.P. O'Connor, *Memoirs of an old Parliamentarian* 2 vols. (London, 1929), I: 143.

73 Moirin Chevasse, *Terence MacSwiney* (Dublin, 1961); Terence MacSwiney, *The Revolutionist* (Dublin, 1914).

74 Leon O. Broin, *Frank Duff* (Dublin, 1982).

75 Murphy, in *Catholic Fiction*, underestimates de Blacam's anti-modernism and millennialism. For a fuller account, cf. Patrick Maume 'Anti-Machiavel: Three Ulster Nationalists of the Age of Devlin and Craig' (paper read to the Political Studies Association conference at Jordanstown, April 1997).

76 O'Brien, *WWWB*, Chapter XXI, 'Lotos-Eater versus Iron-Master'.

77 O'Brien, *WWWB*, pp. 145-7.

78 Murphy, 'A New Voice from Old Conventions' (p. 300), suggests that this union is shown to be abortive by examining a scene in which Ken naively proposes to Mabel and realises she does not want to marry beneath herself. The male participant in this scene (p. 262) is Jack Harold, not Ken, and the accusation reflects Jack's cynicism rather than the author's view. Mabel (ambiguously) commits herself to Ken as he leaves for the intended Rising (pp. 431-3); he saves her life in a scene embodying the longstanding Catholic middle-class literary fantasy of alliance with a reformed aristocracy against the mob, which Murphy wrongly sees O'Brien as disavowing; by the end of the novel the black-clad, griefstricken Mabel is totally committed to Ken (pp. 548-9). O'Brien idealises English cross-class marriages such as that of the ironmaster Joshua Neville and his aristocratic wife (pp. 203-5).

79 O'Brien, *WWWB*, pp. 89-92, 331-3. (He is clearly a Liberal; he favours limited disendowment of the Church of Ireland [p. 90].) C.f. also the failure of a railway funded by 'that wildly romantic being, the British shareholder' to transform West Cork (pp. 8-9).

80 O'Brien, *WWWB*, p. 123.

81 O'Brien, *WWWB*, pp. 518-9; see also Warwick-Haller, *William O'Brien and the Irish Land War*, p. 126.

82 O'Brien, 'Introduction', *WWWB*, p. viii.

83 Bew, *Conflict and Conciliation*; Bull, *Land, Politics, and Nationalism*; O'Brien, *An Olive Branch in Ireland and its History* (London, 1910).

84 Sheehan letter read at election meeting reported in *Cork Free Press* (30 May 1911), p. 5.

85 Heuser, *Canon Sheehan*, pp. 309-12.

86 O'Brien, *Olive Branch*, pp. 353, 397, 437.

87 'The National Convention', *Irish People* (23 June 1900), pp. 5-6; 'A Patriot Priest' *Irish People* (23 June 1900), p. 7.

88 Sheehan, 'The Dawn of the Century', *The Literary Life* (Dublin, n.d.); Garvin, *Nationalist Intellectuals*, p. 62.

89 Heuser, *Canon Sheehan*, pp. 116, 139.

90 Michael O'Riordan, *Catholicity and Progress in Ireland* (London, 1905); for Sheehan's review, see Heuser, *Canon Sheehan*, pp. 210-12.

91 Sheehan, *Geoffrey Austin*, pp. 62-3; poem quoted in M.P. Linehan, *Canon Sheehan of Doneraile* (Dublin, 1952), pp. 142-3.

92 E.g. Sheehan, *The Blindness of Dr. Gray* (London, 1909), pp. 306-9.

93 Heuser, *Canon Sheehan*, pp. 250-1.

94 Suzanne Day, *The Amazing Philanthropists* (London, 1916), p. 146.

95 E.g. O'Brien, *Grattan's Home Rule, Gladstone's, and Asquith's: An Answer to a Boast* (Cork, 1915); Sheehan to Holmes (25 February 1913) in David H. Burton, *Holmes-Sheehan Correspondence* (Bronx, NY, 1993), p. 85.

96   Sheehan, *The Intellectuals* (London, 1911), pp. 211-4, 227-9, 373.

97   Sheehan, 'The Moonlight of Memory', *Literary Life* (Dublin, n.d.).

98   Some plot elements (notably the appearance of the son of the hero's former love and his old enemy as the political ally of his old age) may derive from Daniel Corkery's play *The Embers*, performed by the Cork Dramatic Society in 1908, though Corkery's handling of the old Fenian is very cynical.

99   Sheehan, *Graves*, pp. 26-9, 36-9, 44-8.

100 O'Brien, *WWWB*, pp. 422-3.

101 Sheehan, *Graves*, pp. 49-55, 95, 105, 119-44.

102 O'Brien, *WWWB*, pp. 343-5.

103 Sheehan, *Graves*, pp. 345-55.

104 Sheehan, *Graves*, pp. 360-73.

105 Cf. his ballad 'The Emigrant's Return' in Heuser, *Canon Sheehan*, pp. 355-9.

106 Sheehan, *Graves*, pp. 58-60.

107 Sheehan, *Graves*, pp. 65-9.

108 Sheehan, *Graves*, pp. 133-44.

109 Sheehan, *Graves*, pp. 149-57; O'Brien, *WWWB*, pp. 540-4.

110 Sheehan, *Graves*, pp. 150-3, 220.

111 Sheehan, *Graves*, pp. 47-8, 74.

112 Sheehan, *Graves*, pp. 32-3.

113 Sheehan, *Graves*, pp. 220.

114 Sheehan, *Graves*, pp. 241, 273.

115 Griffith's *United Irishman* regularly reports OGU activities.

116 O'Brien, *WWWB*, pp. 196-8.

117 Sheehan, *Graves*, p. 29.

118 O'Brien, *Recollections*, p. 55. For more information on Sullivan see Rev. Fergal McGrath S.J. *Father John Sullivan S.J.* (London, 1941), pp. 12-21.

119 O'Brien, *Recollections*, pp. 221-3.

120 O'Brien, *Recollections*, pp. 231-3.

121 O'Brien, *Recollections*, pp. 227-9; see also Sheehan, *The Intellectuals*, pp. 197-201.

122 Sheehan, *Triumph*, pp. 240-56. Compare the accusations against Parnell described in Callanan, *The Parnell Split*, pp. 121-8, 167-8, 187-91.

123 Sheehan, *Graves*, pp. 220, 266-73; Patrick Maume, *D.P. Moran* (Dundalk, 1995), p. 33. This view of Belfast business methods was not entirely confined to nationalists; cf. F. Frankfort Moore, *The Ulsterman* (London, 1914).

124 Sheehan, *Graves*, pp. 235-6.

125 Sheehan, *Graves*, Chapter XXXVI.

126 Review by 'Fenian', *An Gael* (12 February 1916), pp. 15-16.

127 O'Brien, 'Introduction', *WWWB*, p. xv.

128 Fr Robert O'Loughran, *Cain's Rival* (London, 1916), pp. 127-8.

129 Sheehan, *Graves*, pp. 372-3.

130 Brendan Clifford (ed.) *Reprints from the 'Cork Free Press' 1910-16: An Account of Ireland's only Democratic Anti-Partition Movement* (Belfast & Cork, 1984); Brendan Clifford, *Canon Sheehan: A Turbulent Priest* (Aubane Historical Society, Millstreet, 1990).

'our own good, plain, old Irish English':

Charles Macklin (Cathal McLaughlin) and Protestant Convert Accommodations

Christopher J. Wheatley

'Sir, you took Lodgings in the name of "Macklin," and here, yesterday, a person came, and called you by some strange name – *"Maclotlin!"* or *"Maclottin!"* Indeed, it is impossible to pronounce it'.

> Spoken by an English landlady attempting to evict Macklin because of his apparent use of an alias.[1]

When, in the early eighteenth century, Charles Shadwell and William Philips incorporated a Gaelic heritage in their plays it was partly a response to patronage, and, consequently, the aristocracy; Butlers (the dukes of Ormond were patrons of the Shadwells) and O'Briens (the earls of Thomond and Inchiquin were patrons of Philips) were either descendants of, or were related to the pre-Norman aristocracy that had converted prior to the eighteenth century and whose place in the post-revolutionary settlement was therefore assured. Another, more recent, group of Protestants came from the lower reaches of the gentry and consisted of converted Catholics, pressured by the penal laws into changing religion either to preserve family lands, or to achieve access to the professions. These converts' attitudes toward the revolutionary settlement remained ambivalent. No doubt the conversion of some was purely pragmatic and had little effect on their identity (that is, they continued to be 'culturally' Irish and even attended mass covertly). But for some, conversion meant a genuine belief in protestantism (or, at least, a rejection of Catholicism), and an adoption of the Ascendancy's attitudes toward the native Catholics.

Still, this group of converts perforce could not accept racist stereotyping of the Irish, while at the same time it was difficult for them to support Irish nationalism as they could not afford to be suspected of disloyalty. The embarrassments of accommodation are thus a part of the Protestant identity in Ireland. Converts could, with complete honesty, embrace historical arguments about Irish political independence from England; after all, they were the descendants of the original Irish. They also, however, needed political cover to save them from accusations of covert sympathy with the disaffected elements of the Catholic community, and the 'Patriot' movement provided that shelter precisely because many of its leading figures remained anti-Catholic. In short, converts of the mid-eighteenth century are transitional figures that pave the way for the complete identification (political, historical, and dramatic) of the patriots with Irish culture that occurs in the 1770s.

Charles Macklin, as a convert, embodies the diverse allegiances of this group, complicated by a few internal conflicts that were a consequence of his personality: proud, hot-tempered, physically powerful (he killed one man and beat the actor James Quin savagely during the interlude of a performance), yet insecure because of his Irish, lower-class background. His plays portray warmhearted and loyal Irishmen, and satirise English attitudes toward the Irish, while at the same time espousing 'patriot' political attitudes. However, he substitutes for the Irish a Scottish scapegoat. Immediately after his death, an obituary describes why he changed his name: 'The real name of the family, however, was M'Laughlin, which to render more pleasing to an English ear, was familiarised to Macklin'.[2] Macklin's plays, like his name, retain Irish roots, but are 'familiarised' to English and Irish Protestant ears. His life represents the uneasy consolidation of the Irish and the English of Ireland into a shared identity as 'Irishmen'.

In the eighty-six years after 1703, five thousand five hundred Catholics in Ireland conformed to the established church.[3] This relatively small number is at least partially a consequence of the elites' recognition that wide-spread conversion was not desirable.[4] Reasons for conformity included a desire to enter professions barred to Catholics (such as the bar or armed services) or to retain family land. The former created competition for scarce positions and the latter limited the availability of land to upwardly mobile members of the Protestant interest, thus intensifying social conflict.[5]

Those who converted were also divided amongst themselves. L.M. Cullen argues that 'rising families not only conformed outwardly to the Established Church, but identified themselves wholly with its aims'. The most prominent example of this identification is John Fitzgibbon, Earl of Clare.[6] On the other hand, Kevin Whelan proposes that 'it can no longer be safely assumed that "converts " were a loss to the Catholic interest'.[7] Some converts were exploiting legal loopholes, and others even represented a parliamentary interest sympathetic to Catholics.

Thomas Russell's family represents the divided loyalties of the converts. His great-grandfather had had to choose between his wife's Protestant relatives and his own Catholic, Gaelic relatives for guardians for his children:

When Mr. O'Clear was considering of making his will he sayd: 'if I
leave my brother O'Clear guardian to my children, as he is a dissi-

pated man he will spend their fortunes but he will educate them in my
religion (he being a Catholick and wife of the reform'd religion); but if
I make my brother Bradshaw (his wife's brother) their guardian, he
indeed will preserve their fortunes but they will lose their religion.'
This divided him for a long time, but at last he dicided in favor of
property and made Bradshaw guardian, leaving to each of his children
500£, esteem'd not an inconsiderable fortune in these days.[8]

The cultural product of this decision, Russell himself, was a pious Protestant
(as evidenced by his self-recriminations when he indulged his propensity for
wine, women, and song), yet sympathetic towards the Catholics. His divided
psyche is also indicated by his progression from serving officer in the British
army to leader of a revolution striking for Irish independence.

All converts remained unmistakably Irish. Even a distinguished parliamentarian such as Edmund Burke, whose father converted in order to practice law,[9]
could be slighted by a patriot rabble-rouser like John Wilkes for his Irishness
alone; Wilkes dismissed Burke's oratory, saying it 'stank of whiskey and pota-
toes'.[10] Contempt for the Irish cannot be accounted for solely on the basis of
religion, although dislike of Catholics was part of the English psyche. Novelist
Henry Fielding, fervidly anti-Catholic and a good friend of Macklin (who had
acted in his plays), is sympathetic to the plight of the poor Irish in London.
In *Amelia* (1751), the Irish victim of a bully is charged by the assailant with
battery:

> The Justice asked the defendant, What he meant by breaking the
> king's peace – To which he answered, – 'Upon my shoul I do love the
> king very well, and I have not been after breaking any thing of his that
> I do know; but upon my shoul this man hath brake my head, and my
> head did break his stick; that is all, gra.' He then offered to produce
> several witnesses against this improbable accusation; but the Jus-
> tice presently interrupted him, saying, 'Sirrah, your tongue betrays
> your guilt. You are an Irishman, and that is always sufficient evidence
> with me'.[11]

Fielding, himself a magistrate, clearly regards the Irishman as the victim of
prejudice and ignorance.

Nevertheless, Fielding also accepts stereotypes about the Irish as duelists
and fortune hunters, and the Protestant landed gentry are special objects of
his satire. In *Tom Jones* (1749), Mrs. Fitzpatrick describes to Sophia her life as
the captive wife of a jealous and ignorant Irish squire. Sophia offers condo-
lence: 'Indeed, Harriet, I pity you from my soul! – But what could you expect?
Why, why, would you marry an Irishman?' Fielding allows Mrs. Fitzpatrick a
rebuttal:

Upon my word... your censure is unjust. There are, among the Irish, men of as much worth and honour, as any among the English: Nay, to speak the truth, generosity of spirit is rather more common among them. I have known some examples there too of good husbands; and, I believe, these are not very plenty in England.[12]

Unfortunately, this statement of tolerance is radically undercut by the novel. Several chapters have detailed that Fitzpatrick is a vile and self-interested brute (both a duelist and a fortune-hunter). Nor is Mrs. Fitzpatrick a good character witness for the Irish. Aside from the fact she is an adulteress, her defense of the Irish seems primarily motivated by her desire not to appear a complete fool for marrying an Irishman.

And Fielding is one of the most tolerant and urbane voices in eighteenth-century literature in English. The ordinary bigoted Englishman must have indicated his contempt for the Irish more overtly. R.B. McDowell has argued that working-class Irish immigrants to England did not feel themselves to be aliens.[13] Macklin's experiences make this claim dubious, as he experienced significant social problems, despite enormous talent and the legitimate fear his ability as a pugilist inspired. When Macklin attempted to make money independently of the stage through a combination of lecturing and sales of refreshment, a part of what limited success the venture had came from the comic Samuel Foote's mockery of him. Macklin's lecture on the causes of dueling in Ireland was interrupted by a question about the time. Told half past ten, Foote said,

'about this time of night, every gentleman in Ireland, that can afford it, is in his third bottle of claret, consequently is in a fair way of getting drunk: from drunkenness proceeds quarrelling, and from quarrelling, dueling, and so there's an end of the chapter.' The company seemed fully satisfied with this abridgement; and Macklin shut up his lecture for the evening in great dudgeon.[14]

Macklin's annoyance may be an act. The anonymous *M-ckl-n's Answer to Tully*, (not by Macklin) indicates how indebted Macklin was to Foote's comic relief.[15] But other critiques of Macklin's lectures were straightforwardly antagonistic: 'How inimitable are your Criticisms on the Works of that Sublime Spirit, the doubly immortal *Shakespeare*!... How does he receive that Honour which you, tho' born in *Ireland*, condescend to bestow [on] him, by calling him your Country-man?'[16] Appreciation of Shakespeare is exclusive, and even the second best Shakespearian actor of his age, if an Irishman, should not pretend to understand what he portrays.

Some of this embarrassment shows up in Macklin's early play *The New Play Criticiz'd, or the Plague of Envy* (1747). Sir Patrick Bashfull, travelling in London, denies his heritage: 'I am originally descended from the Fitz-Bashfulls of France – tho' indeed our Family was of Irish Distraction first of all.' On the one hand, Sir Patrick is proud of being Irish, while on the other he wishes to conceal his heritage to avoid slights:

Harriet   Then you have several good Poets in Ireland.

Sir Patrick Yes, to be sure, Sir, there is hardly a gentleman there but knows every one of the Ninety Nine Muses, and can speak all the Mechanical Sciences by Heart, and most of the liberal Languages except Irish and Welch.

Harriet   And how happens it that they don't speak their own Language?

Sir Patrick Because, Madam, they are ashamed of it; it has such a rumbling Sound with it. Now when I was upon my Travels I liked the Language so well that I learned it.[17]

The comic errors make Sir Patrick likeable, rather than an object of scorn (he is so nervous that he also calls Heartly, the male lead, 'Madam'), but his defense of the Irish language and Irish learning invoke pathos because the erroneous boasts are a function of insecurity. He immediately sings an Irish song which draws praise, but must claim that Irish is not his native language. Macklin, who was a native Irish speaker, is perhaps drawing on his experience in England for this scene.

In England, then, the problem for immigrants was Irishness irrespective of religious belief. Meanwhile in Ireland, Catholic converts remained objects of suspicion and patriot agitators insisted on drawing a line between Protestants and Catholics, one which the English were increasingly inclined to ignore in connection with the Irish. This left converts in a grey area. Charles Lucas attacks unspecified converts, comparing them disadvantageously with the professed Catholics: 'There are none so dangerous, as those, who, in Publick, are *Protestants* by Profession, in Private, *Papists*, in Policy and Practice. Those, who from Conscience, profess the *Popish* Religion, openly and honestly, deserve tenderness and Pity, and are much less dangerous to the establishment'.[18]

Thomas Sheridan, by contrast, represents the insecurities of the Protestants of Irish descent. The Kelly riot in 1747 illustrates not just class tension – part of Sheridan's problems come from his claim to gentlemanly status, to some an insufferable assertion from an actor, whatever his descent – but insecurity and religious tension.[19] An anonymous pamphlet suggests that Lucas advised Sheridan to defend himself by playing off sectarian anxiety:

And he came unto L—-s and said, what shall I do, for the men of *Conaught* are upon me.

And L—-s said unto S———n, fear not neither be thou dismayed: Are there not Papists in the Land of *Conaught*? and are not the Papists Rebels?[20]

Paul Hiffernan, political controversialist and enemy of both Sheridan and Lucas, mocks Sheridan because of his hysterical assertion of Protestant purity:

But the cream of the jest is, his declaration, that if he thought himself indebted to the MECHEL'S dancing for any part of the extraordinary receipts of this winter, as they are *Papists,* and subjects to the *French* king, he would instantly refund, or rather apply it to some *public* charity, to shew his *love* to the *present establishment,* and have the exquisite pleasure of inserting a *dear* paragraph in the journal.[21]

The barb is directed at contradictory attitudes. Sheridan booked a Catholic act and then worries over the possibility that they may be responsible for his profits. It does not really matter if the charge is fair; Hiffernan's satire only makes sense if Hiffernan thinks Sheridan is nervous about being suspected of Catholic sympathies (or thinks that the public will believe that this is so).

Sheridan is a convenient target for anti-'Patriot' polemicists because the 'Patriot' politicians actually were conflicted about incorporating a heroic Irish past into political arguments and over the apparent necessity of sympathy for the Catholics who represented the legacy of that past.[22] Lucas found it necessary to apologise for his public suspicion that the Kelly riots might represent the tip of a Catholic plot.[23] He also recycles the argument (dramatised in Charles Shadwell's *Rotherick O'Connor* [1719]) that the Norman invasion was an attempt to help the oppressed Irish:

Lastly, consider to what End have our *Ancestors,* brave free-born *Britons,* left their native Climate, to settle in this *remote,* and then *uncultivated Isle?* Was it not at the request of an oppressed King, and injured People, to restore their *Rights* and *Liberties,* and to impart a *free* and generous Spirit to the *Whole?*[24]

The whole of Ireland, of course, was not participating in the rights and liberties of the British constitution. But the argument for those constitutional rights, that the Normans had come to preserve the Irish from tyranny, implied that they should.

Lucas was even prepared to accept the possibility that Irish Catholics had some justification for their outbreaks of rebellion. Certainly the Irish were justified in overthrowing the Danish conquest: '[T]he *Irish*, in general, were, ab-solutely treated worse, than the *Victims* of the most *Savage Barbarians*; as bad, as the *Spaniards* used the Mexicans; or, as inhumanely, as the *English*, now, treat their Slaves, in *America'*. The political code is in the equation between the Danish domination of Ireland and the English domination of America. England and Denmark are related through metonymy, with oppression as the shared term. With Ireland as the modern victim of foreign domination, the English become universally as oppressive as the ancient Vikings.[25] But it is hard to see how Lucas could have avoided the application of this same metonymy to the Protestant oppression of Catholic Ireland, which carried the same poten-tial threat that the Irish represented to the Danes: 'No wonder they [the native Irish] should have become *implacable Enemies* to their *lawless, inhuman, per-fidious,* their *worse,* than *Savage Oppressors*: when we find the *deluded Wretches,* always treated, worse, than *a good man* could treat *Brutes!'*[26]

I am not accusing Lucas of inconsistency; the confusion in his attitudes is closer to multiple personality disorder. On the one hand, he claims the Irish victory over the Danes as a noble example of patriotism, while on the other hand, he remains unwilling to allow their descendants, the Catholic Irish, any share in Irish political power. The religion of the Catholic Irish is the problem, not their culture, in contrast to the English, who regarded Catholic and Prot-estant Irish as nearly equally culturally deficient. Playwright, essayist, and novelist Henry Brooke shares the same dual consciousness. Brooke whips up Protestant hysteria against Catholics during the Jacobite rising in Scotland in 1745 by invoking 1641:

> They say to us, *had we lived in the Days of our Fathers, we would not have been Partakers with them, in their Oppressions and Massacres: But herein they confess themselves to be the Children of those Men,* by whom our Maidens were polluted, by whom our Matrons were left childless; by whom our Grandsires were butchered, and their Infants dashed against the Stones.[27]

By the 1760s, Brooke is writing in defense of Catholics at the instigation of Charles O'Conor, although Brooke's need for money assuredly played a role in his authorship of *The Tryal of the Cause of the Roman Catholics*. Subsequently, Brooke would go on to edit the anti-Catholic *Freeman's Journal*.[28]

Yet Brooke too professes enthusiasm for Irish antiquities, publishing a *Prospectus of a Work to Be Entitled Ogygian Fables* (1743) and *A History of Ireland from the Earliest Time Proposed* (1744).[29] An anecdote, published after Brooke's death, suggests that he could be as flattered by Irish praise as English:

> A young man, of the name of Dary, or Mac Dary, who lived on the banks of that river, addressed some verse to him in the Irish language.

He was so highly pleased with this little nosegay of native flowers, that he resolved to learn the Irish language, a resolve, with many others, which he never put into execution.[30]

Like the unwritten fables and history, good intentions toward the Irish do not result in any real rapprochement – at least in his own life. But it should not be forgotten that his daughter, Charlotte Brooke, published the important early collection of translations of Irish poetry, *Reliques of Irish Poetry* (1789), and Brooke was responsible for her early education.

In this atmosphere of ambivalence towards things Irish, both in those of Irish descent and in Anglo-Irish 'patriots' espousing reformation of the Irish political structure as well as legislative and juridical independence, Macklin's own experience becomes politically charged, especially because his sympathies were with the patriots, both in England and Ireland; he was, for instance, a friend of Wilkes.[31] At the same time, Macklin becomes, with success, almost ostentatiously unashamed of his Irish past. Sir Callaghan, the Irish lover of *Love à la Mode* (1759), while comical, is the most admirable character in the play, and his Irish descent informs his courtship of Charlotte (of Norman stock):

Sir Theodore is my uncle only by moder's side, which is a little up-start family that came in vid one Strongbow but t'other day – lord, not above six or seven hundred years ago: whereas my family, by my fader's side, are all the true old Milesians, and related to the O'Fla-herty's, and O'Shocknesses, and the McLaughlins, the O'Donnegans, O'Callaghans, O'Geogaghans, all the tick blood of the nation – and I myself, you know, am an O'Brallaghan, which is the ouldest of them all.[32]

The mild brogue and inclusion of Macklin's own family the M'Laughlins, plus the ultimate success of O'Brallaghan's wooing, reveal an unwillingness to compromise with Irish heritage; the hero is Irish and proud of it. So too O'Dogherty, the wise patriot of *The True-born Irishman* (1762), refuses to allow his wife to Anglicise him: 'And pray, above all things, never call me Mr. Dig-gerty – my name is Murrogh O'Dogherty, and I am not ashamed of it'.[33] Nor was this affectation on Macklin's part. The sale catalogue of his library shows a substantial Irish collection, along with a manuscript play, presumably by Macklin, called *Love is the Conqueror, or the Irish Hero*.[34]

In the latter part of his life, Macklin also ceased to apologise for being a native Irish speaker. In 1765, Samuel Johnson and Macklin engaged in a round of linguistic one-upmanship. As Johnson tried various languages on Macklin to humble him, Macklin managed to keep up his end of the conversation in each:

Johnson, growing more determined from the failure of his attempts, at last addressed him with a string of sounds perfectly unintelligible. 'What's that, Sir?' inquired Macklin. 'Hebrew!' answered Johnson. – 'And what do I know of Hebrew?' – 'But a man of your understanding, Mr. Macklin, ought to be acquainted with every language!' The Doctor's face glowed with a smile of triumph. *'Och neil en deigen von-shet hom boge vaureen!'* exclaimed Macklin. Johnson was now dumfounded, and inquired the name of the lingua. 'Irish, Sir!' 'Irish!' exclaimed the Doctor. 'Do you think I ever studied that?' 'But a man of your understanding, Doctor Johnson, ought to be acquainted with every language!'[35]

Even if the story is apocryphal, something like it is true, or should be. Johnson and Macklin had too much in common not to have argued: proud, strong, self-made men, they were unlikely to have deferred to each other. Importantly, however, Macklin is asserting that Irish is a language with which the learned should be familiar, a position a long way from Sir Patrick Bashfull's unwillingness to acknowledge that he is a native speaker.

Yet in an uneasy pairing with Irish pride, Macklin's plays consistently espouse the calls for political reform common to sporadically anti-Catholic writers such as Lucas and Brooke. In *The School for Husbands* (1761), Townly is chastised by Angelica for wooing when he should be seeking a way to reform the philandering Lord Belville: 'Sir, you were called into our cabinet to assist us in punishing my lord, and in redressing this lady for the general weal – and like a selfish minister you would neglect the business of the nation to gratify your own private passion'.[36] Private morality and public morality are thus closely related, an important patriot creed. In *The Man of the World* (1781), Sidney castigates Sir Pertinax for his self-interested approach to politics:

Indeed, sir, I believe the doctrine of pimping for patrons, as well as that of prostituting eloquence and public trust for private lucre, may be learned in your party schools – for where faction and public venality are taught as measures necessary to good government and general prosperity – there every vice is to be expected.[37]

In *The True-born Irishman*, Macklin attacks the Castle through Count Mushroom, a fop who abuses O'Dogherty's hospitality by trying to have an affair with his wife and who, according to Cooke, was meant to ridicule *'Single Speech Hamilton*, who was then Secretary to the Earl of Halifax, Lord Lieutenant of Ireland'.[38] The English as a whole are abusing the Irish, and some of the Irish are aiding them. Referring to the practice of buying parliamentary votes, O'Dogherty says sourly, '[W]e have a great many among us that call themselves patriots and champions, who, at the same time, would not care if poor old Ireland was squeezed as you squeeze an orange – provided they had but their share of the juice'.[39]

Macklin's patriot politics made him popular in Dublin, but also connect him with the virulent anti-Catholicism of some of the patriots, a position that may well have made him uncomfortable. He was not alone in this awkward area of supporting patriots while probably regarding their sectarian views as lamentable; Charles O'Conor of Belanagare, defender of Catholic rights, was moved to support Lucas as well.[40] Macklin, to his credit, never gives in to the anti-Irish-Catholic virus. In his first play, *King Henry the VII, or The Popish Impostor*, he calls attention to Irish inactivity in the 1745 Stuart rebellion. Sevez, the papal legate, asks Frion, a rebellious Scotsman, about Ireland's support for Perkin Warbeck (an analogue for Charles Stuart). Frion responds:

> Th'Apostate Slaves are fallen off from *Rome*,
> And firmly fixt in the Usurper's Cause;
> *Kildare*, *Clanrikard*, with many others
> On whom we built absolute Assurance,
> Have, at their own Charge, arm'd their Friends and Followers
> And join'd the *English* General, *Poinings*.[41]

The mention of existing loyal Irish noblemen in connection with the name Poinings reminds an English audience of loyal Irish subordination to the law that gave the English Privy council the right to amend Irish bills. The Kildare and Clanrikard families were, of course, Protestant in Macklin's time, but he depicts the Irish (and by extension Catholic converts) as more loyal than the Scots, who are willing to turn traitor for any plausible pretender. Macklin's politics show the uneasy compromise being worked out between Irish nationalism and some limited relief from paranoia about Catholic insurrection.

In the same vein, he tweaks British hypocrisy about the presence of Irish soldiers in the military. Lord Belville is humbled in *The School for Husbands* (1761) by a press gang. When they lay hands on him, he protests that he is a lord, and the corporal responds, 'O be quiet – be aisy, my dear soul, for if you was the lord leeftenant of Ireland you must go when you are commanded'.[42] While Irish Protestants were allowed to serve in the cavalry, neither Catholics nor Protestants were allowed in the infantry, since they supposedly were a threat to discipline. The manpower demands of the Seven Years' War, however, forced regiments to find manpower wherever they could, and violations of the restrictions assuredly occurred – an eighteenth-century version of 'don't ask, don't tell'.[43] Irish and English audiences are not being challenged here, but they are being reminded of the gap between the law and practical necessity.

Tolerance toward Irish Catholics was, in some ways, more possible in England than in Ireland. Hugh Reily's defense of Catholics, originally published in 1695, was reprinted in London in 1762. In it, Protestant schemes for the conversion of Ireland, emphasising conversion, exile, or death, are attacked as unchristian:

> Here we have a hopeful Scheme of a Protestant *Thorou' Reformation*, where knocking Arguments are urged, not to convince People's Judgments, but in effect to beat out their Brains, a Practice never thought of, much less used by the most renowned of our Primitive Christians towards the very Heathens.[44]

Apparently unfamiliar with the conversion of Norway, Reily's Catholic apologia praises Catholic fidelity to the church of St. Patrick and accuses Luther and Calvin of 'new Revelations'.[45] The late reprint of his work implies increasing confidence in England that Catholics were not a danger to public security. Irish Protestants were not so sanguine.

Macklin's background is crucial to understanding his Irish patriot politics. Modern commentators point out that the early biographies of Macklin are unreliable, but what is striking about them is the ubiquity of his Irish identity. Whether or not the stories are true, memorialists were unable to separate Macklin from them. The anecdotes reveal an Irishman abroad, facing slights, and likely to respond dangerously when treated with disrespect. Macklin was somewhat unusual, no doubt: his achievements as actor, director, and playwright, as well as his temper and ambitions exposed him more to ridicule. Moreover, because of his success, we have more information about him than most Irish actor/playwrights. Still, the tone of the commentaries, their awareness of the effect of history and geography on events, implies a wider applicability than just to Macklin's experience abroad. Family, class, and nation figure repeatedly in the biographies of Macklin published shortly after his death.

Macklin died in 1797, yet immediately a mythology developed about his connections with the Irish aristocracy and their displacement. A restrained obituary merely describes loyalty to the pre-revolutionary order: 'The M'Laughlin's, originally respectable, suffered greatly from an unfortunate attachment to the Stuarts; and the fortunes of the family were at the lowest ebb before our hero saw the light'.[46] There is no heat in this identification – Jacobite fears had been extinguished generations before, at least in England – but there is an inference that Stuart loyalty is crucial to understanding Macklin. On one level, this account explains why he became an actor, as poverty forced the landed gentry into trade, crafts, or entertainment. But there is more to it than that, as Kirkman's biography makes clear:

The circumstance of CHARLES MACKLIN'S having been carried away, in a turf-kish, from the scene of action, near the Boyne, on that memorable day which gave freedom to Ireland, and transferred the property of the old possessors to new masters, is still spoken of by those, whose grandfathers, if living, could scarcely remember the event, but who have had it from father to son by oral tradition.[47]

This story, to which Kirkman wholly subscribes, despite the fact it would make Macklin 107 at his death, makes Macklin a transitional figure. His family's loss is Ireland's (and ultimately the stage's) gain, but the echo of the Moses story suggests that Macklin will be forced to serve a country other than his own.

Macklin's divided loyalties receive further elaboration in another early biography. William Cooke claims that Macklin told him that

at the celebrated siege of that city [Derry] in King William's time, he had three uncles within the walls, and three without, who distinguished themselves, though on opposite sides, with a bravery (to use the old man's phrase) 'that kept up the honour of the blood of the M'Laughlins'.[48]

Again, there is no shred of evidence supporting this story; it reads like a novel by Sir Walter Scott wherein kin is forced to fight against kin because of political upheaval. But the story reveals both kinship divisions and acceptance that bravery and honor existed on both sides of the divide, a sort of pseudo-biographical *Battle of Aughrim*, Robert Ashton's 1728 play, which presented both Catholics and Protestants as heroic. Kirkman also describes Irish pride in a pre-conquest past when discussing Macklin's antecedents:

At that time family pride ran as high in Ireland, as it ever did in any part of the world; and the families of M'LAUGHLIN, or O'KELLY, would not have thought themselves very much honored by an union with those of LLEWELLIN, DOUGLAS, or HOWARD.[49]

Diminishment has occurred in that Macklin the actor is incomparably inferior socially to his ancestors; recollection of that aristocratic past remains.

Sliding social status has a specific cause, and Cooke reminds his readers of the penal laws and their consequences:

His mother, by the restraining laws of Ireland at that time, which gave to the next Protestant heir the inheritance of every landed property from the Popish possessor, provided the latter did not conform to the Protestant religion, lost her little farm by the operation of this cruel law.[50]

In this account, the disinherited are objects of sympathy because they are victims of intolerance. Kirkman draws the connection between religious belief and social degradation. Macklin's destitute mother married Luke O'Meally, a Williamite who owned the Eagle Tavern on Werburgh Street.[51] This accommodation merely increases her worries as her growing son turns into a rogue and vagabond, '*Charles a Mollucth*; or, in English, *Wicked Charlie*'[52]: Macklin's mother 'began to be indifferent what line of life her son moved in; no matter how low or how contracted, provided she could persuade him to preserve his morals untainted and his religion unchanged'.[53] Ambition and Catholicism conflict; to choose fidelity to religion means accepting poverty and social contempt. Thus when Macklin converts around the age of forty, despite his own claim that his protestantism was 'as staunch as the Archbishop of Canterbury, and on as pure principles'[54] – a claim that should be treated with serious skepticism, as Macklin may never have married the mother of his children[55] – the emotional baggage of conversion is psychologically linked to betrayal of family for financial and social acceptance.

Further, Macklin is both from the lower class and afflicted, at first, with an Irish accent. Aspry Congreve's biography of Macklin mentions another incident that serves to type the actor:

> A late Irish Judge, however, has been frequently heard to declare, that he remembered him a very inferior servant in Trinity College, Dublin; where he used to stand in the menial capacity of errand boy on the students and fellows of the seminary.[56]

Despite the patronising overtones echoing in the judge's declaration, Macklin came to be able to joke about his early employment. Cooke argues that part of the success of Macklin's plays in Dublin was a consequence of this service, 'what he used jocularly to call himself – a *College man* (being a badge-man to the College,) and from this situation could remember the ancestors of most of the people of distinction in and about Dublin'.[57] This, of course, cuts two ways. If Macklin could remember their grandfathers as students, the Protestant gentry presumably could not forget that he was originally a menial. Macklin's success and protestantism, while making him less threatening, could also not erase the historical legacy of Irish Catholic dispossession. Insofar as Macklin's plays support the patriot agenda, this past made that agenda inclusive, but his social, ethnic, and (formerly) religious compatriots still outnumbered the Protestants and Macklin's joke about being a 'college man' reiterates the exclusivity of Protestant rule.

Macklin's allegiance to his own Irishness, apparent in his plays, is in contrast with the practical necessity of losing his accent. Kirkman writes, 'With the judicious, his Irish accent was an objection which they allowed his acting in a great degree, counterbalanced; – with the lower order, his being an Irishman was an objection, however admirably he might act'.[58] Macklin succeeded in shedding this identifying, and, for an actor, disabling, Irish characteristic. Actors need multiple accents, and Macklin developed them. In a revival of Charles Shadwell's *Humours of the Army* for Macklin's benefit night in 1746, Macklin played the Welsh officer Cadwallader, rather then either of the Irish officers.[59] Two of his best roles were the Scotsmen Sir Archy Macsarcasm and Sir Pertinax Macsycophant in *Love à la Mode* and *The Man of the World* respectively.

Indeed, Macklin could play an Englishman well enough for Cooke to claim that the genesis of Sir Callaghan O'Brallaghan was a meeting with an Irish officer in the Prussian service:

> [H]e was so extremely simple and unsuspicious, that when Macklin (who passed himself off for an Englishman all the while) attributed his successes with the ladies as from having a *tail behind*, as common to all Irishmen, he instantly pulled off his coat and waistcoat, to convince him of his mistake, assuring him, 'that no Irishman, in *that respect*, was better than another man'.[60]

Again, there is no reason to believe this story is true. Kirkman offers an entirely different version; a brother of Macklin's mother, Captain O'Flanagan, recruiting in Ireland for the 'German service', almost persuaded Macklin to join him.[61] But Cooke's version implies that Macklin was not above denying a common heritage to make his countryman the butt of a joke. Cooke goes on to suggest that the model for O'Brallaghan was 'educated in the simple manners of the interior part of Ireland, where an unsuspicious temper, courage, generosity, and fidelity, are qualities that seem particularly congenial to that soil'.[62] These are, of course, particularly valuable qualities in a servant, or a subject people, and the marked condescension of Cooke's praise reinforces denigration of the Irish, rather than working against it.

Fortunately, O'Brallaghan transcends these stereotypes. His bulls usually show either wit or virtue:

Sir Callaghan	Ho! to be sure, madam, who would be a soldier without danger? Danger, madam, is a soldier's greatest glory, and death his best reward.
Mordecai	Ha, ha, ha! That is an excellent bull! death a reward! Pray, Sir Callaghan, no offence, I hope – how do you make out death being a reward?
Sir Callaghan	How? Why, don't you know that?
Mordecai	Not I, upon honour.

Sir Callaghan	Why, a soldier's death in the field of battle, is a monument of fame, that makes him alive as Caesar, or Alexander, or any dead hero of them all.[63]

The Jewish suitor, lacking honor, assumes a contradiction where none exists. The Irish suitor, possessing both courage and honor, parries smoothly. O'Brallaghan is also not a fortune hunter. The other suitors are gulled into believing Charlotte is poor; O'Brallaghan shows his decency by standing by his offer: 'Madam, my fortune is not much, but it is enough to maintain a couple of honest hearts, and have something to spare for the necessities of a friend; which is all we want, and all that fortune is good for'.[64]

O'Brallaghan has been made carefully non-threatening to both an Irish and an English audience. As an officer in the Prussian army, he is rather more likely to be Protestant than Catholic. One Scotsman, annoyed at the satire on his nation, pointed out the nationality of O'Brallaghan's regiment:

An *Irish* officer in the *French, Spanish,* or *Austrian* service, would have been more agreeable to the general received notions of mankind. But such an incoherent medley of heroics and stupidity as *O Brallaghan* is dished out here by his countryman, never has been exhibited before, nor ought to be borne by any audience that would lay a claim to rationality.[65]

In fact, that O'Brallaghan is not the typical stage Irishman draws attention and criticism. The Scottish critic is relying on religious antipathy; France, Spain, and Austria were Catholic countries with numerous Irish soldiers. But whichever anecdote about the genesis of the play one prefers, Macklin is calling attention to Irish soldiers serving in Protestant foreign armies because they could not serve in the English. Where the critic wants to remind his readers of the threat that the Irish represent, Macklin portrays them as loyal exiles who deserve better.

Macklin was fighting an uphill battle. After his death, another anonymous biographer charged him with reverse discrimination in *Love à la Mode*:

Though this piece does not want character and satire, yet it must be observed, his partiality for his country has transported him a little from the strictness of drama; for, out of four lovers, he makes an Irish officer the only one that is disinterested. – A character so widely different from what experience has, in general, fixed on the gentlemen of that kingdom, that, although there are undoubtedly many amongst them possessed of minds capable of great honour and generosity, yet this *exclusive* compliment to them, in opposition to received opinion, seems to convey a degree of prejudice, which as a dramatic writer, and a countryman, he should be studious to avoid.[66]

In short, Macklin's violation of stereotypes is an aesthetic offense because the stereotypes, based on general experience, are more or less true, despite occasional exceptions. Since drama is concerned with the probable, in the opinion of this neo-aristotelian critic, O'Brallaghan's generous and altruistic love is an example of reprehensible bias in favor of the Irish.

Yet this critic's comment is more subtle than just knee-jerk bigotry against positive Irish characters. Macklin's problem is exclusivity. If he wishes to dramatise the exceptional Irishman, contrary to normal expectations of character development, he should have also not have limited the exception to the Irishman. That is, if cultural stereotyping is objectionable, then it should always be objectionable, and Macklin should not have relied on it in connection with the oafish English country squire, the ignoble Jew, and the grasping Scotsman. Macklin has merely substituted a different scapegoat to get the Irish off the hook.

This charge is largely true. Sir Archibald Macsarcasm is a pale object of contempt compared to Macklin's attack on Scottish politicians in Lord Bute's administration with the character of Sir Pertinax Macsycophant in *The Man of the World*.[67] The hero Egerton (Macsycophant's son, but raised by an English uncle) represents patriot politics:

Egerton (With a most patriotic warmth)   I own I do wish – most ardently wish for a total extinction of all party – particularly that those of English, Irish, and Scotch might never more be brought into contest or competition; unless, like loving brothers, in generous emulation for one common cause.

Sir Pertinax   Hoo, Sir! do ye persist? what! would ye banish aw party, and aw distinction between English, Irish, and yer ain countrymen?

Egerton (With great dignity of spirit)   I would, sir.

Sir Pertinax   Then damn ye, sir – ye are nai true Scot. Aye, sir, ye may leuk as angry as ye wull; but again I say – ye are nai true Scot.[68]

O'Brallaghan is a virtuous Irishman. Egerton can only be virtuous because raised by the English. In the former case, altruism and benevolence are natural, in the latter acquired, since Egerton could not have inherited them from the wholly vicious Macsycophant. Egerton's desire for equality in the empire recalls Charles Shadwell's allied soldiers in *The Humours of the Army,* and as in Shadwell's play, the discordant note is struck by the Scotsman. But Shadwell's Hyland is at least silent under correction; Macsycophant, foiled in his plans for greater political power through the marriage of his son, storms off unreconciled saying 'my vengeance leeght upon ye aw together'.[69] Disinterested justice is not possible for 'a true Scot'. Macklin, the victim of racism, succeeds in English and Protestant Irish society but having done so, substitutes another object for victimisation.

Kirkman attributes Macklin's anti-Caledonian tendency to a desire for profit. In connection with *Love à la Mode* he writes,

> Some gentlemen of North Britain were, during the first run of the Farce, highly exasperated at the character of *Sir Archy*, which they imprudently declared was a satire upon the whole kingdom of Scotland. This circumstance turned out exactly as the author imagined it would; the resentment of the Caledonians provoked the mirth of others, and spread the fame of *Love-a-la-Mode* all over town.[70]

Macklin appears here to have appealed to English prejudice by allowing the victims to draw attention to themselves. But this explanation requires that Macklin not only be aware of English prejudice, but aware that complaints about it will only draw laughter from complacent English audiences. In short, Macklin uses prejudice to succeed.

But if Macklin is not a good candidate for sainthood, he is a major influence on increasingly positive portrayals of Irishman on the English stage.[71] In Dublin, he introduces characters whom the Anglo-Irish recognise as their own:

> At the first performance when Messink staggered on as Fitzmongrel, a drunken Irish beau, a gentleman in a box impulsively cried out, 'Why that's me! But what sort of a rascally coat have they dressed me in?' Divesting himself of his own gold-laced one, he called out to Messink, 'Here – I'll dress you!' and flung it to the startled actor amid loud applause.[72]

Comical as this is, it indicates that the cultural idiom of Dublin is no longer West British, for the play only worked with Irish audiences. The English did not identify with these characters while the Dublin audience did.

Moreover, even the English language ceases to identify the English of Ireland. Mrs. O'Dogherty has adopted 'Diggerty' as her name in London and comes back affecting an English accent – unsuccessfully, as she sounds more like a cockney than a member of the aristocracy. To effect reconciliation with O'Dogherty, she must resume her Irish pronunciation:

And as to yourself, my dear Nancy, I hope I shall never have any more of your London English; none of your this here's, your that there's, your winegars, your weals, your vindors, your toastesses, and your stone postesses; but let me have our own good, plain, old Irish English, which I insist is better than all the English English that ever coquets and coxcombs brought into the land.[73]

The introduction of 'stage English' as a source of amusement for the Anglo-Irish reveals that London English is by now merely a variant in the empire, and Dublin English equally defining. Something is lost here, as the Irish language becomes largely irrelevant to an Irish identity in the eyes of an economically comfortable theatre audience. But when an O'Dogherty (who from his social position must be either a convert or the descendent of a convert) praises Irish English, the Catholic converts symbolically both claim a place in the existing Irish power structure, and force the Protestants of English descent to admit that they are sundered from their English co-religionists because they no longer speak identical languages. In short, the English of Ireland are now Irish – or at least think they are – and subsequent playwrights such as Francis Dobbs and Gorges Edmond Howard are able to take the Irish heritage as their own unapologetically.

Notes

1 James Thomas Kirkman, *Memoirs of the Life of Charles Macklin, Esq.*, 2 vols. (London, 1799), 1: 165.
2 *Obituaries of Remarkable Persons; with Biographical Anecdotes* (July 1797), p. 622.
3 J.L. McCracken, 'The Social Structure and Social Life, 1714-60' in *A New History of Ireland, Vol. 4, Eighteenth-Century Ireland, 1691-1800*, ed. T. W. Moody and W. E. Vaughan (Oxford, 1986), p. 38.
4 Thomas Bartlett, *The Fall and Rise of the Irish Nation: the Catholic Question, 1690-1830* (Dublin, 1992), pp. 24-7.
5 L.M. Cullen, *The Emergence of Modern Ireland, 1600-1900* (New York, 1981), pp. 114-5.
6 Cullen, *The Emergence of Modern Ireland*, pp. 115, 125.
7 Kevin Whelan, 'An Underground Gentry? Catholic Middlemen in Eighteenth-Century Ireland', *Eighteenth-Century Ireland* Vol. 10 (1995), p. 10.
8 Thomas Russell, *Journals and Memoirs of Thomas Russell*, ed. C.J. Woods (Blackrock, Co. Dublin, 1991), p. 90.
9 Conor Cruise O'Brien, *The Great Melody: A Thematic Biography and Commented Anthology of Edmund Burke* (London, 1993), pp. 3-4.

10 Quoted in Edmund Burke, *Irish Affairs*, intro. Conor Cruise O'Brien (London, 1988), p. xxviii.

11 Henry Fielding, *Amelia*, ed. David Blewett (New York, 1987), p. 17.

12 Henry Fielding, *The History of Tom Jones*, ed. R.P.C. Mutter (New York, 1989), p. 536.

13 R.B. McDowell, *Ireland in the Age of Imperialism and Revolution, 1760-1801* (Oxford, 1979), p. 142.

14 William Cooke, *Memoirs of Charles Macklin, Comedian* (London, 1804), pp. 208-9.

15 '[P]oor *Sam* died last Night at his House in the *Hay-market*: In that House where he has been labouring Night after Night to serve me and my Family – by hurting us as far as in him lay; Excuse that Sentence from the Orator – consider it as from the *Irishman* – Oh! My Country!' (Anonymous, *M_ckl_n's Answer to Tully*, [London, 1755], pp. 3-4).

16 *An Epistle from Tully in the Shades to Orator Ma——-n in Covent Garden* (London, 1755), p. 10.

17 Charles Macklin, *A Will and No Will, or a Bone for the Lawyers* and *The New Play Criticiz'd, or the Plague of Envy*, intro. Jean B. Kern (Los Angeles, 1967), pp. 54, 65-6.

18 Charles Lucas, *A Sixteenth Address to the Free Citizens and Free-Holders of the City of Dublin* (Dublin, 1748), pp. 31-2.

19 Esther Sheldon describes the incidents of the riot and subsequent controversy in *Thomas Sheridan of Smock-Alley* (Princeton, 1967), pp. 82-99.

20 Anonymous, *The Book of the Prophecies of the Prophet L—-S* (Dublin, 1748), p. 7.

21 Paul Hiffernan, *The Tickler No I. II. III. IV. V. VI and VII. The Second Edition* (Dublin, 1748), p. 12.

22 Neil Longley York, *Neither Kingdom nor Nation: the Irish Quest for Constitutional Rights, 1698-1800* (Washington, D.C., 1994), p. 72.

23 Seán Murphy, 'Charles Lucas, Catholicism and Nationalism', *Eighteenth-Century Ireland* Vol. 8 (1993), p. 86.

24 Charles Lucas, *An Apology for the Civil Rights and Liberties of the Commons and Citizens off Dublin* (Dublin, 1748-9), p. 5.

25 The Viking conquest of Ireland could be appropriated by government supporters as well. In 1753, an anonymous pamphlet comically equates Norway and England: 'Anno T MXXXXXII (for there History begins,) *Magnus* King of *Norway* was in Possession of *Ireland* and the *British* Isles.... He had the love of his *British* Subjects, but the Adoration of his *Irish*, who had prospered more under his equal Government in a few Years, than in any Century before' (*Hibernia Pacata: or, a Narrative of Affairs of Ireland, from the Famous Battle of Clontarf, where Brian Boirom defeated the Norwegians, till*

the Settlement under Henry II. Written originally in Irish and now First Trans-lated by Father Neri of Tuam, and Adorned with Notes by several Hands [n.p., 1753], pp. 6-7). This reversal of the metaphoric identification of England with Viking oppression indicates the author's awareness of the increasing use of the trope by the patriot opposition.

26   Charles Lucas, *An Eleventh Address to the Free Citizens, and Free-Holders of the City of Dublin* (Dublin, 1749), pp. 8, 11.

27   Henry Brooke, *The Farmer's Letter to the Protestants of Ireland* [1-6] (Dublin, 1745), No. 2, p. 8.

28   Bartlett, *The Fall and Rise of the Irish Nation*, p. 54.

29   The best discussion of Henry Brooke's 'colonial nationalism' is Kevin Donovan's '*Jack the Giant Quellar*: Political Theater in Ascendancy Dublin', *Éire-Ireland* Vol. 30 (1995), pp. 70-88.

30   *Brookiana*, 2 vols. (London, 1804), I: 86.

31   William W. Appleton, *Charles Macklin: An Actor's Life* (Cambridge, MA, 1960), p. 209.

32   *Four Comedies by Charles Macklin*, ed. J.O. Bartley (Hamden, Connecticut: Archon Books, 1968), pp. 58-9. All subsequent references to *Love à la Mode*, *The True-born Irishman*, *The School for Husbands*, and *The Man of the World* are to this edition.

33   Macklin, *Four Comedies*, p. 111.

34   In the catalogue are the following titles that indicate Macklin's interest in Irish history: *Laws of Ireland* (1678); Davis, *on Ireland* (1747); *Hibernia Curiosa* (1769); *English Rogue* (1680); Crawford's *History of Ireland* (1783); O'Connor's *History of Ireland* (1766); Vallancey, *Collecteana de Rebus Hibernicis,* (1770); Smith, *Cork, Waterford, and Kerry* (1784); Wynne's *History of Ireland* (1773); Twif's *Tour in Ireland* (1775), Folger Shakespeare Library catalogue number Pn 2598 M2 A3. The relatively late date of most of these books is a function of the fact that Macklin's first library was sunk in an unfortunate crossing of the Irish sea.

35   Quoted in Appleton, *Charles Macklin*, p. 198. Mark Scowcroft suggests that the passage attempts to anglicise 'Ach níl an dídean an bhannsach agan bó agan bhóithrín,' which might mean 'the pen [roof, shelter] is no protection to the cow on the road.' Seamus Ó Maoláin offers the emmendation 'Ach ní haon dídean an bhannsach don bhó agan bhóithrín' as more idiomatic. In fairness to both Dr. Scowcroft and Dr. Ó Maoláin, it must be added that both suggestions are very tentative as neither is familiar with the expression.

36   Macklin, *Four Comedies*, p. 155.

37   Macklin, *Four Comedies*, p. 259.

38   *Memoirs of Charles Macklin, Comedian*, p. 235.

39   Macklin, *Four Comedies*, p. 101.

40 Seán Murphy, 'Burke and Lucas: An Authorship Problem Re-examined', *Eighteenth-Century Ireland* Vol. 1 (1986), p. 156.

41 Charles Macklin, *King Henry the VII, or The Popish Impostor* (London, 1746), p. 3.

42 Macklin, *Four Comedies*, p. 168.

43 I am indebted to Thomas Bartlett for this point.

44 Hugh Reily, *The Impartial History of Ireland* (London, 1762), p. 19.

45 Reily, *The Impartial History of Ireland*, p. 20.

46 *The Monthly Visitor* (5 August 1797), p. 132.

47 Kirkman, *Memoirs of the Life of Charles Macklin*, p. 13.

48 Cooke, *Memoirs of Charles Macklin, Comedian*, p. 2.

49 Kirkman, *Memoirs of the Life of Charles Macklin*, p. 9.

50 Cooke, *Memoirs of Charles Macklin, Comedian*, p. 9.

51 Kirkman, *Memoirs of the Life of Charles Macklin*, p. 17.

52 Kirkman, *Memoirs of the Life of Charles Macklin*, p. 24.

53 Kirkman, *Memoirs of the Life of Charles Macklin*, p. 53.

54 Cooke, *Memoirs of Charles Macklin, Comedian*, p. 76.

55 Phillip H. Highfall, Kalman A. Burnim, Edward Langhans, eds., *A Biographical Dictionary of Actors, Actresses, Musicians, Dancers, Managers & Other Stage Personnel in London 1660-1800* 16 vols. (Carbondale, 1984), X: 24.

56 Francis Aspry Congreve, *Authentic Memoirs of the Late Mr. Charles Macklin, Comedian* (London, 1798), p. 11.

57 Cooke, *Memoirs of Charles Macklin, Comedian*, p. 304.

58 Kirkman, *Memoirs of the Life of Charles Macklin*, p. 64.

59 *The London Stage, 1660-1800, Part Three: 1729-1747*, ed. A.H. Scouten (Carbondale, IL, 1961), p. 1235.

60 Cooke, *Memoirs of Charles Macklin, Comedian*, p. 224-5.

61 Kirkman, *Memoirs of the Life of Charles Macklin*, p. 46.

62 Cooke, *Memoirs of Charles Macklin, Comedian*, p. 232.

63 Macklin, *Four Comedies*, p. 56.

64 Macklin, *Four Comedies*, p. 75.

65 Anonymous, *A Scotsman's Remarks on the Farce of Love À La Mode* (London, 1760), pp. 5-6. Not all the Scots reacted this way, as a later edition makes clear: 'It is singular that it has always been acted with more *éclat* in Scotland than anywhere else; which is a proof that the satire concentrated in the person of Sir Archy does not tell upon the consciences of the natives, and that the national lineaments of the part are true to nature'; (Edinburgh, 1829), p. iv.

66 Anonymous, *An Account of the Life and Genius of Mr. Charles Macklin, Comedian* in *Mackliana*, 2 vols. (n.p.: n.d.) II: 37. Folger Shakespeare Library Catalogue number PN 2598 M2 A3 Cage.

67 J. O. Bartley discusses Macklin's hostility to Bute's administration in the 'Introduction' to *Four Comedies by Charles Macklin*, pp. 29-30.

68 Macklin, *Four Comedies*, p. 218.

69 Macklin, *Four Comedies*, p. 269.

70 Kirkman, *Memoirs of the Life of Charles Macklin*, p. 402.

71 Joep Leersen, *Mere Irish & Fíor-Ghael: Studies in the Idea of Irish Nationality, Its Development and Literary Expression Prior to the Nineteenth Century* (Philadelphia and Amsterdam, 1986), p. 140.

72 Appleton, *Charles Macklin*, p. 130.

73 Macklin, *Four Comedies*, p. 111.

Same Text, Different Story:
Reinterpreting Irish Constitutional Identity

Patrick Hanafin

> The constitution is at once text and nation. It is a document, an inscription, and as such, both the conception of the nation and the material form in which it is manifest. It is the act that founds the nation and the sign that marks it. It is the expression and the annunciation of collective identity... It is an effort to represent what the people are – and hence to record what they have been. It reconstructs, as all such representations do, the present and the past that it records. It reveals, as all such representations do, that those who represent remake themselves.[1]

Introduction

Paul Ricoeur once wrote that the self is a 'cloth woven of stories told'.[2] This narrative concept of the self leads to an evolutionary idea of identity. Richard Kearney has pointed out that:

> The narrative concept of self... offers a dynamic notion of identity... that includes mutability and change within the cohesion of one lifetime... This means, for instance, that the identity of human subjects is deemed a constant task of reinterpretation in the light of new and old stories we tell about ourselves. The subject becomes, to borrow a Proustian formula, both reader and writer of its own life.[3]

This notion of individual identity is equally applicable to the identity of a community or group. As Kearney has noted, 'It is worth recalling here that the story of a society, no less than that of an individual life, is also perpetually refigured by the real and the fictive stories it tells about itself. A society's self-image is also a cloth woven of stories told'.[4] In this context one may argue that the Irish constitutional text reflects a sense of group identity. It is, in effect, a means of expressing group identity in textual form. As Eisgruber has put it:

> In other settings, we give words a representative function that is elaborate and profound, as when we understand ourselves (and think about our choices) through a composition – a myth, a poem or a story – that, however difficult it is to interpret, seems to us to capture our identity better than do simpler expressions.... Constitutionalism is, among

other things, a way for a political community to 'talk out' its political identity.[5]

The Constitution is, to paraphrase Ricoeur, 'a [text] woven of stories told'. Based on Ricoeur's conception of narrative identity as developed by Richard Kearney, this piece analyses how the constitutional story has been reinterpreted to include characters previously excluded from the Irish societal narrative, in effect creating a story with a different ending.

   This could therefore mean that just as with individual identity, the notion of identity reflected in the constitutional text may be deemed to be in a state of constant flux in the light of new and old stories we tell about ourselves as a nation. The Irish constitutional text tells a story about a people, a nation, a national ethos. Thus, it constitutes an apparently common (hi)story. The original reading of the constitutional text portrayed a certain idea of Ireland. The document was the expression of a particular political manifesto.[6] This, I submit, is no longer the case. Through a process of reinterpretation or rereading, the same text tells an entirely different story about Irish society.

The Constitution of Identity in Irish Constitutional Discourse
The traditional model of the Irish Constitution captures a certain idea of Ireland: patriarchal, Catholic, and bound by tradition. In this sense it configures with James Joyce's critique of the paterfamilias. As Hofheinz has noted:

> Joyce's fallen patriarch configures in terms of the Irish Free State because the State institutionalized the patriarchal social philosophy of Catholic Ireland through a long series of prescriptive laws culminating in de Valera's constitution of 1937. These laws enforced the Catholic Church's view of sexuality and generation in marriage by proscribing divorce and contraception, and placed obstacles in the way of working women at a time when economic pressures drove countless men into unemployment.[7]

The political elite of post-independence Ireland created a state which was, in the symbolic domain, both irredentist and patriarchal. This construction of a homogeneous Irish identity constituted an attempt on the part of the ruling elite to inscribe their idea of an imagined Irish community in the imaginary of the new nation. These values became part of public policy through legislative initiatives and in no small part through their official symbolic recognition in the Constitution of 1937. The constitutional text thus conveyed in legal form the framers' conception of the Irish socio-political imaginary. This process is what Paul Ricoeur has termed the reaffirmative function of the socio-political imaginary. In the reaffirmative mode the socio-political imaginary of a community 'operates as an "ideology" which can positively repeat the founding discourse of a society, what I call its "foundational symbols", thus preserving its sense of identity'.[8] However, the reaffirmation of a socio-political imaginary can be transformed 'by monopolistic elites, into a mystificatory discourse which serves to uncritically vindicate the established political powers. In such instances, the symbols of a community become fixed and fetishized; they serve as lies'.[9] In this sense, one could argue that the political elite of post-independence Ireland, in introducing the 1937 Constitution, created a document which reaffirmed the elite's conception of a homogeneous Irish nation. It was thus the case that Eamon de Valera incorporated in a subliminal manner into the constitutional text his ideal of an imaginary Ireland.

Thus, the mythical idea of Ireland as located in the imaginary of the post-revolutionary elite was reflected in the constitutional document. This reflects the way in which myth may be used negatively to uphold a certain idea of nationhood. As Richard Kearney has noted:

> [M]yth may distort a community's self-understanding by eclipsing reality behind some idealized chimera. In such instances, the nostalgia for a golden age of the past... may blind us to the complexities and exigencies of our present reality. Here myth serves as an ideological agency of distortion and dissimulation.[10]

This process demonstrates the way in which a society's perception of itself and its (hi)story can affect the construction of laws. As Katherine O'Donovan has noted:

> Old stories can retain a powerful hold. Stories affect the creation of law and its application. Such laws remain with us and affect our perceptions of realities and truths. The stories influence what we see and what we can see. Our relationships with other human beings at the centre of our lives, are structured by these ancient unchangeable stories and laws.[11]

This attempt to tell a unified story in the constitutional text is open to the criticism which Kearney has articulated in referring to narrative identity generally:

> [S]torytelling can also be a breeding ground of illusions, distortions and ideological falsehoods. In configuring heterogeneous elements of our experience, narrative emplotment can serve as a cover-up. Narrative concordance can mask discordance, its drive for order and unity displacing difference.[12]

However, in recent times, this originary narrative of national identity has been challenged by various counter-narratives. The rereading or reinterpretation of the Constitution by the Supreme Court in recent years has reflected, perhaps subconsciously, the existence of these counter-narratives. In so doing, it exposes the privileging of a particular viewpoint in constitutional discourse. The dominant narrative of a perceived monolithic Irish identity has been, in effect, put in question.

Thus, the manner in which we read or interpret the constitutional text allows us to constitute a certain notion of Irish identity. As Robert Post has noted, constitutional interpretation becomes in a very real sense 'the locus of an overt struggle for the definition of national identity'.[13] This leads one to ask the following question: 'The question facing a court, therefore, is whether it should interpret the Constitution in ways that may express or establish a national ethos, or whether it should do so in ways that may confirm its absence'.[14] One can argue that the programmatic intention of the Constitution (what the author set out to say) differs from the operative intention of the Constitution (what his text ends up saying). We have moved from a master narrative to a reauthored narrative. Thus, while the text of the Constitution remains substantially the same as the document of 1937, excepting of course the constitutional amendments of the intervening years, the story contained therein has been reinterpreted. What has emerged is, in the words of Richard Kearney, 'alternative stories to the official story, emergent stories of marginal or truncated histories, indirect stories of irony and subversion. Such unofficial narratives brush history against the grain. They put the dominant power in question'.[15] In order to expose the privileging of the dominant power, one must reread the constitutional text. This involves questioning the dominant model of a perceived homogenous Irish identity and allowing previously excluded groups to be accepted as part of a heterogeneous and reinterpreted Irish sense of self. These traditionally marginalised groups constitute that part of the Irish self which, to paraphrase Robin West, 'has been trampled, not celebrated by our history, and whose vision has been ignored, not expressed, in the collective communicative texts of our culture's political past'.[16]

In a wider sense, the Constitution is an example of a document which exhibits what Sunstein has referred to as law's 'expressive function'.[17] Law's 'expressive function' refers to the way in which law expresses social values and encourages social norms to move in particular directions. However, the values which law expresses are not necessarily fixed for all time and may change as societal norms and values change. Thus, when a society experiences a 'norm cascade',[18] that is, a rapid shift towards new norms, such norm shifts may be expressed in legal discourse. Thus, one could argue that the 'norm cascades' which Ireland has experienced in recent years may have been incorporated into constitutional discourse through a rereading or reinterpretation of the Constitution's meaning.

Interpretative Strategies and Interpretative Choices

Peter Halewood has identified a number of theoretical modes of constitutional interpretation.[19] If one approaches constitutional interpretation from a theoretical perspective, the traditional model is the objectivist approach[20] which holds 'that right answers are available because we can identify a foundational method'.[21] The objectivist method can be broken down into two strands:

> idealist epistemologies, which base their claims to knowing on a method of abstraction from material processes and an escape into contemplative essentialist insight, and realist epistemologies, whose claims to knowledge are founded on a privileged insight into the mechanisms of material processes and upon having developed an objective verifiable method for plotting materiality's correspondence with or representation in language. In law, the first strand here finds some expression in the natural law tradition, but it is with the second, expressed as legal positivism, that the critical literature is most engaged.
>
> The interpretive stance to which this legal position is traditionally committed might be called 'textual positivism': the view that determinate meaning somehow resides in the text as one of its properties.[22]

In Irish constitutional jurisprudence, the natural law model has been of primary importance.[23] However, it may be seen that there are two competing strains of natural law interpretative models at work; one, which may be called 'strict naturalism', combines an almost originalist zeal with religious natural law theory and another, a less narrow and more secular form which may be referred to as 'moderate naturalism', can be seen as forming the basis of Supreme Court readings of the personal rights articles of the Constitution in its more activist phase, commencing with the decision in *Ryan v Attorney-General*.[24]

The strict naturalist strain in Irish constitutional interpretation favours the traditional model of Irishness. In his judgment in the case of *McGee v Attorney General*,[25] O'Keeffe J. exemplifies this approach: '[O]ne must look at the state of public opinion at the time of the adoption of the Constitution in order to determine whether the effect of its adoption was to remove from the statute book a section of the [impugned] Act'.[26] This interpretative model is also to be found in the judgment of O'Higgins C.J. in the case of *Norris v Attorney-General*.[27] O'Higgins was later to state explicitly the traditionalist approach in a newspaper interview:

> The question merely was whether an Act passed by the British parliament in the previous century was carried over into our law as being

compatible with the Constitution. But what do you find in this Constitution? You find a whole Pauline tract, the whole Christian Preamble.
This is Dev's Constitution. He'd be turning somersaults in his grave if
he were told 'Do you know that your Constitution has been held to
prohibit laws criminalising buggery?' That was the issue.[28]

The consequences of a strict naturalist stance are far-reaching. Under this
model, a certain restricted notion of national identity is favoured. Roderick
O'Hanlon[29] has argued that the Constitution as enacted in 1937 recognises the
superiority of divine law. As such, any legal provisions or, for that matter, constitutional amendments which conflict with the ideals of natural law are
rendered invalid, even if they are technically in agreement with the provisions
of the Constitution. The strict naturalist model of the Constitution limits the
ability of the individual to act autonomously. Thus, a statute such as the Criminal Justice (Sexual Offences) Act of 1993, which decriminalised sexual acts
between consenting males over the age of seventeen; the decision of the Supreme Court in the case of *Attorney-General v X and Others*[30] where it was held
that pregnancy termination was lawful to save the life of the mother in a case
involving a fourteen-year-old rape victim who was pregnant as a result; and
the subsequent amendments to the Constitution on the rights to travel and
information are all invalid according to the strict naturalist conception of the
Constitution. This view echoes that of the American constitutional theorist,
Walter Murphy, who has argued that the Constitution, correctly understood,
expresses a vision sufficiently coherent that amendments radically incompatible with that vision are not law.[31] Under the strict naturalist model proposed
by O'Hanlon, one can see what Feldman has referred to as an 'uncritical commitment to a sacred text',[32] and what Ronald Dworkin has referred to as a
'constitution of detail'.[33] Thus, for example, under such a constitutional paradigm the right to life is seen as more fundamental than other equally valid
rights and is adhered to even when it would interfere greatly with the autonomy of the individual. This is the traditional Irish model. This is also the view
adopted by religious and conservative thinkers who claim that there exists a
certain natural order of things to which we must adhere. Any form of behaviour which does not conform to this ideal is immediately viewed as suspect
and those who engage in such behaviour are not deemed worthy of inclusion
in the constitutional story. Moreover, in the Irish context, by enunciating the
supremacy of natural law in a positivist document such as a constitution, the
framers may be open to a charge of logical inconsistency. Natural law, by its
very nature, is superior to positive law.[34] Thus, as Harris argues:

In some ways, seeking the authorization of a structural approach via
clause-bound positivism is like the Irish Constitution's invocation of

the legal bindingness of natural law, in positivistic terms – an odd kind of realization through self-cancellation. Plain terms might serve as a reinforcement or cue, but if structuralism or natural law are valid constitutional materials or interpretive approaches their validity cannot ultimately rely on, or be concluded by, clause-bound commands. The validity of the contents and / or methods of each must be independently established in a theory of the whole enterprise.[35]

Desmond Clarke uses the following example to demonstrate the paradox of the relationship between natural law and the Irish Constitution:

> The problem is similar in structure to the liar paradox... and arises in the following way. The liar paradox occurs when, in one and the same language we make statements about the truth-value of the statements themselves. If I say 'My brother tells the truth, and I agree with him', I leave myself open to the possibility of my brother saying something which I claim is false. As a result, I both affirm and deny, directly and indirectly, one and the same proposition. A constitution which endorses the contents of an indeterminate, unwritten natural law and grants it a constitutional status which is superior to other provisions of the written text, stands in the same relation to this unwritten law as I do to my truth-telling brother. Such a constitution provides courts with a constitutional basis for appealing to an antecedent and superior law which may be inconsistent with explicit provisions of the written constitution.[36]

It can thus be argued that the adoption of a particular interpretative strategy by the Supreme Court in its deciphering of constitutional meaning is of primary importance to the model of Irish identity which is projected as a result. Thus, under a strict naturalist model, the idea of Irishness which is projected is narrow, traditional, and exclusive. Other models may lead to a more inclusive model of Irishness. Indeed, as Richard Humphreys has contended,

> it is also possible, and perhaps preferable, to take the view that the natural law conception of the Constitution may be regarded as a secular one. Although the Constitution does make occasional references to the existence of God, the natural law origin of human rights is not expressly linked in the document itself to those references.[37]

The Irish Supreme Court's Reading Strategy
The strict form of naturalism has not been favoured by the Supreme Court in interpreting the Constitution and in particular the personal rights articles of the Constitution. The Supreme Court's approach is more in the form of a mod-

erate naturalism or, alternatively, in the words of Robert Post, 'responsive interpretation'. Post points to the classic formulation of such a concept in the writing of Oliver Wendell Holmes:

> When we are dealing with words that are also a constituent act, like the Constitution... we must realize that they have called into life a being the development of which could not have been foreseen completely by the most gifted of its begetters. It was enough for them to realize or to hope that they had created an organism.... The case before us must be considered in the light of our whole experience and not merely of what was said a hundred years ago.[38]

Thus, as Post explains:

> [T]he nature of [constitutional] authority can be captured neither by rules laid down in judicial precedents, nor by notions of original intention. The authority must rather be conceived as flowing from the 'whole experience' of nationhood. That experience legitimately claims our allegiance because we are necessarily included within it, and hence responsible for both what it has been and what it might become.[39]

In the Irish context, the judgment of Walsh J. in the case of *McGee v Attorney-General*[40] seems to fit into the responsive interpretation model. Walsh observed:

> According to the Preamble, the people gave themselves the Constitution to promote the common good with due observance of prudence, justice and charity so that the dignity and freedom of the individual might be assured. The judges must, therefore, as best they can from their training and their experience interpret these rights in accordance with their ideas of prudence, justice and charity. It is but natural that from time to time the prevailing ideas of these virtues may be conditioned by the passage of time; no interpretation of the Constitution is intended to be final for all time. It is given in the light of prevailing ideas and concepts.[41]

As Post notes, responsive interpretation is, in fact,

> a vast umbrella sheltering a myriad of different approaches to the Constitution.... It can be used by those who stress the constitutional priority of democratic decision making and hence who emphasize judicial caution and prudence, as well as by those who stress the con-

stitutional primacy of individual rights.[42]

The ultimate claim upon which responsive interpretation rests is that the Constitution is not 'static and lifeless'. Thus, the ambition and challenge of responsive interpretation is to determine which aspects of our contemporary ethos may be regarded as legitimate 'growth from the seeds which the fathers planted', and hence as bearing 'the essential content and the spirit of the Constitution'. Only these aspects of the national ethos are genetically related to the document and thus may properly form the basis for responsive interpretation. In this sense, responsive interpretation does indeed 'point (backward) toward' the document, in at least as strong a metaphoric sense as does doctrinal interpretation.[43]

In the wake of such cases as *Attorney-General v X and Others*[44] and *Re Article 26 and in the matter of the Regulation of Information (Services Outside the State for Termination of Pregnancies) Bill, 1995,*[45] one can detect a perceptible shift from the confirmation of a monolithic national ethos as espoused by the framers of the Constitution. This may reflect a recognition on the part of the judiciary (albeit subconsciously) that there is no such thing as a monolithic Irish identity, only individuals, various and fragmented. Thus, one could argue that later Supreme Court jurisprudence configures in terms of the fragmented postcolonial self and has moved away from the symbolic overlay of a monolithic Irish collective identity which informed the framers' document. This development has come about through a shift in the Supreme Court's method of reading the Constitution. In its more activist stage since the case of *Ryan v Attorney-General,*[46] the Court has engaged in a number of reading strategies. Initially the supremacy of the natural law as a source of individual rights was assumed by the Court. However, since its explicit rejection of this approach in the case of *Re Article 26 and in the matter of the Regulation of Information (Services Outside the State for Termination of Pregnancies) Bill, 1995,*[47] a new reading strategy has emerged. This new model conforms more to the textual positivist mode, that is, the Supreme Court in adjudicating in the realm of personal rights has recognised that the written text of the Constitution, rather than natural law, is the authoritative source for the determination of constitutional issues.

Thus, in *Re Article 26 of the Constitution and in the matter of the Regulation of Information (Services outside the State for the Termination of Pregnancies) Bill, 1995,*[48] the Supreme Court rejected the strict naturalist model in the following terms:

> [I]t is fundamental to this argument that, what is described as the 'natural law' is the fundamental law of this state and as such is antecedent and superior to all positive law, including the Constitution and that it

is impermissible for the people to exercise the power of amendment of
the Constitution by way of variation, addition or repeal, as permitted
by Article 46 of the Constitution unless such amendment is compatible
with the natural law and existing provisions of the Constitution and, if
they purport to do so, such amendment had no effect.

The Court does not accept this argument.[49]

The Court went on to posit the following novel reading of the place of natural
law in interpreting the Constitution:

> From a consideration of all the cases which recognised the existence of
> a personal right which was not specifically enumerated in the Consti-
> tution, it is manifest that the Court in each such case had satisfied itself
> that such personal right was one which could be reasonably implied
> from and was guaranteed by the provisions of the Constitution, inter-
> preted in accordance with its ideas of prudence, justice and charity.
>
> The courts, as they were and are bound to, recognised the Con-
> stitution as the fundamental law of the State to which the organs of
> the State were subject and at no stage recognised the provisions of the
> natural law as superior to the Constitution.[50]

This move on the part of the Supreme Court has been heavily criticised by
strict and moderate naturalists alike. This stance has been criticised for its lack
of analytical sophistication. It places personal rights jurisprudence in a positivist framework rather than a natural rights framework. The Constitution
qua Constitution rather than an extrinsic source, such as the natural or divine
law, is seen as the source of individual rights. It appears to conform more to a
textual positivist model. In theoretical terms, it has been argued that textual
positivism would be a preferable model on which to base Irish constitutional
interpretation. Gerard Hogan has argued:

> Unless the decisions of the courts can be seen to be based on conven-
> tional legal sources – the text of the Constitution and the traditional
> legal principles that are necessarily therein – constitutional adjudica-
> tion would thereby become politicised and devalued.[51]

Hogan's mode of argument falls into what Brink has described in the following terms:

> It is claimed that in the troublesome cases the Court has exceeded the
> scope of legitimate judicial review because it has invalidated legisla-

tion on grounds not explicitly provided for 'within the four corners' of the document of the Constitution. This claim assumes that constitutional interpretation must be guided by, and cannot exceed, the 'plain meaning' of language which actually occurs in the text of the Constitution.[52]

This interpretative shift on the part of the Irish Supreme Court could be compared to the shift in the American Supreme Court's reliance on natural law as a ground for decision-making in the mid-nineteenth century. As Howard has pointed out: 'By the time of the Civil War, however, such direct invocation of natural law principles had largely died out, and in our age judges disclaim reliance on natural law reasoning, however much their opinions may strike some observers as having all the elasticity of the natural law about them'.[53] However, some commentators have criticised this move towards textual positivism on the Irish Supreme Court's part as being fatal for the protection of human rights. As Binchy has noted:

> Having affirmed the absolute supremacy of the written Constitution, the court then relied on precedents drawn from the earlier contrary jurisprudence to affirm that it falls to the judges of the court in the last analysis to ascertain and declare what personal rights are guaranteed by the Constitution 'in accordance with their ideas of prudence, justice and charity'. The effect of this judicial license is to release the court from any strict adherence to the text of the Constitution....
>
> One suspects that, in its desire to drive from the Constitution a particular school of natural law theory, the Court recklessly destabilised the whole scaffolding of the protection of human rights in our Constitution. The substance and the tone of the judgment betray a willingness to accommodate the exercise of raw judicial and legislative power which does not augur well for the future.[54]

Nonetheless, this move to recognising the superiority of the written constitution over extra-textual sources such as natural law does attempt to overcome the pre-existing paradox of enshrining the superiority of natural law in a positivistic legal document. By rereading the source of rights in Irish constitutional law in such a fashion, the Court may have approximated to Desmond Clarke's proposed solution to the problem or paradox of Irish constitutional adjudication. Clarke proposed the following:

> There is a way of avoiding these problems, just as there was a way out of the earlier paradoxes. It involves either granting a superior status to

the text of the Constitution over that of natural law.... [This] involves saying, in effect: we accept natural law theory as a helpful interpretative tool in constitutional adjudication as long as it agrees with the written text of the Constitution (including amendments). In cases where they are inconsistent, the explicit text of the Constitution prevails.... This resolution is also equivalent to conceding what critics of natural law have frequently urged, namely, that it is too vague and dangerous a standard to provide a useful criterion for decision-making in constitutional law.[55]

A similar approach was taken in the recent *Report of the Constitution Review Group*.[56] The Committee recommended a move away from the natural law model of constitutional interpretation in the realm of personal rights. It was recommended by the Committee that Article 40.3.1 be amended so as to provide a comprehensive list of fundamental rights which could specifically encompass the personal rights that have been identified by the courts to date, as well as those set out in the European Convention on Human Rights and Fundamental Freedoms and other international human rights conventions to which Ireland is a signatory, 'so far as may be considered appropriate, and other personal rights which might be particularly appropriate in the Irish context'.[57] The Committee suggested that the further recognition of fundamental rights by the courts would be limited to those contained in the constitutional text. Thus, the move to textual positivism on the part of the Supreme Court in its decision in *Re Article 26 and in the matter of the Regulation of Information (Services Outside the State for Termination of Pregnancies) Bill, 1995* is reflected in the Constitution Review Group's recommendations in this area. However, the move to textual positivism, whilst promoting certainty, is not without difficulty. As Beytagh has observed:

> Courts in a constitutional system utilising judicial review need more leeway than that, and a variety of checks restrict them in exercising their discretion in this regard inappropriately. Certainty is an elusive goal in the fluid business of construing constitutions, and rejection of Ireland's natural law heritage, however imprecise it might sometimes seem, is to me too high a price to pay.[58]

The wholesale abandonment of the natural rights model may indeed restrict constitutional development. Can one predict that the list of rights enumerated in a new model constitution will not seem dated and constricting to later generations? The advantage of allowing constitutional norms to develop in tandem with societal shifts is that the Constitution remains a living document reflective of the actual experiences of the community. The danger in abandoning a model which has proved flexible and dynamic is that the Constitution's personal rights provisions may become, in Ronald Dworkin's words, 'an antique list of the particular demands that a relatively few people long ago happened to think important... [which may produce] a document with the texture of an insurance policy or a standard form of commercial lease'.[59]

On the symbolic level, one could argue that the recent jurisprudence of the Supreme Court on the source of individual rights evinces an uncoupling from the shackles of authorial intent, if one can state that the de Valerean imaginary was male, Catholic, and traditional. The Supreme Court as authoritative reader is taking on itself the task of revising constitutional meaning in a manner which reflects the new Irish societal paradigm, allowing for a less contrived notion of identity. Thus, in cases such as *McGee v Attorney-General*[60] and *Attorney-General v X and Others*,[61] the traditional model of female identity was questioned, and found wanting. This contrasts with the old model of rejecting in the interpretive process any roles which did not concur with the ideal type Irish citizen.[62] Irish constitutional history has reached a point where the idea of inclusion of previously excluded identities is emerging. There is a move away on the symbolic level from identifying the Constitution with a certain idea of Ireland. The Supreme Court as reader of the text is subverting traditional ideas of what Irish citizenship entailed and questioning the old certainties. The symbolic death of the constitutional author through the reinterpretation of the constitutional text may be deemed to configure with an unravelling of this traditional model of Irish identity. As Barthes has stated: 'We know now that a text is not a line of words releasing a single "theological" meaning (the "message" of the Author-God) but a multi-dimensional space in which a variety of writings, none of them original, blend and clash. The text is a tissue of quotations drawn from the innumerable centres of culture'.[63] Barthes notes the importance of the reader in constituting the text:

> [T]here is one place where this multiplicity is focused and that place is the reader, not, as was hitherto said, the author. The reader is the space on which all the quotations that make up a writing are inscribed without any of them being lost; a text's unity lies not in its origin but in its destination. Yet this destination cannot any longer be personal: the reader is without history, biography, psychology; he is simply that someone who holds together in a single field all the traces by which the written text is constituted.[64]

The Supreme Court as authoritative reader, one may argue, has refigured the text of the Constitution.

Conclusion

In adopting a more dynamic interpretative strategy in the area of constitutional personal rights jurisprudence, the Irish Supreme Court has implicitly reflected the recent 'norm cascades' in Irish society. By linking the Constitution's 'expressive function' to norm shifts in society, the Supreme Court has facilitated the expression of ideals and norms in legal discourse which mirror more accurately the norms of contemporary Irish society. This way of reading the constitutional text allows us to see that previously dominant societal norms can be replaced by new norms and that it is possible to represent such norm shifts at the level of legal discourse. Thus, in the sixty years since its adoption, the programmatic intention of the Irish Constitution differs quite radically from its operative intention via the reading of the authoritative reader, the Supreme Court. In effect it allows us to see that texts, like the individuals and communities which they represent, are being constantly reinterpreted and redefined. This does not imply a wholesale rejection of the Constitution; rather it reflects what Justice Kennedy of the United States Supreme Court has described in the following terms: 'To say that new generations yield new insights and new perspectives, that doesn't mean the Constitution changes. It just means that our understanding of it changes'.[65] Thus the Constitution, which was written in the 1930s, through re-reading takes on a different meaning, yet retains a mystical sameness. The same text becomes a different story. As Steven Winter has noted: 'Because the Constitution is a text to be interpreted, it necessarily changes as new assumptions mediate the reading of its text'.[66]

Notes

[1] Anne Norton, 'Transubstantiation: The Dialectic of Constitutional Authority', *University of Chicago Law Review* 55 (1988), p. 459.

[2] Paul Ricoeur, *Time and Narrative* 3 vols. (Chicago, 1988), III: 246.

[3] Richard Kearney, *Poetics of Modernity: Toward a Hermeneutic Imagination* (Atlantic Highlands, 1995), p. 99.

[4] Kearney, *Poetics of Modernity*, p. 233, note 25.

[5] Christopher Eisgruber, 'The Fourteenth Amendment's Constitution', *Southern California Law Review* 69 (1995), p. 49.

[6] Dermot Keogh, 'The Irish Constitutional Revolution: An Analysis of the Making of the Constitution', *Administration* 35 (1987), pp. 4-76.

[7] Thomas Hofheinz, *Joyce and the Invention of Irish History* (Cambridge, 1995), pp. 37-8.

[8] Paul Ricoeur, 'The Creativity of Language' in Richard Kearney (ed.), *States of Mind: Dialogues with Contemporary Thinkers on the European Mind* (Manchester, 1995), pp. 229-30.

[9] Ricoeur, 'The Creativity of Language', pp. 29-30.

10 Richard Kearney, 'Between Tradition and Utopia: The Hermeneutical Problem of Myth' in David Wood (ed.), *On Paul Ricoeur: Narrative and Interpretation* (London, 1991), p. 65.

11 Katherine O'Donovan, 'Marriage: A Sacred or Profane Love Machine', *Feminist Legal Studies* 1 (1993), p. 90.

12 Kearney, *Poetics of Modernity*, p. 99.

13 Robert Post, 'Theories of Constitutional Interpretation', *Law and the Order of Culture* (Berkeley, 1991), p. 30.

14 Post, 'Theories of Constitutional Interpretation', p. 34.

15 Kearney, *Poetics of Modernity*, pp. 99-101.

16 Robin West, 'Adjudication is not interpretation', in Robert Post (ed.) *Narrative, Authority and Law* (Ann Arbor, MI, 1993), p. 96.

17 Cass R. Sunstein, 'Social Norms and Social Roles', in Robin West (ed.) *Columbia Law Review* 96 (1996), p. 953.

18 Sunstein, 'Social Norms and Social Roles', p. 912.

19 Peter Halewood, 'Performance and Pragmatism in Constitutional Interpretation', *Canadian Journal of Law and Jurisprudence* 3 (1990), p. 91.

20 Halewood ('Performance and Pragmatism in Constitutional Interpretation', p. 91) also notes another broad approach to constitutional theory, the sceptical approach, which holds that no such objective method is possible and that our goal of achieving objective knowledge or decisive interpretation is unattainable.

21 Halewood, 'Performance and Pragmatism in Constitutional Interpretation', p. 91.

22 Halewood, 'Performance and Pragmatism in Constitutional Interpretation', p. 92.

23 See Francis X. Beytagh, *Constitutionalism in Contemporary Ireland: An American Perspective* (Dublin, 1997), pp. 115-8.

24 See, for example, *Ryan v Attorney-General* [1965] IR 294, and *McGee v Attorney-General* [1974] IR 284.

25 [1974] IR 284.

26 [1974] IR 292.

27 [1984] IR 36.

28 Cited in Richard Humphreys, 'Constitutional Interpretation', *Dublin University Law Journal* 15 (1993), p. 63.

29 Roderick O'Hanlon, 'Natural Rights and the Irish Constitution', *Irish Law Times* 1 (1993), pp. 8-11.

30 [1992] 1 IR 1.

31 See Walter Murphy, 'An Ordering of Constitutional Values', *Southern California Law Review* 51 (1980), pp. 703-60.

32 David Feldman, *Civil Liberties and Human Rights in England and Wales* (London, 1993), p. 364.

33 Ronald Dworkin, *Life's Dominion: An Argument about Abortion and Euthanasia* (London, 1993), p. 119.
34 See Declan Costello, 'The natural law and the Constitution' *Studies* 45 (1956), pp. 403-14; Gerard Whyte, 'Natural law and the Constitution', *Irish Law Times* 14 (1996), pp. 8-12.
35 William F. Harris II, *The Interpretable Constitution* (Baltimore, 1993), p. 23, note 18.
36 Desmond Clarke, 'Natural law and constitutional consistency', in Gerard Quinn, Attracta Ingram, and Stephen Livingstone (eds.), *Justice and Legal Theory in Ireland* (Dublin, 1995), p. 35.
37 Humphreys, 'Constitutional Interpretation', p. 69.
38 *Missouri v Holland* 252 US 416, 433 (1920).
39 Post, 'Theories of Constitutional Interpretation', p. 24.
40 [1974] IR 284.
41 [1974] IR 319.
42 Post, 'Theories of Constitutional Interpretation', p. 25.
43 Post, 'Theories of Constitutional Interpretation', p. 32.
44 [1992] 1 IR 1.
45 [1995] 1 ILRM 8.
46 [1965] IR 294.
47 [1995] 1 ILRM 8.
48 [1995] 1 ILRM.
49 [1995] 1 IR 38.
50 [1995] 1 IR 43.
51 Gerard Hogan, 'Constitutional Interpretation' in Frank Litton (ed.), *The Constitution of Ireland 1937-1987* (Dublin, 1988), p. 188.
52 David Brink, 'Legal Theory, Legal Interpretation, and Judicial Review', *Philosophy and Public Affairs* 17 (1988), p. 138.
53 A.E. Dick Howard, 'The Indeterminacy of Constitutions', *Wake Forest Law Review* 31 (1996), p. 385, note 14.
54 William Binchy, 'Abortion ruling one of the most significant legal decisions in the history of State', *The Irish Times* (15 May 1995), p. 15.
55 Clarke, 'Natural law and constitutional consistency', pp. 35-6.
56 Constitution Review Group, *Report of the Constitution Review Group* (Dublin, 1996).
57 Constitution Review Group, *Report of the Constitution Review Group*, p. 259.
58 Beytagh, *Constitutionalism in Contemporary Ireland: An American Perspective*, p. 183.
59 Ronald Dworkin, 'What The Constitution Says', *Freedom's Law: The Moral Reading of the American Constitution* (New York, 1996), p. 74.
60 [1974] IR 284.
61 [1992] 1 IR 1.

62 See, for example, *Norris v Attorney-General* [1984] IR 36.

63 Roland Barthes, 'The Death of the Author', *Image, Music, Text*, trans. Stephen Heath (London, 1977), p. 146.

64 Barthes, 'The Death of the Author', p. 148.

65 Nomination of Anthony M. Kennedy to be an Associate Judge of the United States Supreme Court, [Senate] Executive Report 100-13, 100th Cong., 2d sess. (1988), p. 8.

66 Steven Winter, 'Indeterminacy and Incommensurability in Constitutional Law', *California Law Review* 78 (1990), p. 1507.

THE THIRD
GALWAY CONFERENCE ON COLONIALISM

DEFINING COLONIES

17-20 JUNE 1999

NATIONAL UNIVERSITY OF IRELAND, GALWAY

CALL FOR PAPERS

The aim of this multidisciplinary conference is to explore the meanings of the contemporary and historical entities which are categorised under the rubric of *colony*. Papers should address the question of how colonies have been defined politically, economically, socially, and culturally. Are there any sure signs of coloniality, or postcoloniality? What is the role of ethnicity, race, gender, and social class in different colonial dispensations? Papers might also consider the ever-present danger of generating 'universalist' colonial theory from the specific experience of certain kinds of colonies.

As part of the conference, a round-table discussion will address the question: 'Was Ireland a Colony'?

Confirmed conference speakers include:
Dipesh Chakrabarty, Claire Connolly, Terry Eagleton, Luke Gibbons, David Lloyd, Gearóid Ó Tuathaigh and **Gauri Viswanathan**

Papers should be no longer than 20 minutes. If you wish to contribute to the conference, please send an abstract of not more than 300 words, preferably by email, to the Conference Organisers, Department of English, NUI Galway before the **1 February 1999**.

Conference Organisers

Fiona Bateman, Tadhg Foley, Lionel Pilkington, Seán Ryder, Elizabeth Tilley (Dept of English) and Terry McDonough (Dept of Economics), National University of Ireland, Galway, Ireland
Tel: 353 [0]91 524411
Fax: 353 [0]91 524102

email: colony@ucg.ie

REVIEW ARTICLE

How He Was

Steven Connor

James Knowlson, *Damned to Fame. The Life of Samuel Beckett* (London: Bloomsbury, 1996), 784 pp. £25.00

Anthony Cronin, *Samuel Beckett: The Last Modernist* (London: Harper Collins, 1996), 672 pp. £25.00

Literary biographies are supposed to make an author's life cohere, first with itself, and then with its work. The particular problem for the biographer of Beckett is to put together the diffuse life of restless indolence which Beckett lived before the War with the utterly different life into which he entered after it. Any biography of Beckett must be judged largely on the quality of its account of what happened to produce this transformation. It will also, incidentally, have to cope with the problem of keeping the story going. Up to the beginning of the War, the reader will be hanging on wanting to know what will become of this wisecracking, but feckless wunderkind. Once Beckett came into his own life, by beginning to write the work that defined him, his life also tended disconcertingly to vanish into that work. Neither James Knowlson nor Anthony Cronin are able to do much more with this long aftermath than chronicle the dates of Beckett's publications and productions.

Everything came late for Samuel Beckett. Unable or unwilling to hold down a job or even to pick one up in the first place, the young Beckett was the despair of his well-heeled, austerely Protestant, and utterly non-artistic family, who nevertheless continued to support him financially. Beckett had spent his twenties and thirties drifting back and forth between Paris and Dublin, becoming part of the circle of artists and assistants who gathered around Joyce, giving up a promising academic career at Trinity College Dublin, undergoing a period of psychoanalysis with the young W.R. Bion in London, undertaking a sort of Grand Tour of Germany in order to perfect his German and in vague hopes of turning himself into a connoisseur of painting. During all of this time, Beckett was living the life of a writer in the classic fashion, i.e. not really writing anything, but instead, as he put it in a letter during the period of his analysis, 'boozing and sneering and lounging around and feeling that I was too good for anything else'. By the beginning of the war, the only publications of consequence he had to show for a decade of his shabby vocation were a volume of short stories and a novel. There was nearly a play about Samuel Johnson as well, though the fragment that survives fails even to get Johnson on the stage. (Even in its fragmentary condition, however, *Human Wishes* is actually an extraordinarily fully-imagined piece of drama.)

Anthony Cronin has some very striking pages on why Beckett should have been drawn during the late 1930s to the pessimism of Johnson rather than to that of Swift. He thinks that Beckett found a deeper, more generalising and less personal pessimism in Johnson, who himself criticised Swift for the fundamental egocentricity of his hopelessness. But there might be another turn left in this screw. What if the figure of Johnson represented for Beckett a perverse kind of ego-ideal, formed from the recognition of how rooted his own unforgiving, Swiftian wildness was in a set of very personal glooms and gripes? Beckett is Swiftian rather than Johnsonian also in the fact that it is not sadness but rage that flares most distinctly through his writing of the 1920s and 1930s. This brilliant, but neurotically self-regarding young man was lacerated and nourished by a savage indignation at, well, it is hard to know quite what precisely, but largely at the not uncommon discovery that the world was not shaped according to his needs. This indignation issues both in matchless comic writing and in some of the vilest misogyny to be found in the pages of any writer. I sometimes have an uneasy feeling that only Beckett's indolence saved him from a slide into a more programmatic kind of literary hatred. Had his rage found a convenient gutter of wrath in which to flow, had all that patrician *ressentiment* and carefully distilled disdain been directed into, rather than at politics, one can easily imagine a very different career for him. I imagine such a Beckett rising at best to the wild, misanthropical minority of Wyndham Lewis, whose icily erudite ferocity finds no closer parallel in pre-War writing than *Dream of Fair to Middling Women* or *More Pricks Than Kicks*.

Something happened to prevent this, something absolutely not given in Beckett's temperament or upbringing. In Dublin, during the years immediately following the War, Beckett experienced a kind of revelation that his work would have to be written about and from within a condition of helplessness and impotence. Following this, he wrote in extremely short order the works that established his distinctiveness and on which his fame is certain to continue to rest, the three novels of the Trilogy and *Waiting for Godot*.

I think an argument could be made that the transformation in Beckett's life and writing begins with the period of quite intensive analysis which he underwent with W.R. Bion in 1934-6. Neither Cronin nor Knowlson devote much space to this encounter, possibly because however absorbing and exacting the analysis might have been (nearly two years of weekly sessions, though Beckett remembered it in later years as lasting only about six months), Beckett himself had little to say about it in his many letters to Thomas MacGreevy of the period, and, in fact, he broke off the analysis prematurely. Of course, one must expect biographers to suffer from a certain measure of sibling rivalry with psychoanalysts. Both Cronin and Knowlson confirm the story which Beckett himself frequently recited (and which features in his radio play *All That Fall*) of a visit in the company of Bion to a lecture by C.G. Jung at the Tavistock Clinic, in which Jung described a patient as never having been properly born. However, the evidence of one or two letters to MacGreevy seems to indicate that during these years, Beckett was beginning a process of giving birth to himself. (The stern, somewhat stodgy Bion, who seems to have helped initiate this process, was towards the end of his life to write some extraordinary psychoanalytic dialogues with his own unborn self.) The acknowledgment rather than the disavowal of his own melancholy ambivalence, an acknowledgment that perhaps could not be complete until after the War, would be a crucial stage in delivering Beckett from an art of mutilating rage into one of maimed mercy.

There can be no doubt that Beckett's experiences during the War, first of all working for the Resistance as a translator and collator of strategic espionage, and then, following the betrayal of his cell, hiding in the village of Roussillon in the unoccupied zone, helped make the existence of other people for the first time truly unignorable for him. Here, Knowlson comes into his own, combining the advantages of access to a huge range of previously uninvestigated sources and unpublished documentation with an indefatigable inquisitiveness and a breathtaking capacity for taking pains. Given Cronin's more limited access to materials and necessary dependence upon previously-published accounts, Knowlson's account of Beckett's life from the late 1930s to the end of the War is inevitably the much richer and more nuanced of the two biographies.

Knowlson plays his trumps very liberally in the chapter he calls 'Germany: The Unknown Diaries 1936-7', which is based on notebooks discovered in Beckett's trunk after his death, made available to Knowlson for his exclusive use by the writer's nephew, Edward. And yet there are also times, I feel, when Cronin's relative distance from the material allows him to squint past the trees to the wood. Basing his judgment largely upon remarks made by Beckett in letters to Thomas MacGreevy, Cronin is visibly dismayed by the boredom and apathy with which Beckett responded to the cultural barbarism of Nazi Germany, declining, for example, to make the acquaintance of some contemporary painters who had been the victim of oppression because '[t]hey are all great proud angry poor put upons in their fastnesses and I can't say yessir and nosir anymore' (qtd. in Cronin, p. 244). Knowlson explains that Beckett was tired and depressed when he wrote these words, but even after his return to Dublin he was still complaining (in letters which Cronin quotes, but I think Knowlson does not) about having to listen to 'all the usual sentimental bunk about the Nazi persecutions' and 'the usual bilge about the persecutions' (qtd. in Cronin, p. 246). This is not wickedness exactly, though it is the smallness that makes wickedness possible. It is obvious that Beckett found Nazi ideology intolerable too; but, like many of those lacking in political imagination in the period, Beckett seems to have objected much more to the vulgarity of the Nazis than to what they were actually doing. Knowlson insists that Beckett's diaries show that while he was actually meeting persecuted Jewish artists, 'he felt genuine concern at the constraints under which they were working and at the restrictions that had been imposed on their freedoms' (p. 239). It may very well be that the diaries do show this, but there is precious little sign of it in what Knowlson chooses to quote from them. For the most part, Knowlson's judgments about his subject are as measured and objective as those of a close friend writing an authorised biography can be; but on the question of Beckett's political sensitivities there are times when it seems that he may have known the liberal and compassionate man that Beckett became in his later years too well to be able to take proper measure of the crassness of his youth.

After the War, Beckett volunteered to work as part of a Red Cross mission to the shattered town of Saint-Lô. As usual, Knowlson has the edge over Cronin in the abundance and variety of the testimonies and materials on which he is able to draw. But again, the very thinness of Cronin's fabric lets some of the bony edges poke out that are pillowed by the profusion of circumstance in Knowlson's account. Knowlson alludes only in passing to the 1946 broadcast that Beckett made for Radio Éireann about his experiences at Saint-Lô, asserting blandly that it shows how deeply the experience affected him. Cronin does not flinch from showing us the possibly self-defensive, but still shocking frigidity of that broadcast. Only a knowledge of the humanity of Beckett's later explorations of the inhuman condition could rescue the insufferable, sarky, high-mindedness of stuff like this:

> What was important was not our having penicillin when they had none... but the occasional glimpse obtained by us in them and who knows, by them in us (for they are an imaginative people) of that smile at the human condition as little to be extinguished by bombs as to be broadened by the elixirs of Burroughs and Wellcome – the smile deriding, among other things, the having and the not having, the giving and the taking, sickness and health. (qtd. in Cronin, p. 352)

Was this the important thing? One is tempted to respond to this outrageous assertion in a variation of the authorial rejoinder that closes the story 'Dante and the Lobster': It Was Not. The most emphatic sign of humanisation in the writing that Beckett was already doing in *Watt* by this time would be the ethical dilapidations it wrought (not least with the meddling power of the comma) on the stifled, self-regarding composure of sentences like the above.

The Beckett presented in Knowlson's biography appears much more of a piece, much more a character from the kind of nineteenth-century *Bildungsroman* that the young Beckett despised than the Beckett presented by Cronin, whose life is characterised by rupture and unevenness. This looseness in the joints allows Cronin to make sharper (if also sometimes cruder) distinctions than Knowlson between different bits of Beckett's oeuvre. Writing, for example, about Beckett's first completed play, *Eleuthéria* (which he never translated, and which has only recently been published), Knowlson suggests that had it been staged in 1948, when Beckett wanted it to be, 'it would certainly be talked of now, in spite of its limitations and flaws, as one of the plays that ushered in a new era in avant-garde French theatre' (p. 366). Cronin's rather more robust judgement is, I think, nearer the mark: He reckons that 'if *Eleutheria* had been produced before *Godot* it would almost certainly have been a flop', and, what is more, in seeming 'like an ordinary play gone wrong... might have prejudiced the chances and clouded the strangeness of *Godot*' (p. 367).

I agree with some other reviewers of this biographical pseudocouple who have found that Cronin's account succeeds in summoning up the specifically Irish contexts of Beckett's writing. He has some sharply perceptive things to say, for instance, about the culture of prosperous Protestantism in which Beckett was brought up. He also registers more effectively than Knowlson the horrible (my judgement, not his) maleness of the world which formed him, and which he retained in the form of his friendships and cultural style throughout his life. For a man who wrote so disparagingly about the possibilities of friendship in *Proust,* it is remarkable what a ferocious capacity for friendship he displayed in his life (this is one of the honourable reasons why he could never have been a good critic). But although he was able to have intense friendships with women as he grew older, Beckett was always more comfortable with male butties and drinking partners than with lovers or mothers. Beckett has Molloy imagine a kind of resolution in his tortured relationship with his mother as a relapse into shared decrepitude, in which the crone, as it were, is allowed to become the crony: 'We were so old she and I, she had had me so young, that we were like a couple of old cronies, sexless, unrelated, with the same memories, the same desires, the same rancours'. Both biographers are infinitely more understanding than their predecessor, Deirdre Bair, of the difficulties that must have been faced by Beckett's mother (they could scarcely be less), with Cronin in particular encouraging us to imagine what must have been her exasperation. And both also handle the issue of Beckett's sexual life with honesty and tact, though predictably, Knowlson is much more in the know than Cronin about a couple of affairs and liaisons. But really it is what I once remember a school matron describing as the 'smell of trouser' which hangs most heavily over this life, and which neither biographer really seems to get at.

If Cronin allows himself more robust good sense than Knowlson, he also probably gives in too often to gossip and picture-making to fill the gaps in the record. This is particularly so in the portions of his biography dealing with Beckett's childhood; while Knowlson always sieves his evidence (he, after all, has an abundance to sieve) before concluding that passages from Beckett's work relate to or derive from his life, Cronin shamelessly snitches for his own purposes anything from the work that looks like it might be childhood reminiscence. He also finds it hard to resist comic stories and vignettes, like the account of Noelle Beamish, the tweedy lesbian in Roussillon who claimed to be a cousin of Winston Churchill and whose utilitarian drawers flapping on the line next to the frilly knickers of her partner, he says, caused merriment in the village of Roussillon. Typically, Knowlson both tells us more about this woman and resists the cheap laugh.

Even though the bike he is riding has no lights or brakes, and slews and skids over the terrain that Knowlson treads with such law-abiding circumspection, Cronin often succeeds in being righter than Knowlson. But if one leaves aside Knowlson's propensity for excessive admiration, his style of biography-writing is like that admired by Beckett in early 1937:

> What I want is the straws, flotsam, etc., names, dates, births and deaths, because that is all I can know... I want the oldfashioned history book of reference, not the fashionable monde romancé that explains copious[ly] without telling me anything about Luther, where he went next, what he lived on, what he died of, etc. I say the expressions 'historical necessity' and 'Germanic destiny' start the vomit moving upwards. (qtd. in Knowlson, pp. 244-5)

Knowlson's willingness to let quotation and circumstance speak, if not exactly for themselves, then at least unprodded by the toe of the QED, will probably make his the more lasting of the two biographies. Or rather, come to think of it, the opposite: I must mean that Cronin's book may still be standing illustriously entire on my shelf long after Knowlson's has been thumbed and rifled to venerable tatters.

REVIEWS

Diary Products

James Pethica (ed.), *Lady Gregory's Diaries 1892-1902* (Gerrards Cross: Colin
  Smythe, 1996), 346 pp. £35.00

These diaries chart a pivotal and fascinating period in Augusta Gregory's life,
from her husband's death in 1892 until the diaries begin to peter out in 1902.
This ten-year span witnessed several important transitions for Gregory, as she
changed gradually from a grieving widow and anxious mother of a young
boy to a contented and independent single woman who had successfully
guided her son Robert through adolescence to the age of majority, from a
unionist to a moderate nationalist, and from an intelligent woman with an un-
focused interest in literature to a writer on the verge of being recognised as an
important figure in the Irish literary scene. The diaries do not really change
our general sense of the shape of Gregory's career; rather, they sketch a por-
tion of it in a manner that is, interestingly, both vivid and indirect.

   The early entries outline the conventional life of a titled widow, revolving
around social engagements, visits to sick friends, philanthropic projects
undertaken with other titled women, and the supervision of Robert's school-
ing and social prospects. The diaries convey the impression that this life
is arduous and empty, its difficulties compounded by Coole's precarious financial position and Gregory's determination to improve it before the estate
passes to Robert. As time goes by, she becomes increasingly impatient with the
London social circle she continues to inhabit in order to ease Robert's entry
into social and professional life, and increasingly comfortable in the comparative isolation of Coole. In the later entries, lists of dinner guests have for the
most part been replaced by descriptions of the literary projects in which she is
currently engaged and of the events and squabbles surrounding the beginnings of the Irish theatre.

   About herself, Gregory is intelligently self-conscious, while usually steering
clear of introspection. Even during the early years, her diaries reveal her as
a sharp and funny commentator on the people she encounters. She acidly
describes William Sharp as 'an absurd object, in velvet coat, curled hair, wonderful ties' (p. 154), and makes numerous wry commentaries on friends such
as George Russell and George Moore. Her narration of an encounter with a
suffragist displays an early aptitude for comedy as well as her characteristic reticence in the face of politics: 'Called, in an incautious moment, on Lady
Cork – who expressed gr joy at seeing me – & attacked me to help her in her

crusade for women's rights —— I tried to escape after a time – but she held me with cold fingers & a glittering eye – a regular lunatic' (p. 212). Her constant and uncritical enthusiasm for Yeats, less censored here than in later writings, stands out in particularly strong contrast to this tone of witty detachment. The diaries make it clear, however, that the transformations they track had begun before Gregory met Yeats, and that their friendship, which was cultivated quite deliberately on her part, was as much a result of the changes she was already undergoing as it was a catalyst for future developments.

Many of what seem in retrospect to be the most important events of these years remain unrecorded in the diaries, such as Gregory's visit to the Aran islands, alone, in 1893. James Pethica's excellent introduction supplies a straightforward narrative of various developments that the diaries often merely suggest obliquely. Straightforward but not reductive, the introduction elegantly outlines the major contradictions that shaped Gregory's life and works. For example, on her gradual conversion to Irish nationalism, Pethica observes that 'her philanthropic sympathies and general sense of *noblesse oblige* seem to have challenged the ideological underpinnings of her Union-ism quite directly in the process of completing it' (p. xviii), and he shrewdly comments that collaborative work, in the form of editing Sir William's auto-biography for publication or working with Yeats, helped her to negotiate the conflicting imperatives of creative self-expression and dutiful self-abnegation. The introduction's relative tidiness, its emphasis on the diaries as exemplary of progress and development, is the inevitable goal of a narrative constructed in retrospect, as opposed to an immediate record of events and impressions. As such, it is of course both a major strength and a potential weakness. I found that the most fruitful reading of the diaries proceeded simultaneously under the guidance of and in a certain tension with the introduction. In such a read-ing, other narrative rhythms emerge: the annual summing up of the busy holiday activities at New Year's; the concerns or attitudes that remain constant through these years, such as her determination to stay out of 'politics' even as her politics changed; and pleasantly anomalous moments, such as her 1897 project of learning to ride a bicycle.

Pethica's notes represent a monumental scholarly endeavour, and are very helpful, though some foreign language phrases are translated, while others are not, a puzzling inconsistency considering the massive apparatus included in the volume.

MARJORIE HOWES

Peerless Lives

Ann C. Kavanaugh, *John FitzGibbon, Earl of Clare: Protestant Reaction and English Authority in Late Eighteenth-Century Ireland* (Dublin: Irish Academic Press, 1997) x + 461 pp. £35.00

Stella Tillyard, *Citizen Lord: Edward Fitzgerald, 1763-1798* (London: Chatto and Windus, 1997), xiv + 337 pp. £16.99

In 1798, the Irish lord chancellor, Lord Clare, ushered two grandees, Lady Louisa Conolly and Lord Henry Fitzgerald, into the cell of the latter's brother, the wounded (and dying) Lord Edward Fitzgerald. Clare, then and thereafter vilified as 'Black Jack', is rarely depicted in compassionate guise. Overcome by emotion, however, he apparently retired to dab away his tears. So, one of the newly important in Ascendancy Ireland, clearly a man of feeling, encountered the scion of its leading family, who had striven to overthrow the entire structure. The meeting, with its ironies and pathos, cries for a quartet from Verdi. Although he sometimes aestheticised recent and revolutionary events, Verdi never transformed this scene in the Dublin gaol into high art. Instead, we are left with Stella Tillyard and Ann Kavanaugh.

Tillyard's portrayal of Lord Edward Fitzgerald sometimes aspires to art. The second in a projected trilogy on the late-eighteenth-century Fitzgeralds of Carton, it improves markedly on the first, *Aristocrats*. Yet, to judge from the remaindered copies piled high in the basement of Easons, her study has failed to excite the ordinary reader. It is a strange and arresting story, some parts of which she tells well. At many points, however, she is hampered by sparse or missing documentation. To overcome this problem, the biographer has resorted to varied strategies. Accordingly, her text is bulked out with learned disquisitions on orientalism in eighteenth-century painting, the topography of Nova Scotia, the habits of the Iroquois tribe, dress reform, and horticultural fads. There are fewer set-pieces than in *Aristocrats*, yet the start augurs badly. Carton and its park are evoked, the former characterised as 'dour and square'. Dour some may think it; square it is not, as the accompanying illustration reveals. Next, we have the tiresome Duchess of Leinster, 'her blue grey eyes opened wide, like summer flowers caught out of season'. But soon we are caught up in a rattling good yarn, recounted more in the manner of the now forgotten Carola Oman or Sir Arthur Bryant rather than of Dennis Wheatley or Georgette Heyer, whose authorial voices sounded so loudly through *Aristocrats*.

Tillyard candidly acknowledges the lack of much strictly contemporary testimony for Fitzgerald's life, especially after 1794. She bravely tries to explain his evolution from spoilt brat into fervent revolutionary. Rousseau and Tom Paine enter on cue. Parallel to an intellectual development, the struggle of a weak son to liberate himself from a doting mother is chronicled. The proto-hippy colony at the seaside at Blackrock, where flower power reigned, is followed by the boy's-own-adventure of trekking across North America and sleeping on beds of spruce. Hunting the moose there, not unexpectedly in Tillyard's technique, prefigures the way in which the outlawed Fitzgerald would himself be tracked. The child of the Enlightenment is shaken by sentiment into a romantic. A beneficiary of inherited privilege, although not of any clear role or substantial resources, he eagerly embraced fraternity and equality. He stood, therefore, at the opposite pole from John FitzGibbon, the future earl of Clare and lord chancellor of Ireland. The latter came from a family which acquired wealth and standing only in the time of his lawyer father. But FitzGibbon resembled Fitzgerald in his susceptibility to the intellectual currents of the age. Each searchingly exposed the flaws in the social structures and political systems of Ireland, but reached divergent conclusions. Both succumbed to powerful romantic impulses which attached them to unlikely heroes and unpopular causes.

The difficulties which arise from the meagre evidence for many important passages in Fitzgerald's life are compounded by the way in which it is reconstructed here. Imagining her readers apparently as the successors to the subscribers to Boots' circulating libraries, Tillyard does not trouble them with textual annotations. Thus, although she knows the primary sources intimately and has read widely, few of her statements and none of the quotations can be linked with its source. This would hardly matter had she not, in accordance with a vogue of the moment, levelled the boundaries between what conventionally are regarded as fact and fiction. Of late, many historians, the best of them always a sceptical clan, have admitted that what had passed as fact may be mutable and contested. Nevertheless, it is possible to trust scrupulous historians to tell of the varying alloys from which they have fashioned their accounts. Tillyard, keen to enliven her narrative, fleshes out the devoted black servant, Tony Small. He existed; he was painted: but little more is known of him from the extant record. Yet we meet him wandering on the battlefield near Eutaw Creek, inevitably 'like a wraith', where he saves the injured Lord Edward. Thereafter, he recurs as a choric figure to comment on the turns of fate which touch his master. Perhaps surprisingly, Tillyard eschews any homoerotic bond between the black and white. Otherwise her Tony Small could be a character from a story by Colin Macinnes rather than a plausible inhabitant of an eighteenth-century aristocratic establishment (black servants had been kept in the smartest Irish houses at least since the seventeenth century, their novelty value seconded by humanitarian and sentimental inclinations on the part of their employers). John FitzGibbon, we also learn, 'loved' other men. The worship which he lavished on the chief secretary, William Eden, later Lord Auckland, surprises Kavanaugh, as it must surprise anyone familiar with that dull dog. Such idolatry, Kavanaugh insists, was innocent of any homosexual content. Since both FitzGibbon and Fitzgerald were serial adulterers in the mould of a Clinton or a Kennedy, their passionate male friendships probably speak of no more than the prevalent sensibilities of their age, in which fraternity received effusive literary and even physical, but not sexual, expression.

The *mores* of late-eighteenth-century Dublin, London or Paris, essential background to the outlook, value, and actions of the two men, are perfunctorily sketched. Each comes across as an animated marionette from a Gillray cartoon, with minimal trappings to suggest the physical actuality of the worlds in which he lived. The suspicion that Tillyard's Lord Edward Fitzgerald is a thoroughly modern type who has happened to stray onto a late-eighteenth-century stage is not allayed by the supporting role accorded to the largely invented Small in her costume drama. Those used to more austere kinds of scholarship cannot but be disquieted. Fuddy-duddies will be reassured by Kavanaugh's more orthodox approach. FitzGibbon's public career has deposited enough traces to generate nearly 400 pages of text, all of which rest on a massive substructure of scholarly reference. Clare never emerges entirely from the bulky chrysalis of the doctoral dissertation to wing his way with Fitzgerald into the empyrean. An estimable desire to omit nothing accords the trivial and epoch-forming equal attention. However, in order to avoid revisiting scenes already familiar from other histories of the 1780s and 1790s, Kavanaugh often concentrates on more obscure incidents, particularly those in which FitzGibbon was embroiled as law officer of the crown. 1798 and 1800 pass quickly by, on the reasonable grounds that they are too familiar to need rehearsal and that, in any case, FitzGibbon's part was minor. Despite its bulk, the narrative is effectively controlled by Kavanaugh. Mordant quips and astringent analysis, including the melodrama which invariably enveloped Lord Edward, show what she could do if given the same brief as Ms. Tillyard. Unfortunately, Clare, a more influential figure than Fitzgerald, has not been identified by the market research of publishers as a likely best-seller. Poor Kavanaugh is allowed no illustrations: a pity when FitzGibbon, like Fitzgerald, attached great importance to cutting 'the grand figure', whether in dress, equipage, or housing. As a result, the strutting dandy so reviled by contemporaries goes unseen.

Both biographers strive conscientiously to penetrate the carefully fabricated exteriors of their subjects. However, Fitzgerald's and FitzGibbon's interior lives and so their beliefs, the spurs to otherwise willfully impetuous actions, remain elusive. Kavanaugh, in pursuit of the inner man, dutifully considers what FitzGibbon collected. Tillyard delves into Lord Edward's gardens, in the hope of uncovering the motors of his career, but unearths only surpassing silliness. It is telling, as Kavanaugh notes, that FitzGibbon belonged neither to the Dublin Society nor to the Royal Irish Academy. Furthermore, the books which he is known to have purchased had the utilitarian function of completing his mastery of law and history. These skills were used subsequently to rout adversaries in the courts and parliament. The sheer aggression which all too frequently disturbed the polished behaviour of FitzGibbon disconcerted allies and opponents alike. Those who prided themselves on their civility and affability, notably the Whig peers over whom he presided as lord chancellor in the upper house, attributed these coarser traits to his obscure and recent origins. The swagger which descended into hectoring sat oddly with a character capable, as Kavanaugh amply shows, of politic calculation and private generosity. She rejects as too obvious the explanation that he was drunk with power. Rather, he may literally have been drunk, downing large draughts of alcohol and perhaps dying from the effects. Drink and its impact on Irish history have occasionally been considered in the aggregate, with totals imported and annual consumption computed. But their effects on individuals are seldom included in the dynamics of day-to-day politics. Much of the rashness and miscalculation in the activities of both FitzGibbon and Fitzgerald could readily be explained by judgments clouded by drunkenness. Certainly, Kavanaugh provides an astute and, within reason, a generous vision of an unhappy and discontented man.

What in the end mystifies is not how FitzGibbon scrambled into high office but how he clung on to it. A similar mystery enfolds Fitzgerald. Despite commonplace views, he was propelled into the leadership of a projected revolution. In Lord Edward's case, the glamour of his name, the pre-eminence of his family, and the chance removal of alternatives largely explain his position. For FitzGibbon, the law advanced him, as it had his father and many of his contemporaries. He had, moreover, been bought both a Dublin and an Oxford education. Once installed in office, first as attorney-general, then lord chancellor, he displayed an industry which recalled his equally controversial predecessor back in Queen Anne's reign, Sir Constantine Phipps. Indeed, in his ability to entrench himself, to cow and then see off critical lords lieutenant, and to create a formidable political base he emulated the overmighty lord chancellors of the late seventeenth century: Porter, Archbishop Michael Boyle, and Sir Maurice Eustace. Kavanaugh pleads convincingly for FitzGibbon as an upright, though combative judge. Any legist who presided over his court with a huge Newfoundland dog by his side must have had his attractions.

Not all accepted FitzGibbon at his own high estimation. First an English lord chancellor had tried to stop his appointment; later a second humiliated FitzGibbon, now a member of the United Kingdom House of Lords, for his uncertain grasp of legal principles. Herein lay the ultimate irony. Behind FitzGibbon's fulminations against popery, reform, and rebellion lay a consistent belief in the necessity of the British connection for Ireland's well-being. Cast adrift after the Union onto the open seas of the imperial legislature, those talents which had served him so well in the restricted waters of Dublin looked feeble. Throughout the 1790s, he had survived the several attempts by aggrieved lords lieutenant to be rid of him because of his ability to catch and mouth the sentiments of the generally inarticulate conservative majority in the Irish parliament. That conservatism has been most searchingly anatomised by Anthony Malcomson. But now, alongside his brilliant study of Speaker Foster, we can gratefully set Kavanaugh's study of the Speaker of the Lords, Lord Chancellor Clare.

TOBY BARNARD

Nothing But the Same Old Story?

John N. Molony, *A Soul Came Into Ireland: Thomas Davis, 1814-1845* (Dublin: Geography Publications, 1995), 385 pp. £20.00

Ellen Shannon-Mangan, *James Clarence Mangan: A Biography* (Dublin: Irish Academic Press, 1996), xix + 413 pp. £35.00

It is an interesting coincidence that these biographies – dealing with two of the most important nineteenth-century writers in Ireland – should have appeared almost simultaneously. Although neither biographer has much to say about the relationship between these two men, the pairing of Thomas Davis and James Clarence Mangan is a potentially useful framework for describing the complicated and contradictory dynamics of Irish cultural nationalism. Davis's industrious, earnest, missionary idealism could hardly be more different to Mangan's protean, evasive, desperate eccentricity, yet ironically both writers were canonised by that nationalist tradition which produced the modern Irish state. In these two writers we see clearly the tension between, on the one hand, the need for nationalism to believe that identity is something transcendental, capable of unifying Irish culture (Davis's position), and, on the other, the more unsettling possibility that all identities are always artificial and ideologically-bound, and therefore non-transcendent (Mangan's implicit position). Davis's writings fluctuated between two related strategies concerning Irish identity: the first demanded the recovery of a fundamental, pre-existing national identity which had been lost or suppressed, and the second called for the promotion of a modern, pluralist, transcendent Irish identity 'which may embrace Protestant, Catholic and Dissenter, – Milesian and Cromwellian, – the Irishman of a hundred generations and the stranger who is within our gates'. The latter is a powerful rhetorical solution to the material and ideological problems of sectarian, class, and historical conflict, and while this latter argument relies on quite a different, more materialist conception of nationality to the 'spiritual essence' of the first claim, both arguments assume that singular, authentic national identity is a desirable and achievable end. Plurality is understood to be merely a stage on the way to unity. By contrast, Mangan's version of plurality is always point-ing in more unnerving directions, since for him identities are inevitably masks of a sort, constructions whose claims to permanence, transcendence, or authen-ticity are always undermined by their rhetorical or ideological nature. No identity, least of all a national one, is firmly grounded or self-evident; and atom-istic alienation rather than pluralist integration is usually the existential norm in Mangan's writing.

The process by which such apparently incompatible perspectives as those of Davis and Mangan could be so smoothly absorbed into nationalist tradition has yet to be fully researched. David Lloyd pioneered the way in his work on Mangan and cultural nationalism, where he showed how the circulation of a highly selective canon, combined with nationalist biographical exercises like John Mitchel's 1859 account of the poet, all worked to cast Mangan as a na-tional 'type'. It is true that Mangan wrote many of his most popular poems for *The Nation* and the *United Irishman*, but such gestures by themselves do not erase the very radical critique his work as a whole poses for the 'identitarian' politics of nationalist ideology.

Recent critical and historical work from Seamus Deane, Terry Eagleton, Joep Leerssen, Maria Luddy, Tom Boylan, and Tadhg Foley, not to mention the nu-merous new works on the Famine, have also been valuably re-thinking the complicated discourses which shaped the cultural and ideological movements of the nineteenth century. Unfortunately, both the biographies under review seem unaware of such contemporary critical and historiographical debates. One may or may not approve of the recent arguments, but they cannot simply be ignored. This lacuna is especially evident in the case of Shannon-Mangan's biography, which is extraordinarily unreflective about its methodology or function, apart from a brief statement in the preface: 'This is a straight-forward biography with a traditional chronological structure... I have thus avoided con-fronting the revisionist questions currently being asked about the art and purpose of biography' (p. x). But why? Ironically, a writer like Mangan, who rejoiced in the epithet of 'The Man in the Cloak' and occasionally passed off original poems as translations from other writers, might be considered especially problematic as a subject for 'straight-forward biography'. The 'straight-forward' assumptions with which traditional biographers have worked – that subjectivities are coherent, that empirical method is objec-tive, and that a 'definitive portrait' (Shannon-Mangan's blurb) is a sustain-able aim – are all notions which Mangan himself appears to have doubted, and which his own work seems certainly to critique. To translate a life into a biography can no longer be the unselfconscious activity it might have seemed once; too much has happened in the realm of biographical and literary theory since D.J. O'Donoghue produced the last 'definitive' biography of the poet in 1897.

But even if we leave aside these theoretical problems, and consider the books on their own chosen ground of traditional biography, both remain disappointing. Partly there is a material problem: Mangan, for instance, left very little manuscript material behind him – a crucial resource for the biographer in search of an 'authentic self' – while Davis's private life was brief and relatively uneventful, unlike his contemporaries Gavan Duffy or John Mitchel. As a result both biographers must rely to a heavy extent on Mangan's and Davis's published writings for their raw material, with the result that Shannon-Mangan is often found searching Mangan's poetic and fictional texts for evidence of the poet's 'inner life', while Molony produces little more than an extended summary of Davis's intellectual progress. In such conditions, the evidence of witnesses becomes especially important, and here it must be said that Shannon-Mangan's biography is a valuable resource, publishing for the first time some of John O'Donovan's and Thomas Larcom's fascinating correspondence relating to Mangan. In fact, as a digest of the few facts concerning Mangan's life which have emerged during the last one hundred and fifty years, Shannon-Mangan's work will prove very useful to readers, though it is not entirely complete – there are for instance, interesting memoirs of Mangan by Martin MacDermott, John Kells Ingram, and others which appear in O'Donoghue's 1897 biography but for some reason are not reproduced here.

Yet while Shannon-Mangan does an admirable job of trying to estimate vital material details such Mangan's earnings and the conditions of his early life, her determination to construct a traditional biography out of scarce resources sometimes produces absurdities, like this entry in the prefatory chronology: '1813-17: Family calls young James "mad" due to his eccentricities' (p. xi). There are frequent impressionistic passages for which no direct evidence is cited ('he was undoubtedly precocious' (p. 14); 'probably attended Mass faithfully' (p. 13); 'he surely realized that he was good-looking' (p. 60). There are, in fact, far too many speculative passages containing the phrases 'must have' or 'probably' which at their most serious produce downright contradiction. Writing of Mangan's mother's death, for instance, the biography states that 'her loss was devastating for him', while several sentences later admitting that 'No letter, no poem, by Mangan about his mother exists to testify to what her loss meant to him' (p. 333). Unjustifiable generalisations abound, betraying a lack of sustained reflection, and detracting from the genuinely useful information which the book sometimes provides. Absurdly reducing the complexity of Mangan's nationalism, for example, Shannon-Mangan writes that 'as soon as any movement was afoot to rid his nation of English abuses and abusers, he took part in it' (p. 75). Can this be an adequate summary of a poet who signed an anti-Union petition in the 1830s while contributing to a Protestant evangelical magazine (*The Friend*), or who could write for *The Nation* and the staunchly pro-Unionist *Irish Monthly Magazine* within weeks of each other? Shannon-

Mangan seems not to have fully grasped the deeper implications of Mangan's elaborate use of pseudonyms and masks, which cannot simply be reduced to a lack of artistic confidence, as she would have it, but in fact served a rich variety of functions: sometimes as an enabling device, sometimes a gesture of resistance, often a method of evasion, very often a provocative joke.

The absence of biographical facts and of interpretive sophistication also leads Shannon-Mangan into very basic psychoanalytic readings of Mangan's writing, construing the work as a series of veiled references to traumatic events such as the (purported) loss of a brother in childhood. Such readings are not helped by the fact that the psychoanalytic sources Shannon-Mangan cites are nearly all over thirty years old – she takes no account of more recent developments, especially in the vast field of psychoanalysis and literature. Such readings also tend to downplay the fact that Mangan, even at his most miserable, was frequently following or playing with convention rather than being personally expressive in any simple sense. Gloom and spiritual agony were rhetorical gestures as well as personal outpourings in the nineteenth century. What is fascinating is not simply what such writings may or may not reveal about his inner life, but also what they say about Mangan's facility with form and voice, and about his extraordinary relationship to the culture of nineteenth-century Ireland, whose contradictions also shaped fellow literary desperadoes like Fr Prout and William Maginn.

At times Shannon-Mangan's narrative does become compelling, particularly in the last chapters, where Mangan's slide into serious illness and death takes place against the chiaroscuro backdrop of Young Ireland fervour and Famine devastation. The 1840s are, as it happens, the best-documented period of Mangan's life, which enables Shannon-Mangan to replace speculation with more solid evidence, while allowing Mangan's contemporaries to speak about him, and him to speak about them. Indeed, as a source and digest of information about the poet, the book will be necessary reading for students of Mangan – for historicist reflection on the deeper meaning and function of the poet's biography, however, David Lloyd's work remains indispensable.

While John N. Molony's biography of Thomas Davis does not lapse into the kind of speculative generalisation found in Shannon-Mangan, its concentration on Davis's public and political life means that Molony is really writing intellectual history rather than biography. Molony's book clarifies many aspects of the early part of Davis's career, debunking the myth that Davis travelled in Germany and the assumption, first put about by Gavan Duffy, that Davis never published a line of poetry before he wrote for *The Nation* (in fact he published several anonymous poems in the *Dublin Monthly Magazine*; he even reviewed one favourably in an early issue of *The Nation*!). Molony makes it clear that Davis's nationalism was well-developed at a very early stage in his public career and that his intellectual migration from liberalism to nationalism was not a Damascene conversion. Yet much of the book is preoccupied with detailed accounts of public controversies and debates in which Davis was involved – ground that has already been covered before. Here might have been an opportunity to sketch out something of 'Davis the man' – yet any sense of Davis's personality seems strikingly absent from the book. One would hardly guess that, as Gavan Duffy's 1890 biography of Davis shows, very many of his contemporaries were utterly devoted to him as a person, not just as an inspiring intellect. Part of the problem is that Molony often insists on summarising and paraphrasing Davis's own writing, evidently believing content to be more important than form, but thereby excluding the telling details of style and self-representation which we need to formulate a sense of a writer's personality. Davis's engaging and passionate prose is translated into a historiographical discourse which is inevitably dull by comparison. It is also striking how little weight Molony gives to the significance of poetry, oratory, and the discursive aspects of nationalism in assessing Davis's writing. This is especially important since much of the meaning of Davis's work is inextricably related to his choice of medium, be it journalism, historical writing, or balladry.

Molony's relative singularity of purpose (the book is described on its dust-jacket as an act of 'thanksgiving for the life of an Irish patriot') prevents him from being very curious about alternative, critical perspectives on Davis provided by his contemporaries, such as Thomas MacNevin's criticism of Davis's emotionalism, or the Young Irelanders' high-spirited mocking of Davis's enthusiasm for Irish. There is no sense of debate about Davis's role or significance in Irish history, nor is there any attempt to explore the roots and consequences of his particular obsessions (such as military history, Wolfe Tone, Afghanistan, British imperialism, J.P. Curran, Owen Roe O'Neill). It is in these areas that new ground might have been broken; but they unfortunately lie outside Molony's ken. In fact, it seems to me that despite the praiseworthy intentions of reviving interest in these two crucial figures, both of these new biographies represent lost opportunities. Neither of them has attempted any serious re-thinking of the significance of Mangan and Davis, and neither strays very far from the agendas set by those hagiographic biographies of Mangan and Davis produced almost exactly a century ago by D.J. O'Donoghue and Charles Gavan Duffy.

Sean Ryder

Regional News

David Brett, *The Construction of Heritage* (Cork: Cork University Press, 1996), 172 pp. £32.00

Jim Mac Laughlin (ed.), *Location and Dislocation in Contemporary Irish Society: Emigration and Irish Identities* (Cork: Cork University Press, 1997), 353 pp. £45.00

Cheryl Temple Herr, *Critical Regionalism and Cultural Studies: From Ireland to the Midwest* (Gainesville: University Press of Florida, 1996), 233 pp. £39.95

The Ulster-American Folk Park in Northern Ireland is one of the examples through which David Brett explores the contemporary cultural politics of the heritage industry. This heritage centre takes the visitor on a migrant's journey from Northern Ireland to Pennsylvania and so links the themes of these three books: the construction of the past in the heritage industry, the historical and contemporary migrations that have shaped the Irish-American connection, two places connected through culture and economy. These books trace economic geographies of uneven development and global capital; national, transnational, and subnational political geographies; classed, gendered, and racialised relations of power; and imaginative geographies of identity and belonging – located, dislocated, and mobile. Cheryl Temple Herr charts the economic and cultural interconnections between Iowa and Ireland. Mac Laughlin and his contributors explore not only the nature of Irish migration but also the political implications of different ways of understanding and representing emigration. The spatial vocabulary of scale (local, regional, and global), of core and periphery, of movement and networks, and of location runs through these books, but they also locate their subjects within the history of modernisation: the post-famine emergence of a rural bourgeois made possible through the migration of surplus labour, the nostalgia for the past that accompanies modernity, modern capitalist economic cycles of recession and opportunity that reverberate through farming communities in Ireland or the Midwest.

These books also reflect a stage in cultural studies in general, and in Irish studies specifically, when the deconstruction of essential identities deeply rooted in place has become so central that its orthodoxy is in question. There is a growing sense that the simple celebration of dislocation, dispersal, mobility, and hybridity over location, rootedness, and cultural certainty is as unsatisfactory as its opposite. Keiran Keohane, in his chapter on traditionalism and homelessness in contemporary Irish music in *Location and Dislocation*, articulates an ambivalent but powerful sense of identity. There is, he says, 'a desire for post-national, cosmopolitan identification, to escape from the bonds of tradition to a free, but fearfully lonely, existential condition of rootlessness and at the same time, a desire to return to, to re-collect and re-live in the tradition(s) of 'real' (that is to say imagined) Ireland(s)' (p. 302). Brett writes of a tension between the 'sedentary' local/historical, the 'rooted', with all its essentialist and secure connotations, and the exhilarating and painful 'nomadic' global/simultaneous senses of identity and location. Herr opens the tool box of cultural studies to find metaphors for a non-polarised discourse between distance and identification: the space-between, interbeing, dialogism, difference, nomadic space, intertextuality, hybridity, the assemblage. In different ways, these books are attempts to weave other perspectives out of a rejection of the polarised choice between condemning or celebrating location or dislocation. Cheryl Temple Herr's offers a model of critical regionalism and cross-regional vision; Brett advocates critical popular histories for the heritage industry; Mac Laughlin and his authors denaturalise as well as differentiate Irish migration. The authors eschew the appeal of simple explanation for a critical sense of the complex interplay of large structural processes of capitalism or colonialism and specific local conditions and traditions.

Fintan O'Toole writes in *Location and Dislocation* that 'the notion of America itself is an Irish invention, the notion of Ireland an American invention' (p. 175). Herr's critical regionalism maps these projections of desire and imagination between Ireland and Iowa, traces the flows of people, culture, and capital between them, and examines their place within the global workings of capital. The region, she suggests, offers a scale of investigation that brings into focus the abstract and sometimes incomprehensible nature of the New World Order. Linking two regions in order to illuminate their specific and mutual shaping through economic logics of accumulation offers openings in which fruitful forms of engagement, solidarity, resistance, and empowerment may be possible 'without falling prey to recidivist longings or the induced paralysis of an ever consolidating market economy' (p. 12). Enlisting in the first chapter Adorno, Deleuze, and Kenneth Frampton's architectural manifesto of critical regionalism, Herr gives us a sense of the possibilities of this bifurcated cross-regional vision in the chapters which follow. Linking Ireland and Iowa releases a wonderfully rich narrative of two-way connections in local histories, poetry, film, novels and memoirs, agrarian texts, business publications, and newspaper reports: the 'Little Ireland' settlements of Iowa, the iconic presence of Iowa in a Paul Durcan poem, Arensberg's anthropological imagination of a stable Irish rural world as the Dust Bowl and Depression ravaged the Midwest, an Iowan architectural student's plan for a new united Ireland parliament building. Observing the links between the two regions (migration and farming patterns and their experience of global trade agreements), Herr traces, in both Ireland and Iowa, cycles of settlement, dispossession, migration, renewed hope and decline as capital co-opts desire for its own ends, harnessing the hopes and heroics of fathers, mortgaged on the pain of oppressed children and wives. Herr shifts from detailed reading to more troubling rhetorical sweeps. While she never really examines what treating Ireland as a whole leaves out – Ireland appears a peculiarly homogenous land of deserted farms – her interweaving of two places and their cultural and economic geographies is persuasive. She succeeds in bringing together detailed contextual cultural readings and a sense of global political economy. In this, she endorses the implicit sense that Irish studies is never about Ireland alone.

The study of migration makes this evident. In his three chapters, Jim Mac Laughlin reviews the history of post-famine mass migration that accompanied the growth of an Irish rural bourgeoisie content to endorse migration of surplus labour for the sake of economic aggrandisement. Challenging the continued naturalisation and normalisation of migration as an inevitable part of Ireland's modernisation, Mac Laughlin advocates world-systems theory, with its language of core and periphery, to ground explanations of migration in economic disparity. These points are made strongly but sometimes repetitively. The costs of both a colonial legacy, the economic and social conservatism of post-independence Ireland, and anti-Irish racism are embodied: in tables of statistics that Bronwen Walter examines on the relative deprivation of Irish people in London, in Liam Greenslade's stories of men working themselves to early death to counter the racist stereotype of Irish indolence, in descriptions by Marella Buckley of women traveling back and forth across the Irish sea paying for sexual freedom, and in Mary Corcoran's discussion of the vulnerability of Irish workers trapped in New York's informal economy. The chapters by Mac Laughlin, Gerard Hanlon, and Ian Shuttleworth challenge a rosy picture of a 'New Wave' of migration of skilled Irish graduates freely leaving, flourishing abroad, and returning (more skilled) to Ireland. In turn, Breda Gray importantly points out that the apparently progressive notion of an Irish diaspora not only masks the economic and political problems underlying migration, but so far has been strikingly neglectful of the gendered experience of migration, or the implications that revised versions of Irishness have for versions of Irish womanhood. Again, questions of gender do their challenging work. Raising issues of race and whiteness in the context of Irish migration to the States, Eithne Luibheid asks the crucial question: 'What place do mixed marriages, and racially-mixed children, have in the Irish diaspora?' (p. 271). *Location and Dislocation* is an important collection which performs a multi-directional critique of the acceptance of the emigration solution in Ireland as well as of anti-Irish racism in England, a critique that tries to map out the structural forces and personal hopes that shape migration, its general patterns and differentiated nature, and which speaks of ambivalent longings for home and abroad.

For Brett, senses of location and dislocation may be held in fruitful tension by popular forms of local history that are commemorative as well as critical. His book is both a genealogy of the cultural phenomena of heritage and an attempt to develop a methodological framework for promoting critical, ethical, and popular histories. Brett is not anti-heritage. He highlights the ways depoliticised story-telling allows an imaginative, detached, and irresponsible retreat from the uncertainties of the present and the troubles of the past. He avoids the reductive opposition between authenticity and inauthenticity while retaining a critical perspective on the kind of stories told and not told in heritage sites. In part, this means historicising the heritage industry through its precedents in the nostalgic cults of the past that accompanied nineteenth-century modernity. Instead of applying the language of postmodernism, Brett traces the modern aesthetic traditions and technologies of representation though which heritage works and reads their legacies within it. He analyses the picturesque and sublime as aesthetic and artistic categories through which the world itself was increasingly understood by middle-class tourists; categories that now inform the representation of the past as an aesthetic diversion, rather than a realm of human struggle for material survival and meaning. The contemporary heritage industry is located within a continuum of developments in image reproduction, especially in the illustrated press, and within spectacular traditions of display and exhibition (including the Great Exhibitions but also the panorama, diorama, and waxworks of nineteenth-century Britain).

Brett brings this astute sense of traditions and technologies to bear on his five case studies, exploring their modes of pictorial convention, their devices of simulation, and the paths they offer the visitor, literally and conceptually. For Brett, the five examples (with the exception of the Famine Museum, Stokestown, Co. Roscommon) mask complex histories or fail to explore the critical potential of their historical subjects: histories of enterprise, mercantilism, speculation, and imperialism in the case of Fountains Abbey in North Yorkshire; the meaning and use of the myths of Cúchulain surrounding the ancient earthworks of the Navan Fort Centre by Pearse or loyalist paramilitaries; the idea of the Celtic at the ancient field systems of the Ceide Fields Centre. Only the Famine Museum presents both a more critical and a more unsettled version of history, emphasising its uncertainties as well as highlighting the visitor's active engagement in producing meaning. It is in this simultaneously critical and deconstructivist approach to popular history that Brett sees hope for the future.

These books do many things, but at one level at least they represent both an effort to imagine concepts of identity between location and dislocation and a kind of self-conscious and critical recuperation of tradition, complicated by the frequently oppositional nature of tradition and identity. They negotiate the problem of matching broad critique with the confusing complexity of different histories and experiences. In terms of heritage or of the histories of migration, this means acknowledging the absences in figuring the Irish tradition or Irish diaspora as endlessly Catholic. To return to the Ulster-American Folk Park, Brett reads there a story of spiritual rebirth and civilising mission as the Old World is abandoned for the New. For Brett, the problem with this tale is not that it commemorates the journeys of Presbyterian migrants, but that by remaining unspecified it elides the mass migration of Catholics whose histories are also part of the region. But it also elides its own important place within Irish history. These other stories of regional identity and difference are critical.

CATHERINE NASH

Incensed

James H. Murphy, *Catholic Fiction and Social Reality in Ireland 1873-1922* (Westport, Connecticut and London: Greenwood Press, 1997) x + 172 pp. £43.95

Ruth Fleischmann, *Catholic Nationalism in the Irish Revival: A Study of Canon Sheehan, 1852-1913* (London: Macmillan, 1997), xiv + 188 pp. £42.50

Mike Cronin, *The Blueshirts and Irish Politics* (Dublin: Four Courts Press, 1997), 220 pp. £19.95

The dominant self-image of Catholic-nationalist Ireland for much of the twentieth century was a relatively classless society united by shared Catholic and nationalist values. The three books under review give important insights into the worldview of a social group not fully acknowledged by this paradigm; the various sections of the Catholic middle class and clergy who saw themselves as natural leaders of the Irish people.

James Murphy discusses a forgotten genre, the late-nineteenth-century, Irish, upper-middle-class novel. Associated particularly with Fr Matthew Russell's *Irish Monthly* and written by authors who wished to assert the compatibility of Irish Catholic identity with respectability in British terms, this genre attributed Irish problems to Anglo-Irish misunderstandings rather than genuine conflicts of interest. It presented an idealised picture of the peasantry (knowing English readers took too little interest in Ireland to differentiate between social classes) and used the stock devices of romantic comedy as metaphors for its project of reconciliation through goodwill between the classes, or, even more improbably, through the substitution of a Catholic ruling elite for the Protestant one. (The view that a Catholic elite, having experienced persecution, would naturally show paternalist sympathy for their poorer co-religionists was most strongly articulated in Rosa Mulholland's novel *Marcella Grace* [1889].)

This genre was extremely bland and evasive in its portrayal of Irish society. George Moore's *Drama in Muslin* (1886), by contrast, with its emphasis on the mercenary parasitism of the upper-class marriage market, can be seen as a criticism of such evasions. The *Irish Monthly*, in fact, criticised future Catholic icons like Kickham and Sheehan for paying too much attention to the darker sides of Irish life; yet Murphy shows how later eulogies of these writers saw them through an interpretative grid emphasising invocations of communal harmony (while ignoring depictions of materialism, insecurity, fear, and hatred).

Murphy argues that as the Catholic upper middle class was displaced by an assertive lower middle class, this genre, associated with the former, declined, to be replaced by an oppositional intelligentsia novel which challenged the values of the dominant Catholic lay and clerical elites. Writers of this school advocated modernisation through various means, ranging from political, cultural, and religious reform in the hopeful days of the Revival to individual emancipation and flight as established values proved more firmly entrenched than had been expected.

Some of Murphy's readings of individual novels can be challenged (the sympathetic presentation of 1848 rebels in Justin McCarthy's *Mononia* [1901] does not necessarily imply extreme nationalism, since constitutional nationalists and even Unionists could present the actions of former rebels as justifiable because of past abuses, while denouncing those of the contemporary variety of rebel). Murphy underestimates the traditionalism of some intellectuals such as Aodh de Blacam, underplays the survival of a self-conscious Catholic ruling class mentality in post-independence Ireland, and ignores the 'organic intelligentsia' which presented de Valera's Ireland (with decreasing plausibility) as fulfilling the Utopian hopes of the Revival. Nonetheless, Murphy's acute decoding of the literary conventions of the period opens up a new field of enquiry. This book gives a clearer idea of what the major figures of the Irish Revival reacted against. Suggestively, many of the authors discussed are women.

Ruth Fleischmann provides a detailed analysis of an author touched on by Murphy: Canon Sheehan. Readers of Murphy will recognise certain themes; Sheehan's belief that Jewish and Masonic conspiracies were behind European secularisation and that the secular Queen's Colleges led to irreligion and damnation echo Murphy's account of the earlier priest-novelist R.B. O'Brien, while the ideal (in *My New Curate* [1889]) of pious, contented peasants ruled by Catholic aristocrats awakened to their duties by priestly admonitions is reminiscent of the *Irish Monthly* (the Land League never appears, though the novel is set in the 1880s).

Fleischmann provides some interesting close readings of Sheehan's inconsistencies and selective viewing. (For example, he sees made marriages as spiritually delightful submission to parental authority and as free from unwholesome sentiment, ignoring the material interests involved; his glorifications of suffering and poverty sentimentalise them away.) She particularly dislikes his confinement of women to roles associated with suffering and sacrifice and justified by religious fervour which she sees as based on infantile submission, self-hypnotic devotional incantation, and Manichaean fear of reality. Fleischmann argues that Sheehan's lasting importance lies in his exploration of the fears and frustrations of the Edwardian Irish priesthood.

Unfortunately, Fleischmann's limited historical knowledge leads her to miss some of Sheehan's contemporary allusions and dismiss some of his views more hastily than they deserve. The Fenian critique of the Land League and its successors, which Sheehan echoes, was not merely based on social conservatism but on the accurate perception that the League benefited a section of the farming class while doing little for small farmers and labourers, and was often abused in situations involving personal disputes (as in the boycott in *The Blindness of Dr. Gray* [1909]). Griffith supported the co-operative movement and often criticised the misdeeds of rural traders and their clerical and political allies; Fleischmann's statement to the contrary (p.154) is mistaken. The rapid spread of the religious revival in *The Triumph of Failure* is not implausible (as the 1859 Ulster Revival shows); the transitoriness of such phenomena provides better grounds for criticism. Sheehan does not identify uncritically with the Catholic middle class; one of his central fears is that they will rebel against clerical control and come under Protestant influence.

Sheehan's central concern regarded the qualities required of priests if their social leadership was to be maintained in a changing Ireland; he tried to promote an ethos of service and social impartiality among the clergy. Sheehan was certainly sincere and worked hard for the welfare of his parishioners, but on a vital point Fleischmann is correct: he evades the dark side of paternalism and does not admit that parishioners might need safeguards against abuses of priestly power. His priests may be flawed by pride, but they never display meaner vices; they do not drink to excess or act unjustly in parochial disputes for financial or family motives. Such evasions made contemporary anti-clerical novelists (discussed by Murphy) see Sheehan as rationalising naked clerical power-seeking, while he saw such dissent as personal wickedness.

Belief in a hierarchical society based on Catholic principles did not die with independence; in the 1930s several prominent Catholic intellectuals associated with the Blueshirt movement argued that elected politicians should forego many social functions which might be assigned to professional elites within a corporate society. What interests did these theories serve? Cronin argues on the basis of government records and interviews with surviving rank-and-file Blueshirts that they were a traditionalist organisation, inspired less by fascism or Civil War loyalties than a rational response to the destructive effects of the

Economic War, although a small minority of committed fascists and quasi-fascist intellectuals was isolated by the conservative Cumann na nGaedheal leadership.

Cronin has fascinating local material on Blueshirt social activities, local confrontations, and membership figures. Unfortunately, he draws on a narrow range of sources. Little use is made of the local press (unfortunate, given his emphasis on local politics) or journals of opinion. The insistence of the noxiously pro-Fianna Fáil *Catholic Bulletin* that the Blueshirts were only bogus fascists and de Valera was the true Irish Mussolini is relevant to the question of how far Fianna Fáil as well as the Blueshirts had fascist tendencies, while D.P. Moran's *Leader* shows the Economic War convincing a veteran Irish Irelander and critic of Cumann na nGaedheal economic policy that de Valera was leading the country to ruin and establishing a Fianna Fáil dictatorship.[1]

Yet Cronin's thematic (rather than chronological) structure hinders contextualisation, and his abstruse discussions of whether the Blueshirts were fascist are largely irrelevant, since the central issue is not whether the Blueshirts were fascist but whether they were anti-democratic. His interviews, though useful, fall into the same trap as much German 'everyday history' of the Third Reich; the material is not interrogated enough. Blueshirt rhetoric at the time and present-day interviewees compare the genuine suffering inflicted on farmers by the Economic War to the Famine and the Land War. (The Land War trope, similar to the ritual invocation of the Penal Days to secure Catholic solidarity as discussed by Murphy, could backfire; when O'Duffy told Ballinrobe Blueshirts they would defeat de Valera as their fathers defeated Captain Boycott, the pro-Fianna Fáil *Mayo News* pointed out that the meeting was chaired by a grazier whose family 'grabbed' the demesne land when it was sold and lived in Boycott's former residence.)

This is accompanied by venomous hostility to Fianna Fáil's poorer supporters (whose attitudes are ascribed to parasitism, begrudgery, and free beef). Complaints of preferential treatment for Fianna Fáil supporters should be matched by awareness of similar complaints by Republican sympathisers against Cumann na nGaedheal, and a Blueshirt rank and file initiative unmentioned here – demands to receive preferential treatment from Blueshirt employers.

Cronin points out that the Blueshirts followed traditional organisational patterns rather than continental fascist models. For example, Blueshirt mobilisation of women (who constituted twenty-five percent of the membership) and even children has fascist parallels, but also recalls the Ladies' Land League with its associated Children's League, Cumann na mBan and Fianna Eireann. But Cronin neglects Tom Garvin's discussion of the extent to which these patterns and Irish society in the period were undemocratic. The willingness, for instance, of rank-and-file Blueshirts and their IRA opponents to use violence

extended far beyond those who called themselves fascists. Until 1922, nationalist politics were based on a single-party ideal; divisions were equated with
disloyalty and dominant local factions freely intimidated dissentients. There
were regular suggestions during the 1920s that Ireland's problems could be
solved by reuniting the old Sinn Féin in a party of perpetual government.
(Fianna Fáil inherited much of this ethos.) Similarly, Southern Unionists
claimed an untutored majority should not prevail against an enlightened elite.
Protestant participation in the Blueshirts remains unexplored despite Conor
Cruise O'Brien's discussion of 1920s ex-Unionist admiration for Mussolini and
President Erskine Childers's suggestion that participation in the Blueshirts
helped to integrate ex-Unionists into the political mainstream.

The corporatist and quasi-fascist ideas discussed by Cronin did not die with
the Blueshirts, and were more widespread among intellectuals than he realises. Only after the Second World War did the idea of rule by a paternal
Catholic elite, as superior to 'English' liberal democracy, lose all intellectual respectability. Murphy's suggestion that its displacement marked the revival of
a (secularised) upper-middle-class ethos is intriguing, though questionable.

PATRICK MAUME

[1] Patrick Maume, *D.P. Moran* (Dundalk, 1995).

Famine Fields

Robert J. Scally, *The End of Hidden Ireland: Rebellion, Famine and Emigration*
(New York: Oxford University Press, 1995), x + 266 pp. £21.50

Christine Kinealy, *This Great Calamity: The Irish Famine 1845-52* (Dublin: Gill
and Macmillan, 1994), xxi + 450 pp. £17.99

These two important contributions to historical writing on the Irish Famine
take what at first appear to be highly divergent points of focus and stylistic
approaches. Scally's book is a microstudy, an exercise in 'history from below'
that attempts to describe and empathise with the experience of a specific townland community from the beginning of its 'rebellion' against proprietorial
control in the mid-1830s, to its clearance and dispersal in 1847-48. Conscious of
the limitations of his sources, Scally's style is often imaginative and vivid, and
his mastery of literary and theoretical sources makes for a stimulating and
provocative read.

The basis of the study is an almost unrivalled collection of papers relating to
the Crown estate of the Ballykilcline in County Roscommon during the period
of the thirteen-year rent-strike that followed the end of the townland's lease to

Lord Hartland in 1834. The survival of the estate papers of the adjoining Stroke-
stown estate, site of the notorious assassination of Major Denis Mahon in 1847,
make this a particularly rich area for a local study. The author admits that the
'hidden' world of the townland's inhabitants can only be dimly seen through
the 'dusty panes' of the sources, but from what is available he constructs a persuasive impression of the multiple layers of rural society, its overt and covert
structures of power, patronage and collective activity, and the texture of the
lives of the rural poor who participated in the Ballykilcline 'rebellion'.

  Some problems arise from the juxtaposition of the specificity of Ballykilcline
and the more schematic framework through which the author relates this to
wider histories. Scally describes the situation of the Ballykilcline community
through a series of polarities: 'native' against 'colonial', 'townland' against
'town', 'peasant' against 'rural bourgeois'. The 'hidden Ireland' which Ballykilcline is taken to represent is largely isolated from an outside world, whose
economic structures and institutional manifestations are moulded by colonialism; the 'rebellion' of the townland's cottier-tenants is thus, for Scally, the
manifestation of traditional communal solidarity against the encroachments of
external authorities. The evidence he presents bears this out to some degree,
but also suggests that there may be a dimension missing from his account. The
practice of the Ballykilcline 'Defendants' appears, in fact, to have been rather
non-traditional in many respects. Acts of violence were rare (and solely re-
active), despite the calculated alarmism of the estate's agent and the local Protestant squirearchy. The 'rebellion' was primarily 'legalistic and pacific', featured a sustained appeal to the courts and, as Scally observes, 'an apparent
conviction... that the law would uphold their rights' (as, indeed, it did, tem-
porarily, in 1844). No explanation is offered as to why a townland community
should be quite so enthusiastic (even idealistic) about litigation as the primary
means of protecting their rights to land and life.

  Perhaps the reason for this may lie in what is unaccountably absent from
Scally's narrative: politics. While the author admits that a 'nascent political
consciousness' was awakened in the townland, he attributes this solely to a reaction to Crown encroachment. Yet surely O'Connellite popular politics must
have had some impact on communities like Ballykilcline. 'Catholic' political
organisation in Co. Roscommon dated from 1826, when the forty-shilling free-
holders of that county were mobilised by priest and schoolmaster (two classes
represented in Ballykilcline) in the cause of Catholic emancipation. Roscommon was represented between 1831 and 1847 by a Repeal MP, the O'Conor
Don, who presented the 'Defendants' petitions to Parliament in 1846. Perhaps
most important of all, the 'monster meeting' of the summer of 1843 at Roscommon town (less than 15 miles from the townland) apparently attracted over
one hundred thousand people (more than a third of the county's population, if
anyway accurate).

It is possible that Ballykilcline was untouched by the popular political mobilisation of the 1830s-40s. Yet combine the presence of typical O'Connellite 'agents' in the townland, the literacy of its more prominent tenants, the neglect of conspiratorial violence, and the resort to litigation (itself reflecting both O'Connell's political objective of 'popularising' the law and the widespread popular mythology surrounding 'the Counsellor'), and there seems at least an *a priori* case to answer. The rhetoric of 'fixity of tenure' that became prominent in Repeal politics in 1843 can only have appealed to the 'Defendants' and offered an alternative to the tradition of resort to agrarian violence.

Scally's neglect of the political extends to his rather glancing references to the government administration that ultimately determined the fate of the Ballykilcline community. Lord Monteagle is erroneously referred to as the Chief Commissioner of Woods and Forests in 1847 (in fact he was in open opposition to the government at this time), and the second commissioner, Charles Gore, is wrongly re-named 'Gore-Booth'. These errors appear minor, but they epitomise the author's indifference to what might be called the 'high-political' dimension of the incident.

Scally observes the relative moderation of the commission in its treatment of the 'rebellion' – the deliberate sidelining of the malign recommendations of the local agent, the repeated attempts to find a compromise short of clearance, and the relatively generous emigrant bounty paid to the tenants on top of their passage-money to New York. All these gestures may seem grossly inadequate given the ultimate destruction of the community by mass eviction and the attendant suffering; yet, as the author admits, the Ballykilcline tenants were relatively advantaged during the Famine to a degree that meant, for most, the difference between life and death. To find the reasons for the 'special treatment' of Ballykilcline, one needs to consider the nature of the Department of Woods and Forests. This was no backwater, but what Peter Mandler has called the 'public works department of the early Victorian age'. It was, moreover, the political base of some of the British politicians most committed to 'popular' measures in Ireland. The post of chief commissioner was held by O'Connell's friend Lord Bessborough in 1835-41 (he was Lord Lieutenant 1846-7) and by the former reforming chief secretary Lord Morpeth in 1846-50. Both were more knowledgeable about Irish rural conditions than most British politicians, and were adherents of conciliatory policies. Again, it seems possible that Ballykilcline's history was intimately related to its very exceptionalism as a high-profile Crown estate (this is what drew Monteagle's attention in the House of Lords). Political sensitivity about its treatment changed with the advent of a new, harder line Lord Lieutenant in the spring of 1847, and (as Scally describes) with the assassination of the proprietor of the neighbouring estate later that year.

Christine Kinealy's *This Great Calamity* is, in contrast to this intimate local study, a general narrative of the Famine catastrophe, offering an overview of conditions throughout the island and placing particular weight on the perceptions and failings of the British administration. As such, it invites comparison with Cecil Woodham-Smith's much maligned 1962 survey, *The Great Hunger*. Kinealy's book redresses some of the weaknesses of the earlier account, particularly by incorporating much of the recent writing on Irish economic history into her analysis of the Famine's causation. The text is bolstered with a number of useful quantitative tables and appendices (although a few, such as the table that omits Mayo and Sligo from the counties above the national average for mortality in 1847, might have required more explanation). The author has also been particularly successful in utilising the scattered records of local boards of guardians and other administrative bodies. The result is by far the most comprehensive account of the mechanisms of Famine relief yet published, dealing as confidently with the chaos and despair in the localities as with the dogmatic certitudes and self-assurance of Charles Trevelyan and his allies at the Treasury.

Perhaps the high point of the book, and the mainspring of the author's argument that the state could and should have done more to preserve life, is the vivid account of the increasingly confrontational relationship in the later years of the Famine between Trevelyan and Edward Twisleton, the chief poor law commissioner for Ireland who was to resign in disgust over government parsimony in March 1849. One need go no further than Twisleton's expert evidence to find ample contemporary endorsement for the conclusion that the low priority accorded by government to humanitarian aid was as responsible as ecological disaster for mass mortality.

If Kinealy's work endorses much of Woodham-Smith's findings, it ultimately fails in a similar important area. Both convincingly indict government for the inadequacies of relief policy, yet neither really explains why this failure took place. Perhaps the central weakness of this book lies in its rather superficial treatment of ideology and political motivation, arising from the neglect of political, as opposed to administrative, sources. While 'political economy' undoubtedly played a key part in constructing the Irish crisis and constraining response, complex and multifaceted phenomena are treated here in a decidedly stereotyped fashion. The unfortunate Parson Malthus is again presented as the malign influence behind British thinking, despite the distinctly anti-Malthusian tendency of the dominant ideological strand in late-1840s British politics. It was Trevelyan's certainty that an Irish economic miracle was both feasible and divinely ordained, rather than any belief that the island was overpopulated, that lay behind the penal aspects of relief policy.

Kinealy tells us much about the workings of the Treasury, but virtually nothing about the political context in which its luminaries operated; we learn little of Cabinet discussions and nothing of the Parliamentary and extra-Parliamentary developments that constrained humanitarian intervention. This neglect of the political leads to minor errors (Lincoln is elevated to the Lord Lieutenancy in 1846, Peel described as leader of the 'Tory Party' in 1847), but also to more serious misreadings of developments such as Peel's repeal of the Corn Laws in 1846. Most importantly, neglecting the 'private' correspondence of ministers such as Russell and Clarendon (and indeed, of Trevelyan), in which protagonists often expressed themselves in less guarded terms than in the 'official' records, leads to elisions in many important aspects of Famine policy – the formulation and reception of policy measures other than those actually implemented, the nature and significance of a 'reconstructive agenda' behind relief policy, and the balance between political calculations and ideological imperatives.

The publishers are to be complimented on producing an accessible paperback edition of this useful book. There, however, praise must end. There are noticeable lapses in proof-reading, a number of cases where the endnote references fall out of sequence for several pages, and some frustrating indexing errors (including some confusion between Lords Lieutenant Bessborough and Clarendon). One suspects that publishing pressure was responsible for the decision to market an extremely good history of the relief administration as a general history. The Great Famine still awaits such a multifaceted 'total' history. Any such history must assimilate both the 'history from below' pioneered in this area by Professor Scally, and the history of folklore and popular memory that has come to prominence in recent years. It is equally important that it not neglect the history of ideas and politics, as no treatment of the subject really can be complete without them.

PETER GRAY

Contributors

TOBY BARNARD is a Fellow of Hertford College, Oxford. He is the author of *Cromwellian Ireland* (1975) and *The English Republic* (1982), and editor of *Lord Buckingham: Life and Architecture* (1994).

THOMAS BARTLETT is Professor of Modern Irish History at University College Dublin. He has recently edited for publication *The Life of Theobald Wolfe Tone* (1998).

CATRIONA CLUTTERBUCK lectures in the Department of Anglo-Irish Literature and Drama, University College Dublin.

STEVEN CONNOR is Professor of Modern Literature and Theory at Birkbeck College, University of London. He is the author of books and essays on Joyce, Beckett, and contemporary literary theory.

PETER GRAY is Lecturer in History at Southampton University. He is the author of *Famine, Land and Politics: British Government and Irish Society 1843-1850* (1998).

PATRICK HANAFIN is Lecturer in Law at the University of Sussex and is currently (Fall 1998) visiting Fellow in the Human Rights Program at Harvard Law School. His publications include *Last Rights: Death, Dying and the Law in Ireland* (1997) and (with David Tomkin) *Irish Medical Law* (1995).

MARJORIE HOWES is Associate Professor of English at Rutgers University. She is the author of *Yeats's Nations: Gender, Class, and Irishness* (1996).

PATRICK MAUME is a British Academy Research Fellow at the School of Politics, Queen's University of Belfast. He is the author of *Life That Is Exile: Daniel Corkery and the Search for Irish Ireland* (1993) and *D.P. Moran* (1995) and is currently completing a book on Irish nationalist political culture 1891-1918.

CATHERINE NASH lectures on cultural geography and Irish Studies in Royal Holloway, University of London. Her research interests are in the historical and contemporary interconnections between geography, gender, and Irish identity.

SEAN RYDER lectures in English at the National University of Ireland, Galway and has co-edited *Gender and Colonialism* (1995) and *Ideology and Ireland in the Nineteenth Century* (1998).

ROBERT SULLIVAN is Associate Professor of History and Senior Associate Director of the Erasmus Institute at the University of Notre Dame. He is the author of *John Toland and the Deist Controversy: A Study in Adaptations* (1982) and is working on a book entitled *Modern Stories*, a study of competing meta-narratives of modern history.

CHRISTOPHER J. WHEATLEY is Associate Professor at the Catholic University of America and is the author of *Beneath Ierne's Banners: Irish Protestant Drama of the Restoration and Eighteenth Century* (forthcoming) and *Without God or Reason: The Plays of Thomas Shadwell and Secular Ethics in the Restoration* (1993).

Bullán Subscription Form

General Editor: Ray Ryan   **Co-Editors:** Rónán McDonald, Jim Smyth

Advisory Editors: Toby Barnard, Seamus Deane, Terry Eagleton, Roy Foster, Christopher Fox, Seamus Heaney, John Kelly, Bernard O'Donoghue, Tom Paulin, Fiona Stafford, Jon Stallworthy

Previous issues of *Bullán* have featured Seamus Heaney's last lecture as Professor of Poetry in Oxford, Terry Eagleton on the Anglo-Irish novel, Charles Townshend on the 1916 Rising, and reviews and essays from, amongst others, Donnchadh Ó Corráin, Toby Barnard, Siobhán Kilfeather, Brendan Bradshaw, Paul Bew, Tom Garvin, Clair Wills, R.B. McDowell, Bernard Crick, Julia Briggs, Elizabeth Cullingford, Margaret O'Callaghan, W.J. McCormack, Robert Crawford, Peter Gray, Bob Purdie, Keith Jeffery, Robert Young, Robert Kee, Paul Arthur, David Norbrook, Steve Bruce, Cormac Ó Gráda, Thomas Kilroy, and Joanna Bourke

Future contributors to *Bullán* include Jonathan Allison, Brendan Bradshaw, Maurice Bric, Terence Brown, Matthew Campbell, Joe Cleary, Seamus Deane, Nicholas Grene, Liam McIlvanney, Christopher Morash, Margaret O'Callaghan, Jane Ohlmeyer, Kiernan Ryan, and Carol Tell

'Bullán *is indispensable. It offers theoretically and culturally informed writing by the most provocative scholars in the field. Such a journal was urgently needed;* Bullán *fills the gap.'* - Elizabeth Cullingford

----

I would like to subscribe to *Bullán*. Enclosed is my check, money order, or charge in the amount of £/$ _____ , payable to University of Notre Dame Press.

Charge to my   ❏ Mastercard   ❏ VISA

Credit Card # _____

Expiration Date _____

Phone # _____

Signature _____

Name _____

Title _____

Institution _____

Address _____

City _____

State _____ Zip _____ Country _____

Subscription Rates
(incl. p&p):
Please circle applicable rate:

U.K. & Ireland
Individuals - £7.50 per issue
  £15.00 per year (two issues)
  £25.00 per two years
Institutions - £25.00 per year

U.S.A.
Individuals - $15.00 per issue
  $30.00 per year (two issues)
  $55.00 per two years
Institutions - $50.00 per year

Please send to *Bullán*, c/o University of Notre Dame Press, 310 Flanner Hall, Notre Dame, IN 46556 USA